"In *The Way of the Mysterial Woman*, Suzanne Anderson and Susan Cannon present their brave, pioneering, richly-informed proposals for the advance of womankind. This is a big and unique set of proposals, which is bound to enlarge our thinking about both the thwarting and liberation of our greater potentials. It's time now for women to get out of jail. Reading this book, I say 'hurrah'!"

—**Michael Murphy**, co-founder of the Esalen Institute and author of *The Future of the Body*

"*The Way of The Mysterial Woman: Upgrading How You Live, Love, and Lead* is awesome! Here I am at 85 reading it with recognition of so many growth potentials still to come in my own life! The 'Mysterial Woman' offers a new source code for our culture. Beyond equality and empowerment lies the evolving woman, a new archetype I have named the Feminine Co-Creator. It is a new map for women. She's in the midst of an evolutionary move, between mystery and manifestation at the edge of a new world. With great compassion and wisdom we are guided through dynamic steps toward a new level of wholeness. Highly recommended."

—**Barbara Marx Hubbard,** The Foundation for Conscious Evolution and author of *Conscious Evolution: Awakening the Power of Our Social Potential*

"In their excellent book, *The Way of the Mysterial Woman*, Susan Cannon and Suzanne Anderson describe sophisticated yet user-friendly leadership models and techniques that are empowering for women and men alike. *The Way of the Mysterial Woman* reveals the full complexity of the mature Feminine essence, providing a new *source code*—a fundamental set of inner instructions for personal and professional growth. Highly recommended!"

—**Steve McIntosh,** author of *The Presence of the Infinite*, and president of the Institute for Cultural Evolution

"In their new book, Suzanne Anderson and Dr. Susan Cannon engage a recognition that could not be more timely and significant: current images of realization for women, those that in recent decades have provided more equal roles and essential new freedoms, while important, are not in themselves enough. The book's sensitive inquiry into what more must lie ahead is richly pertinent not just to the lives of women, but also to broader questions of what will be needed if humanity as a whole is to progress in ultimately rewarding ways."

—**Charles Johnson, M.D.**, author of *Cultural Maturity: A Guidebook for the Future,* and founder of the Institute for Cultural Maturity

"*The Way of the Mysterial Woman* presents a code, a sequence of experiences that, if followed in order, delivers a woman to a place of wisdom, love, and power beyond any prior accomplishments in business or service or personal life. This transformational pathway is rooted in the co-authors' collective years of graduate studies, coaching, research, and leading cohorts of intelligent and soulful women. Anderson and Cannon have mapped what could be called a rite of passage for women who are ready to draw up the love of *being* from the well of the Feminine and combine that with the creative *action* of the Masculine in ways that are both powerful in the world and nourishing in their personal lives."

—**Vicki Robin,** author, *Blessing the Hands that Feed Us* and *Your Money or Your Life*

"*The Way of The Mysterial Woman* is an amazing compilation of wisdom and practice. Our most successful leaders will recognize this book's guidance as akin to what they follow. What Anderson and Cannon provide is a well-researched, practical roadmap for how woman can consciously develop this capacity to positively guide the future. Men should read this—and not enough of us will. We all, male and female, need to *lean in* this book's direction and become our deeper, truer selves. The next generation will be very grateful that we did!"

—**Geoff Bellman**, consultant and author of *Your Signature Path*

"Ever longed for a more fulfilling, joyful life, enriched by deep relationships and satisfying accomplishments? Anderson and Cannon offer an original roadmap for achieving such a dream. Derived from their own life journeys, years of research and work with women, they draw together myth, psychology, complexity science, and more. The resulting alchemical mix is a nuanced, comprehensive, and actionable approach that changes how women live, love, and lead, with exciting implications for us as individuals and as a society."

—**Peggy Holman**, author, *Engaging Emergence: Turning Upheaval into Opportunity* and co-author of *The Change Handbook*

"*The Way of the Mysterial Woman* brings health, depth, and clarity to the rising feminine voice. Flip through it, you'll catch the vision. Read it, you'll feel the challenge. Work through it and you will grow."

  —**Rev. Samuel G. Alexander,** author of *Evolving Christianity, Life After Faith Crisis*

"What a rich book! Like the wise women they are, Anderson and Cannon take us by the hand and guide us confidently through the transformation that is already underway for thousands of women—and men—who have felt the tug of the Mysterial potential within. In delineating five clear stages and multiple practices to support the maturation of integral capacities at each stage, the authors have created an elegant map for a brave new emerging model of leadership. Brava!"

  —**Belinda Gore, PhD,** senior faculty at The Deep Coaching Institute,
  author of *Ecstatic Body Postures: An Alternate Reality Workbook* and
  The Ecstatic Experience: Healing Postures for Spirit Journeys

"This book provides a compelling, overarching theory of human, and particularly women's, development. It weaves multiple psychological, sociological, futurist, and philosophical systems into a stunning arc of individual and societal development. But the book goes beyond theory. This is a working manual. You can feel the traction given this work by the ten years of on-the-ground training, coaching, and consulting that were the cauldron from which the vision and methods emerged. As a man, I learned more about myself and about women, and I completed this book inspired and hopeful. There is little doubt that the emergent feminine power is sadly and deeply needed in our atomized and hierarchically damaged world. If there is one thing to take from this book, it is the confident and well-etched vision of feminine capacity fully realized and its potential influence on our world's future."

  —**Gregory Kramer,** co-creator of Insight Dialogue, founder of the Metta Foundation,
  and author of *Insight Dialogue: The Interpersonal Path to Freedom* and
  Dharma Contemplation: Meditating Together with Wisdom Texts

"Let's face it. The masculine leadership that has run the world for millennia is a double-edged sword. Its focus on hard science, economic growth, military might, and political dominance has left us a world that, despite the consumer cornucopia produced by its powerful technologies, is coming apart at the seams from war, greed, climate change, and over-exploitation of resources. And until now, much of the world's female political leadership has gotten where it has by governing in the same way and with the same priorities. But *The Mysterial Woman*—using carefully developed new paradigms and illustrative case studies—uncovers a new way of female leadership capable of bringing about the 'great transformation' our world so deeply needs. In this book, Susan Cannon and Suzanne Anderson bring all of their insight together in one volume. Beautifully written and clear, this is a book for both men and women who believe that another world is possible and much needed.

—**John de Graaf**, co-author of *Affluenza* and *What's the Economy for, Anyway?*

"Original, dynamic, compelling, and eminently practical, *The Mysterial Woman* is a blessing of a book for any women whose inner guidance system is nudging her to grow into her authenticity and wisdom to make a powerful contribution to the world, one that is hers alone to make. Rich with lyrical content, as well as down-to-earth action, Cannon and Anderson's book is a step-by-step guide to recognizing and freeing ourselves from our limiting beliefs and patterns. This is one of those books you'll want to keep as a reference, but also one you'll recommend to others, so buy several copies!"

—**Kerul L. Kassel**, author of *The Thinking Executive's Guide to Sustainability*

"Anderson and Cannon had me when they used the expression 'the long emergency.' They were talking about the world situation, but I felt they were looking at my life. And so it continued, page after page. They were by my side on a journey through the book—my companions as I saw through a new lens, analyzed from a new perspective, and made choices using a new way of knowing. Perhaps you, yourself, are experiencing 'the long emergency.' Perhaps you are at one of life's critical intersections and unsure which way to go. Perhaps you are feeling stuck without even knowing why. *The Way of the Mysterial Woman* will help you answer the question: *What next?* It can help you to decide mindfully and spiritually, and then to move forward with confidence, courage, and hope."

—**Ruth Middleton House, EdD**, president of Middleton-House & Company and author of *It's Time to Change the Way You Change*

"*The Way of the Mysterial Woman* is a powerful, resonant, and original offer to the world. I loved every chapter—especially when I followed the "Mysterial Sequence" and found myself in all the archetypes and their fascinating shadows. Think of this as a transformational guidebook—as life changing as *The Artist's Way*, anchored in a conversation as groundbreaking as *Women Who Run With the Wolves*. This is our time and this is our book."

—**Gail Hudson**, writer, life coach and co-author with Jane Goodall of *Hope for Animals and Their World: How Endangered Species are Being Rescued From the Brink* and *Seeds of Hope: Wisdom and Wonder From the World of Plants*

THE WAY
of the
MYSTERIAL
WOMAN

Published 2016
Printed in the United States of America
ISBN: 978-1-63152-081-5 pbk
ISBN: 978-1-63152-082-2 ebk
Library of Congress Control Number: 2015959048

For information, address:
She Writes Press
1563 Solano Ave #546
Berkeley, CA 94707

Cover and interior design by Tabitha Lahr
Interior graphics by Brad Reynolds www.integralartandstudies.com
Cover painting © Lynda Lowe

She Writes Press is a division of SparkPoint Studio, LLC.

We are deeply grateful to a sister Mysterial, Lynda Lowe, for the use of her powerful painting "Boundless" as our front cover art. Archetypal symbology is often found in Lowe's art. In this painting, the vessel may be viewed as both sacred bowl and familiar domestic object, as container for body or soul. The image of flying birds appearing and disappearing into surrounding space furthers a link between the embodied and the spirit. Reconciling and making wholeness out of complementary forces within and without is a theme frequently brought to Lynda Lowe's artistic practice. More of her art may be seen at her website www.lyndalowe.com

THE WAY
of the
MYSTERIAL
WOMAN

Upgrading How You Live,
Love, and Lead

SUZANNE ANDERSON, MA *and* SUSAN CANNON, PhD

SHE WRITES PRESS

We dedicate this book to women all over the world who are awakening to the Mysterial potential within that is urging them to the edge of their own evolution. Your upgraded wisdom, love and power are desperately needed now. We bow to your courage and commitment to fulfill your own soul's longing and become a change agent positively shaping our common future.

This book is an offering to the women who are yet to come. May the willingness of women today to 'wake up and grow up' blaze a wide and welcoming trail for your Mysterial emergence.

CONTENTS

PART III

PART I

INTRODUCTION

When you are transformed the world will be transformed,
for you are the world and the world is you.
—The Gospel of Mary Magdalene

Women have enjoyed decades of liberation and empowerment that were unimaginable just half a century ago. In the US in 1960, it was socially acceptable and perfectly legal to refuse to hire a woman—especially for a job with authority or career potential—simply because she was female. If she did land a job, she was lucky to be paid half what a man would make doing the same work. And if she got pregnant? She could be fired, yet abortion was a felony and birth control pills were either unavailable or regulated as strictly as narcotics. It was common for medical, law, and business schools to admit only one or two women to a class (the thought being that two could keep each other company[1]). Harvard, Yale, and Princeton didn't admit women, period. If a woman dared apply for a bank account or credit card, the bank required her husband to co-sign. Having the audacity to wear pants might get her shamed in public or sent home from work to change.

What a difference a couple of generations make when the time is right. Marriage and childbearing have become not only optional (although still highly valued) but possible to delay. In the extreme, a woman can freeze her eggs for the future, make a withdrawal from a sperm bank, or hire a surrogate womb. Biology is no longer destiny. Today, women are making inroads and contributions in every conceivable occupation and profession: exploring space, diving inside Antarctic icebergs, winning NASCAR races, running linear accelerators, unlocking genetic codes. They are building innovative businesses, as well as influential charitable and civic organizations, setting records of physical skill and endurance, inspiring humanity through artistic expression and public acts of moral courage and sacrifice.

Through micro-lending and other alternative financing methods, women are liberating whole communities from the tyranny of chronic poverty. They are being ordained as ministers, priests, and monks as never before, while initiating the conversation in traditions that still prohibit female ordination. As of January 2015 a record number of women simultaneously presided as heads of state. Women are winning elected offices all over the world and making a vast difference in how societies are governed. Technology has made it possible for some to spend more time at home involved in the crucial task of caring for family and community, while staying in the paid workforce and even continuing to educate themselves.

Clearly, the playing field has become, while not level, a whole lot closer to level. And the world is far better for it. Yet something else has been stirring under the surface of our apparent emancipation.

And this brings us to a perplexing observation. Many women are starting to name a dissatisfaction that has been building for years in the wake of such historic accomplishment. A woman today is still expected to excel in her profession while caring for children, a home, and aging parents; being a sensitive, smart, and sexy intimate partner; contributing to her community; and managing a social life—not to mention a socially networked life. And she is doing all of this in a world that, unlike 1960, can reach her 24-7. These routine demands on women have all too often come at a cost of deteriorating health and well-being—a flashing red alarm that something is not right.

Societal attitudes and systems, while considerably more enlightened and friendlier toward women in many places in the world than in 1960, still create barriers and disadvantages. Women describe their struggle within oppressive systems of power that drain their last drop of life energy while constraining what is best in them. They have lost confidence and trust in authorities and leaders at all levels that seem ever more incapable, confused, and even corrupt.

These same women pour out their passionate longing to be fulfilled and make a difference in the world. Many are no longer satisfied to simply "make it" by the socially defined measures of position, money, image, and power over others. They are connecting with their natural impulse to evolve.

"We want a different way!" they plead, not quite able to articulate what that might be, or how to get there. They can find no appealing role models—men or women—in their milieus. They scan fervently for answers to this longing of their soul, devouring books, getting therapy, makeovers, hiring personal trainers and trying diets, seeking spiritual guidance, taking endless workshops.

Many are tired of dabbling in self-improvement experiences that excite them then fade. They are left, yet again, with a dull ache inside.

This is what we began to hear over and over again from women. They were sensing that their ways of being and engaging with themselves, others, and the world were just not adequate to meet the challenges and opportunities of these times. And they were right.

Yet if their true hearts' desire to make a contribution actually were to manifest, this world could become a far more just, sustainable, peaceful, and beautiful place. Clearly it was time to hit the evolutionary button again and grow in a revolutionary way that could have a huge impact on society—*upgrading how we live, love, and lead.*

A Masculine Epoch

The old models for living, loving, and leading are based on a cultural worldview that *for more than five thousand years* has been continuously tilted in the extreme toward Masculine values, styles, and ways of making sense of reality. It is not just Masculine, but has become *Hypermasculine*. All of our existing paradigms for living a successful and fulfilling life are therefore naturally aligned with *the way that men develop and evolve.* This was not a mistake. As we will show you, it was exactly what had to happen, in the appropriate time, for humanity to evolve. But the Hypermasculine paradigm of wholeness is no longer sufficient for the full emergence of our potential as women today. We need another image of the future.

This book is not against men or the Masculine, nor is it political. We are not predicting or advocating that women will or should rule the world, or that they have been wronged, are better than men, or have been unfairly left out for so long. We are simply looking at what is, what that means in the context of how human systems evolve, and where women fit in this picture. We are certainly not the only ones who are noticing that the Hypermasculine saturation of today's world is resulting in intense evolutionary pressure to rebalance with the conscious, mature Feminine.

A key distinction we make is between *gender* (female, male) and *essence* (Feminine, Masculine). Our stance is that women as a group have a foundational essence that is grounded in the Feminine. Not every single woman, of course, but a very high percentage. Therefore, this evolutionary pressure to rebalance is felt *even more urgently within women*. Fortunately women have spent the last half-century breaking into the Masculine systems and structures and building a solid foundation of skills, power, and infrastructure from which to do this.

We believe that women are in the midst of a profound rite of passage. Evolution seems to be urging us forward, demanding that we meet the immediate pressure for a planetary rebalancing of the prevailing Hypermasculine essence with the full complexity of our mature Feminine essence. This deep impulse is the stimulus of much of the inner discontent, yearning, confusion, pain, and depression experienced by women. A new world, and our new identity as women leaders, is seeking birth.

And that birth requires a new *source code*, a fundamental set of inner instructions for growth.

How Did The New Source Code Emerge?

We, the co-authors of this book, did not set out to invent a new source code for the way women live, love, and lead. The source code found us, in the mysterious way these things happen when history and higher purpose align. It was hiding in plain sight, ripe for discovery when the right conditions would finally present themselves.

One of those conditions was our own personal readiness to evolve, which we experienced, as do many women today, as a deep and gnawing inner discontent. Though we came from quite different professional and academic backgrounds, both of us were innovators of transformative learning, change, and leadership. As such, we were used to following the call to transform in the spirit of poet Guilliame Apollinaire's often-quoted stanza:

> *Come to the edge, Life said.*
> *They said: We are afraid.*
> *Come to the edge, Life said.*
> *They came. It pushed them . . .*
> *And they flew.*

We had been to the edge many times in our lives. In fact, coming right to the edge, peering down into the abyss, feeling that nervous, excited ripple of energy in the belly—this was a familiar story for us. It was our common identity. The edge was the place where we learned, where we could shake ourselves up enough to see beyond consensus reality.

Before we met, we had made our marks in our careers, and felt confident in the world. We took risks, made crazy mistakes, and pursued edgy alternative life paths that fed our souls in a way that work alone could not. We got graduate degrees to further our purpose more than our position, and sought out the most transformative ideas for making a difference. We stretched ourselves to be part of global events and make history.

Some edges were closer to home. We married, divorced, relocated, miscarried, lost loved ones, and grappled with the pain and messiness of life. Every time we came to the edge, we trusted the inner impulse and flew.

But there came a time in both of our lives when it was different. We were tired. Where was this all headed? Was there a "there" to get to? And if we did get there, would we even like it? At the close of the twentieth century, we each in our own very different ways had run out of runway. We were no longer sure we could fly. And we started to notice we weren't alone. We began to seek out others.

From our first chance meeting in the waning days of the twentieth century at an Open Space conference for women's leadership, we co-authors agreed that the leadership models women were being encouraged to adopt were still fundamentally Masculine. This wasn't wrong—it just wasn't a complete fit, especially for women.

And it wasn't adequately preparing anyone for the dramatically new world that we were recognizing even then was well on its way.

We had both grown up as "father's daughters" in the '60s and '70s, eschewing the domestic lives and roles to which our mothers had been unwillingly constrained, and admiring the achievement and power our fathers experienced. Yet we weren't satisfied copying our fathers either.

The central inquiry that remained constant for each of us, while many other things changed, was this:

How can I be all of myself? How do I resolve a deep inner tension between two differing parts of myself—one that is more Masculine, able to achieve, focus, create order, control, and powerfully bring things into form in the world, and the other part that is more Feminine—receiving, wild-spirited, intuitive, embodied, creative, loves the mystery, and speaks the language of the heart? And how can I be of most service to the world without losing myself?

We had no quick and easy answers. But we were willing to explore the questions together.

Each of us brought something different to the table. Suzanne, a Canadian fluent in French and Italian, had a background in art and architecture, and a graduate degree in psychology focused on Masculine and Feminine integration in women's development. Having earned her livelihood consulting and executive coaching in Fortune 500 companies, while simultaneously living in an intentional spiritual community, she knew what it meant to put on a game face and suit up. After a powerful experience of spiritual awakening while vacationing in Bali, Indonesia, she left this lucrative consulting work to find out what it meant to "midwife the re-emergence of the Deep Feminine on earth." She began a thriving private coaching practice in Paris for professional women seeking to reclaim their Feminine nature. Suzanne eventually moved to Seattle, bringing with her a psychological view of the individual, and an understanding of how to create a transformative sanctuary for women.

Susan, an artistically and scientifically talented American, also knew what it meant to navigate Hypermasculine environments. She had worked as an engineer and manager in semiconductor and defense systems manufacturing, a senior executive in the construction industry, and operated an air charter service between Alaska and the Soviet Union during the Cold War. That path came to an abrupt end when toxins from a classified missile project damaged her health. Following a mystical call, she earned a doctorate in Integral studies and transformative learning and change in human systems from a holistic institute in San Francisco that honored the Deep Feminine. After experiencing firsthand the epic collapse of the Soviet Union, and writing a doctoral dissertation on the future of the United States, Susan brought the cultural and large systems view of the emerging future to the forefront. Her research showed that the most positive and desired future scenarios were the ones where society had significantly rebalanced toward Feminine values, such as care for the environment and all beings, collaboration, decentralization, and a valuing of the true economic contribution of "women's work."

Our two areas of inquiry meshed perfectly together—blending the individual and collective dimensions of a woman's transformation. Both of us had come to the same conclusion that one of the most potent and timely opportunities to make a positive difference was to focus on helping women evolve as leaders. But not leaders who would be limited to or defined by the Hypermasculine model. Rather, a radically different kind of Feminine leader who could effectively meet and respond to the new world we were facing.

In short, we believed that women had the potential to be a kind of natural tipping point force toward a more positive future outcome for us all. But how would this happen?

A New Map for Women

In all of our research neither of us could find any adequate leadership models of a new way of being and doing for women that would be a match for the increasingly complex and fast moving demands of the times. Nor could we see any transformative paths designed for women that were integral, or complete enough to ensure that we were addressing all the domains of a woman's experience.

It began to dawn on us that maybe there was no map and pathway already laid out. We would need to be the explorers and create it ourselves. And so we set forth.

Starting in the year 2000 in Seattle, we launched our first Women's Integral Leadership Circle. By word of mouth, it quickly filled and soon became a series of highly successful university certificate programs. Clearly, a hunger was aching to be satisfied.

It would be a nice story if we could say that everything clicked into place immediately, and that we understood exactly how to set free this new woman of the future. But that was far from the case.

Life experience and our own studies had taught us a lot about what didn't work, and we were determined to find what would. Circle after circle, the map began to reveal itself with far more intricacy and beauty than we had ever imagined. Over the years many women from all walks of life, leadership styles, and capabilities found their way to us and participated in this ongoing research in action.

We, and the women we were guiding, were being simultaneously pushed and pulled into uncharted territory by that sense of suffering and longing that was sometimes hard to articulate. All of us shared a profound disenchantment with the old models we had struggled to fit within for years, both at work and at home.

Exhaustion, illness, anxiety, or depression seemed a troublingly common pattern among women who were drawn to our work. Despite their worldly success and hard-won achievements, we found that they commonly experienced a pervasive and unsettling sense that they weren't enough, and that they didn't really belong somehow in the world the way it is. This persistent background static was amplified by the speeding up of the world's rapacious demands on them to do more and more to prove their value. Yet a yearning for fulfillment and a desire to make a difference in the world, to set their souls free and be who they really are, everywhere, all the time, was adding even more pressure to their (and our) systems.

As the years passed, something was being catalyzed in us and in our students as we uncovered the steps of a developmental pathway specifically designed for our unfolding potential. The women were dramatically shifting their sense of identity and how they were able to engage in the world.

After the tenth year of continuous improvement of our university certificate programs with women leaders—through much trial and error, research, and synthesis—we had the amazing experience that we can only describe as akin to witnessing a new "species" of woman come into being.

Why We Call Her Mysterial

At first we tried to define this newly emerging woman using more recognizable language. We thought of "*Authentic,*" "*Full Presence,*" and "*Integral.*" None of them quite fit. None of them captured fully enough the enigmatic, beautiful nature of this radically new way of being.

Her name finally came to us through a kind of linguistic gymnastics when we accidently merged two key abilities of this evolving woman.

She has a remarkable ease with the unknown, chaotic, and ambiguous realities of these uncertain times: she sees herself as a co-creative partner with the *Mystery.*

And she is able to bridge between diverse worlds and polarities, between radical differences—self and other, conscious and unconscious, Feminine and Masculine—manage reactivity, and find a creative middle way in challenging situations. She is a *Medial.*[2]

When Mystery and Medial came together the evocative word **Mysterial** was created.

Once the word popped out we realized that given this is an evolutionary move women are in the midst of now, it made sense that there would not already be a word in our current language to describe this way of being. Of course, the Mysterial woman is much more than the sum of the two words that gave us her name: she is a radically new way of being.

The Way of the Mysterial Woman is a wise, loving, and powerful way of being that arises when our unique Yin and Yang essences are moving freely through body, heart, and mind in a creative partnership with the mystery of life.

The personal pathway that we had finally uncovered to bring us to the Mysterial Woman—the developmental *source code* that offers what you actually need to do, and in precisely what order—we named **The Mysterial Sequence.** The corresponding transformative "technology," or personal practice, that generates the change is called **The Mysterial Change Process**.

Although we uncovered The Mysterial Sequence and developed The Mysterial Change Process as we designed and facilitated our university certificate programs, this book is not an attempt to reproduce those programs. We are not providing a recipe to be copied by rote, but rather, a pattern to be activated in your own life in the manner that is most effective for you.

What to Expect From This Book

The Way of the Mysterial Woman offers you an image of the future that is radically different from previous models of women's wholeness. Our intention is that the image itself will begin to activate the Mysterial Woman who is being called forth in you and in women around the globe.

This book will guide you through each dynamic step of The Mysterial Sequence, exploring the Feminine and Masculine (also known as Yin and Yang) characteristics and potentials that reside in every woman. You will see how they relate to familiar archetypes in surprising ways. We will explore ways to see and transcend the "shadow" aspects of our feminine psyches that keep us from developing into our full Mysterial Womanhood. Along the way we offer inspiration, guiding questions, and specific practices that will help you create a more lasting change and transformation.

With each step of The Mysterial Sequence you will find yourself developing greater skills and capacities to engage with life in ways that finally feel fulfilling, meaningful, artful, joyful, and whole.

In **Part I**, we will introduce enough theoretical background about human development so that you can better understand the Mysterial Woman and The Mysterial Sequence—the pathway for activating this powerful evolutionary, psychological force within. We will reveal why the Mysterial Woman is arising at this critical juncture in history, and actually couldn't have done so until now. We will also introduce you to our signature transformative technology, The Mysterial Change Process, so that you can prepare for the journey to come in Part II.

In **Part II**, we will first lead you through a compelling preparation and initiation process, and explain why the alchemy of initiation is relevant for contemporary women. You will meet women, composites of our actual students, as case studies. We will then take you step-by-step through their experience to the threshold of becoming a Mysterial Woman. This represents the core of the book, and is also the core of our developmental work with women. This powerful and specific journey through archetypes and shadows has the power to dramatically change and improve your life. Each chapter will include practices that you can use to begin your own Initiation. By the end of Part II, you may even begin to notice Mysterial transformations "activating" within you.

In **Part III**, you'll experience the profound and sacred alchemy that brings forth the Mysterial Woman. You'll learn more about sustaining and applying your emerging strengths and abilities after completing the Mysterial Sequence. And we will look into our collective Mysterial future. What will society be like ten to fifty years from now, when many of us are Mysterial? That day will come, and we make some grounded and inspiring predictions about that future!

The Mysterial Woman is shaking up ingrained beliefs about who we can become, and where we are going. Perhaps she's already shaking up your world as well.

One thing we know for sure: we have only glimpsed the beginning of her emergence.

Chapter 1

THE CALL OF THE MYSTERIAL WOMAN

We all have the extraordinary coded within us, waiting to be released.
—Jean Houston

Signs of Mysterial Emergence

The Mysterial Woman is not something we invented. She is a natural phenomenon we discovered and named. We believe she is being called forth now from within women to meet this extraordinary era of human evolution. Think of her as the natural next step in women's development. You could even say she is a force within women that cannot be suppressed.

In days gone by, change happened by revolution—by toppling the old order and installing the new order in its place. Mysterial women are catalysts for a more graceful way—the surgical thrust and parry of revolutionary disruption embraced within the persistent and organic unfolding of evolutionary change over time. As philosopher Alfred North Whitehead has been poetically paraphrased, "evolution is the gentle movement toward God by the gentle persuasion of love." Mysterial women will upgrade the way we live, love, and lead.

How do we know this?

First, let's examine the personal level. What we know from our years of experience is that many, many women in all walks of life are sensing a "call" to grow and develop. This call often shows up as an uncomfortable inner urging to change ways they are living, loving, or leading, and sometimes all three.

See if you recognize any of these signs.

Maybe you . . .

* Feel a painful gap between who you are on the inside and what you are able to express in the world.
* Wonder where your playful spirit went and how life became such hard work.
* Long for a relationship where you can feel met and received for all of who you are.
* Are tired of constantly giving to everyone else and having nothing left for yourself at the end of the day.
* Are exhausted and feeling soul-dead, and possibly depressed even though you have achieved your career goals.
* Feel pulled to discover and share your unique gifts, and make a contribution, but you can't see how.
* Feel alone and alienated from the mainstream and are afraid to share what you see with others.
* Want to be an inspired role model for your daughter or leave a legacy for future generations, but are not sure how to do that.
* Feel a constant low-level anxiety or depression that doesn't go away even when things are going well.
* Are overwhelmed by everything that you are responsible for and are wondering how you will survive, let alone thrive.

This call is often experienced as a growing dissatisfaction with the way things have become, like trying on a favorite outfit that no longer fits, and even worse, has gone out of style. "I remember ten years ago when I was so motivated to be climbing the career ladder," said Kerry, a senior IT manager who participated in our Mysterial Leadership Program. "I was proud of the all-nighters, the miles traveled, seeing our goals met, making more money. But now . . . I don't know, it doesn't feel worth it. I'm tired. I got the success I wanted, all the material stuff, but why am I not happy? There are so many things I just don't like about my life. It scares and depresses me to think that it wasn't worth it."

This call can also feel like an unrequited, frustrated longing for something a woman really wants but feels she can't have. "Why is it that I can't seem to get my consulting business off the ground?" asked Gabriella, another student of ours, who was a teacher and K-12 educational consultant. "I know I can really help the way kids learn. Something just always seems to be holding me back, like I'm running through mud on an obstacle course."

A woman might not even be able to articulate what that longing is. She just senses something is missing. "I know there's something I came on this earth to do, some way of giving back to society," sighed Rachel, a highly educated stay-at-home mother. "I'm dying to find my purpose in life, to be in touch with what I'm passionate about, but I just don't know what it is and it's driving me crazy!"

If these experiences resonate with you, maybe you have been interpreting these uncomfortable feelings and dissatisfactions as signs of your own incompleteness. Maybe you've worried that you have gotten out of step, missed the boat, or failed in some way. But that is not true. They are actually early signs of your Mysterial Emergence calling you to grow.

When we reach the limits of a way of being or a worldview that is no longer a match for the demands and stage of our lives, it starts to get very uncomfortable. Rightly so. This is the signal that growth is required. We are being prompted to evolve a more complex "inner operating system" to meet the conditions of our lives. This impulse is similar to a crawling baby's inner directive to begin walking. The difference is that we might choose to question or even ignore the urge (which will, of course, make it worse).

Discovering that the turmoil in our lives could be an invitation to grow instead of a sign of failure is often a deep relief for women. You may be experiencing this discomfort as something intensely personal, just your own life crisis. But it is much bigger than that. We can assure you that you are in very good company with women all over the world. But why is it that so many of us are being called to change now?

Let's look at the collective or cultural picture.

The roots of this Mysterial Emergence lie deep in the past, and only now have the conditions ripened enough for this beautiful and much needed potential to be expressed on a significant scale.

The Bigger Picture: The Good, the Bad, and the Ugly

We can probably all agree that we live in unusual, perplexing, even dangerous times. A lightning-quick review of what's being written in futures/foresight studies, professionally researched scenarios, think tanks, and government research on global trends is pretty sobering. Some of the most talked about trends include abrupt climate change, sudden global economic or financial disruption, and unsustainable production and consumption that rapidly and dangerously degrades our biosphere: runaway pandemics, catastrophic water shortages over large parts of the earth, and spreading armed conflict/failing states/terrorism—potentially with weapons of mass destruction.[1] Phew!

These are but a few of the more likely probabilities. What's truly mindboggling is that they are all catalysts for even more change! They could drive a whole host of secondary trends all over the earth, such as mass refugee migrations, the potential collapse of urban population centers due to food and resource supply chain disruption—the gloomy story goes on and on. The 2013 State of the World Report aptly named this growing intensity of intertwined economic, environmental, and social challenges "the long emergency."

You may be tempted to change the channel at this point. You may be asking, "What can I, as one person, do in the face of so much potential calamity?"

The good news is that we are not in this alone, and we do, surprisingly, have the wind in our favor. Innovative thought leaders have been telling us for at least the past thirty years that something new and never before seen is trying to birth itself on the planet to deal with global challenges that appear unsolvable. Birth, as we know, comes with a lot of upheaval and disruption. The signature of evolutionary change is exactly this phenomenon—when something novel, something never before seen *emerges out of necessity,* disrupting the status quo.[2]

Mass change doesn't happen because everyone agrees it's a nice idea. It happens because it must. Because it's time. The great thing about evolutionary change—whether it is for one person or a whole planet—is that it *wants to happen for the better.* If we take the long view, over time humans have inexorably become better fed, sheltered, healthier, entertained, protected, and also more sensitive and welcoming to each other, and have extended justice more broadly.

As we'll show in a moment, humanity has seen similarly dramatic tipping points catalyze mass novelty by necessity before. And we have seen how these exciting but disruptive breakthroughs have guided us through similar dire situations in the past.

Like the discomfort that signals the Mysterial Emergence in an individual woman, all this disruption is not necessarily bad news. It may be uncomfortable. It may create instability. But it almost always leads to a change that needs to happen—a change that has been stirring and yearning to materialize for some time.

For example, In 2010, almost on cue, people all over the world suddenly woke up to challenge Hypermasculine authoritarian structures and leaders. Yet only a few years earlier, these same people were perhaps too afraid to challenge the status quo, or couldn't see it as a problem. Many had resigned themselves to live with it. From the Arab Spring uprisings, the Occupy movements in the West, to protests against anything "big"—big business, big government, big oil, big pharma, big agriculture, big media—people began to take action. This happened collectively, almost spontaneously. It wasn't something any one person or group could plan.

And at the same time, novelty born out of *opportunity* is emerging through more people, more quickly, and with more creative diversity than ever before. A village midwife in Africa with a cellphone has far more computational power and connection to life-saving information than was used to land the first spacecraft on the moon. Sitting in a mud hut next to a woman in labor, she has more global access than the president of the United States had twenty some years ago sitting in the White House.

The bad, scary news may get more attention, but there is plenty of good news out there too. We actually live amidst a wild upwelling of empowering knowledge, in a flowering of spiritual resources, and with the means to be in constant creative connection with one another and the world.

The Leadership Conundrum

But at the end of the day, who is it that will help guide us through all this disruption, out the other side to the most positive future possible? Whose steady, wise hand is on the rudder or weaving wonders behind the scenes? All this emerging novelty by necessity is hard for most people to wrap their heads around, let alone consider tackling.

In terms of leadership challenges, we could liken our times to a planetary perfect storm: complexity is increasing, change is accelerating, and uncertainty is a constant companion. According to research on adult development and leadership, such conditions are already exceeding the mental and emotional capacities of most leaders today.[3]

We looked at a sample of four recent global studies on current and future senior leadership needs,[4] and they generally concluded that there is a lack of "higher-order capacities" to meet the complexity of today's challenges. Examples of such capacities might include an ease with ambiguity and uncertainty, building strategic relationships across organizational or cultural boundaries, or having the emotional and intuitive intelligence to sense the crucial undercurrents that have remained unspoken amongst the individuals at a meeting.

Such capacities are valuable whether a woman has a formal leadership position, or is extending informal leadership in her sphere of influence. And they are very much in keeping with the Way of The Mysterial Woman.

How do we get to such nuanced higher-ordered capacities? We all know what it's like when our computer's operating system is out of date. The system slows down and gets buggy. We install an exciting new application that promises to solve all our problems, and it just doesn't run very well, if at all. Eventually the system crashes for good, and we are forced to install an upgrade or even replace the whole computer.

The Mysterial Upgrade

You can think of the Mysterial Woman as someone who is running on an upgraded personal operating system. Her upgrade gives her access to the higher capacities required to meet the evolutionary challenges upon us. This inner template allows her to live in the eye of the current storm—at peace with whatever comes her way, skillfully unfolding a life that is accomplished, creative, and beneficial to all.

The Mysterial Woman is not trapped inside old patterns of identity that were built by the more toxic elements of Hypermasculine culture. This "Patriarchy" as it is sometimes called, has a lust for power and control over others, and is uncomfortable with the more collaborative and co-creative nature of Feminine power.

Driven by fear and greed, The Patriarchy has an insatiable need for endless growth and achievement, keeping it on the treadmill 24-7 without any sense of natural restorative cycles. Nothing is ever good enough for it, and it is highly suspicious of women's ways of knowing. It delights in pure win-lose competition, blind to unintended consequences. It has no problem with the exploitation and destruction of planetary resources and other people for the sake of enriching itself beyond any reasonable need.

Despite excruciating pressure to change—manifesting in punishing forms such as mega-storms, economic chaos, and widespread misery—this inheritance from our past maintains itself in great part through the self-serving efforts of major media, institutions, and corporations that fear they have something to lose if things change.

The Mysterial Woman is grounded in a different kind of consciousness. As we will show, the Mysterial Woman is literally embodying a consciousness of the future that is not yet shared by the masses. And because it is consciousness, individual and collective, that shapes our worldview, she can begin to create a different reality here in the present.

Mysterial Capacities

A key distinction of the Mysterial Woman is her access to the full spectrum of her being. All of us, whether we are men or women, have both Feminine and Masculine aspects of our nature.[5] They coexist. The Mysterial Woman is deeply connected with the Feminine ground of her being, and a deep sense of sufficiency. And she is equally connected to the Masculine aspects of herself that empower her to bring her gifts out into the world. She neither rejects the Masculine, or as often happens in contemporary life, allows herself to be driven by its unbalanced and extreme version, the Hypermasculine.

Specifically, the Mysterial Woman has elegantly upgraded her embodied Feminine and Masculine capacities. By elegantly, we mean that she has access to the *most essential* set of effective Feminine and Masculine capacities necessary to meet the challenges and opportunities of this time with grace and ease. And most importantly, she is able to bring them all together into a seamless whole, *a higher ordered synthesis*.

With her innate wholeness and adaptability, the Mysterial Woman's approach to leadership is especially suited to the constantly shifting ground that organizations and institutions are experiencing today. To get a feeling for this, the chart on the next page compares some Traditional Leadership qualities[6] and Mysterial Leadership qualities.

The Mysterial Woman is also not bound to the simplistic idea that we are all separate masters of our own destiny, bouncing off each other like individual billiard balls, able to create any future we want as long as we have a strong enough intention. She knows that we are deeply interconnected through subtle fields of energy, emotion, and thought, as well as through our dense global ecosystems of communications and exchange. She understands that reality is complex, far beyond the grasp of rational knowing.

The Mysterial Woman creatively attunes her intention and stewardship of her destiny, and the destiny of the whole, with the unfolding evolutionary forces themselves. She embraces this great cosmic adventure that by its own nature remains a great and wonderful Mystery, moment to moment.

This makes her a *natural leader*, whether or not she aspires to a formal position of authority and power. And as we have shown, the world is hungry and ready for a new kind of leadership to emerge.

Traditional Leadership Qualities	Mysterial Leadership Qualities
Command and control decision making style. Micromanages; leader expected to have all the answers.	Solicits input from the group and cultivates group coherence that results in exceptional collective intelligence. Trusts employees to make decisions within their doman of authority, and takes responsibility for decisions that are hers to make. Is a life long learner.
Drives self and others to the point of burnout to accomplish goals and tasks; coercive.	Works with a rhythmic drive and flow that allows for physical, mental, emotional, and spiritual restoration, which ultimately results in greater sustainability and higher performance.
Lays out a highly linear project plan; tends to rigidly stay the course.	Able to understand the structure and timing of a creative process, organically knowing when to act and when to let factors ripen for the best possible outcome in the situation for all.
Strategizes 3–5 years out; plan is cast in stone.	Holds a vision that includes the influence and impact on future generations, while able to dynamically steer a 5-year strategic plan to adapt as conditions change.
Most strongly motivated by desire for personal success.	Strongly motivated by service and higher purpose; including the higher altruistic purpose for organization, which has alignment with the leader's higher purpose.
Employees are set up to vigorously compete against one another.	Creates team environments that develop and reward collaboration while recognizing and mentoring individual contribution.
Focuses on being a technical expert and "in charge."	Focuses on continually learning and developing self and others, creating conditions for employees to shine and express their own leadership.
Exclusively focuses on numbers and quantitative measures of performance to steer the organization.	Takes into account both quantitative and qualitative measures, including cultural cohesion, customer feedback, employee engagment, and community/global impact; draws on multiple intelligences.
Wears a "mask" and projects an image of authority and power designed to command respect and subservice.	Has an authentic embodied presence that inspires trust and empowers others.
Required to be two different people at home and at work; the worlds are kept highly separated. At work keeps "game face" on.	Recognizes that life and work are of a whole, and that greater productivity and satisfaction arises from flexible stewardship between the two.

Why Women, Why Now?

From an evolutionary point of view, we propose that women are actually poised to play a leading role in this upcoming human drama. Why is that? It's not because of ideas of fairness or social justice, as important and timely as those are.

We can see it in the patterns. Once the social revolutions of the 1960s began to shake things up, women suddenly left their enclaves of domesticity and streamed *en masse* into workplaces, institutions, and public life. Ever since, we've been climbing to positions of authority, power, contribution, and influence that would have surprised even a suffragette.

When you think about it, fifty-plus years is an incredibly short time for such a monumental transformation. In the evolutionary big picture, you could say that women have been enormously successful in developing themselves and becoming leaders. The planetary impact of women's advancement goes far beyond women who are in traditional leadership roles or positions of power. Research has shown that investment in women's education and well-being, especially in the developing world, consistently produces lasting benefits for everyone. It leads to constructive change for the entire society.

This unprecedented advancement of women has also been a rapid climb up one of history's steepest learning curves. No wonder we're so tired! Most of our energy has been spent not advancing the ball, but by sheer necessity, adapting to the Hypermasculine world that has been in force.

It's clear that women's development and their empowerment is accelerating and we propose that this is *just the beginning of the wave of changes, of the emergence that will come.*

The Presence of our Past

Though the Mysterial Woman is tuned to our future, the past, as they say, is prologue. For the last 5000-plus years, human culture has been immersed in a dominantly Masculine worldview. By transcending that, she is accessing a new and emerging template of being that is more resonant with women.

Yet the Mysterial Woman is not throwing the baby out with the bathwater. Not at all. In fact, she includes the best, the most effective and life-affirming human inheritance from the past—the essential Masculine and Feminine capacities for human thriving. When these are skillfully united, they create a greater, more beautiful, more loving, wise, and powerful whole.

The rise of the Mysterial Woman, as we will show, will be a natural outcome of large-scale shifts in global consciousness and culture, arriving in waves. You can envision it this way: each new wave brings an entirely new and more complex way of making meaning of experience (a worldview), a new economic and technological system to sustain us, and a new form of leadership to govern and manage it. Each wave is not only more complex, but more fluid and capable than what came before. For example, the scientific and creative explosion of the European Renaissance signaled to Medieval society that a new wave of consciousness and culture was on the rise—the Modern worldview.

When a wave of consciousness and culture inevitably ebbs, its innate vitality and strategies for human flowering are spent. Many believe that we are experiencing something like this now, in the form of planetary despoiling and systemic breakdown that is spiraling out of control. To paraphrase Einstein, the level of thinking carried by the consciousness and culture that produced the intractable problems it faces just doesn't have the bandwidth to find their solutions. Then the next wave surges forward to engulf the previous, offering up the next needed solution or breakthrough for humanity's survival and flourishing.

Waves of Human Development

The story of our past, in a greatly distilled form, goes something like this:

Our human family began in the **1ˢᵗ "Archaic" wave** [7] of consciousness and culture, immersed in the quiet, nurturing Feminine essence[8] of the ancient nomadic foragers, dependent like infants on the bounty of Mother Nature. It was the beginning of the **First Feminine Epoch** when The Great Mother Goddess was worshipped. This was the time of informal clan elders, men and women, communing with the forces of nature for collective survival.

In the **2ⁿᵈ "Tribal" wave**, we bonded together in tight circles of safety and kinship, appeasing the spirits and ancestors. We settled down to plant and herd, providing our own sustenance where we wanted it. Men and women worked side-by- side, sharing power and responsibilities for the whole. A Chieftain became the mind and voice of the tribe.

In the **3ʳᵈ "Warrior" wave**, a heroic Masculine essence burst free of the stagnating confines of the Tribal circle, to conquer land and enslave others to plow large fields, store food, and build great empires. The **First Masculine Epoch** had begun, abruptly ending

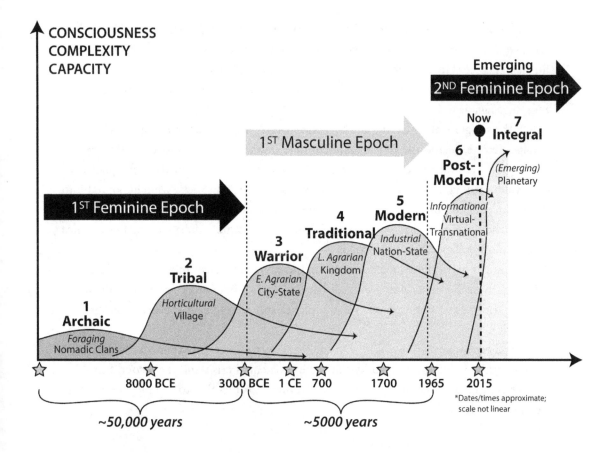

the prevailing Feminine epoch.[9] Fierce god-like emperors had unlimited power. To keep accounts, men learned to read and write. Brute labor often meant miscarriage, so women were confined to the home, bearing the children needed for the empire.

In the **4th "Traditional" wave**, this brutal world was stabilized and organized with a new, more paternal Masculine essence of law and order. The over-reaching Roman Empire collapsed under its own weight, and orderly Medieval society arose after the reboot of a long quiet Dark Age. We looked to the One Right Way of faith and religion under one almighty Father God, more just and powerful than any emperor. Bloodline Monarchs connected to religion enforced the rule of law. Women were still at home, kept under wraps.

In the **5th "Modern" wave**, our rational mind lit up like a torch, and strained against these rigid limits. It perceived that we were masters of our own destiny and all beings were created equal. The 5th wave's fierce yet organizing Masculine essence radiated across the planet like a firestorm, as science, technology, democracy, and commerce created wealth and freedom, as well as the means to exploit and destroy the planet. Governance shifted to term-limited executives chosen by mass election, subject to removal for malfeasance. Dependence on brute labor diminished. Toward the latter part of this wave, women finally emerged from the home, got educated, and became engaged citizens once again.

The social revolutions of the **6th "Postmodern" wave** brought a surge of rebellious, young, creative, relational, and sexual Feminine essence. **The Second Feminine Epoch** had begun. Because an overwhelming Masculine epoch had prevailed on the planet for over five millennia, this dynamic Feminine essence came as a shock. Women poured into the workplace and positions of power, creating quite a stir. The world flattened out, linked up, gave the marginalized a voice and new rights, and became a global village. Governance became more collaborative and shared.

But this world remained contentious and divided, the consciousness and cultures inherited from the many past waves all battling each other into a standstill and worse. Women had gained some power, yet the planet still teetered on the brink of absolute destruction.

So here we are, still living within the breakup-shakeup early transition years of the Postmodern Revolution. The world remains in existential crisis and the second Feminine epoch has just barely begun to register. Clearly, there is something to complete here before we can catch the next wave.

What's Next?

So where are we going now? That is a question that we will be building up to through the course of this book, and will reveal in the final chapter on The Mysterial Future. Don't peek! It will make a lot more sense once you understand the pattern of The Mysterial Sequence.

After five millennia of immersion in Masculine essence, a full rebalancing with the Feminine essence is simply due. In the process of evolution, extremes build to tipping points. The way we project it will play out—based on our model—may surprise you.

You might have noticed that the waves seem to be getting shorter and shorter in duration. This is because we build upon what was learned in the past. Our capabilities keep increasing, our perspective keeps broadening, and thus change accelerates. Now, this of course could reach a point of absurdity . . . new waves of consciousness emerging within weeks, days, or hours. Sometime in the future, some other pattern will reveal itself.

What we can say now is that the revolutionary arrival of the current 6th wave will be followed with a time of consolidation and stabilization. New structures will begin to come into place to solidify our Postmodern culture and make it truly sustainable. The important point is that *women are natural leaders for this*. It is likely that within the next decade or so, we will begin to truly feel that the Second Feminine Epoch is underway.

Mysterial Women, we predict, will begin to arise as a force in society over the next twenty years, upgrading the way women live, love, and lead.

And if this unfolding story of humanity continues as it has, a 7th wave will begin to have influence sometime in this century. It is already showing up in certain "bleeding edges" of society, and in some highly developed individuals. And we can expect the 7th wave to also have a Feminine essence. This is where Mysterial Women are likely to play a pivotal role in the twenty-first century and beyond.

This wave, as you will see later in the book, will carry a different "frequency" from the Feminine essences of the past . . .

For now, we invite you to welcome discomfort and turn toward your suffering and longing as signals of an old world that is passing away, and a new world that is on its way.

And know that it is one in which you belong and have a very important role to play.

Chapter 2

THE MYSTERIAL SEQUENCE—
Liberating Your Archetypal Source Code

In order to change an existing paradigm you do not struggle to try and change the problematic model. You create a new model and make the old one obsolete.

—Buckminster Fuller

I magine yourself right in the sweet spot of the evolutionary wave as it moves forward. You are no longer caught in the churn and tumble of the surf as it hits the beach. Although everything is not perfect you are at peace inside, resting into a deep knowing that you are enough just as you are and that you belong here on Earth. You have the capacities that are needed to meet the challenges of the world the way it is today and to shape the new world to come. Yes, you have the inner operating system that is finally a match for the challenges of life in the twenty-first century.

Nearly every woman we speak with resonates with the idea of needing an upgrade to her *inner operating system*. So many of us feel the gap between our changing inner world and the ability to consistently and sustainably show up in the world in ways that are fulfilling, creative, and effective. Adding some new software, such as an MBA, a new relationship, or a new diet, just doesn't fix the problem—and soon enough our system crashes again.

Yet still we try for the quick fix to make the pain and suffering go away, hoping this time things will be different. If only we had more passion, luck, hard work and discipline we could reach the sun and really succeed and be the superwoman we know lives inside of us. This is the *up and out* approach so valued by the Hypermasculine world.

There is another—though counterintuitive—path to achieve takeoff in our lives. It is **down and in**. After decades of experience guiding hundreds of women, we know that the transformational path that delivers lasting life changes requires us to go toward what's under the surface of our conscious minds in order to tap our hidden potential. The transformation that can result from such deep diving does not happen overnight. It takes time and it takes some effort, but the rewards—sustainable and enlivened Mysterial ways of being in the world—are more than worth it!

An Elegant Way

So how then do we do this upgrade? The Mysterial Sequence is our elegant and efficient pathway that unblocks Mysterial potentiality. We invite you to come with us as we show you a preview of the transformational journey.

The Mysterial Sequence is a guiding series of steps that turn on the developmental tap again. Like a plant that unfolds from seed, to shoot, to leaves and flowers, a woman is able to develop in an organic process that unfolds in identifiable stages, each more complex than the next. These stages build upon one another and, as you will see, none can be skipped.

The order of the sequence isn't arbitrary either. It harmonically mirrors the natural order of the Masculine and Feminine waves, described in the last chapter, which emerged in human consciousness and culture as we evolved over thousands of years.

And perhaps most importantly, The Mysterial Sequence is specifically designed to address the unique nature of a *woman's* developmental unfolding, and to *redress* wounding that occurred at various stages of our emergence into womanhood as we tried to fit into a Hypermasculine culture.[1] As you move through the Sequence today as an adult woman you can integrate those aspects of yourself that have remained stalled or repressed. In doing so, you open the channel for a radically new way of being and doing to emerge—The Way of the Mysterial Woman.

Wrestling with the Feminine/Yin and Masculine/Yang Forces

When we first set out to discover a new pathway of wholeness for women, we knew we would need to grapple with an embodied understanding of the Feminine and Masculine forces that shaped us, and women in general. This turned out to be a much bigger exploration than we ever imagined. It took us twelve years of working together in intensive trial and error research and over seventy-five combined years of wrestling with the Feminine and Masculine forces in our own lives, oscillating wildly back and forth between the two, until we were ripe for this discovery.

As our work with women developed, an understanding of the forces of the Feminine/Masculine shifted dramatically. The popular idea of a single polarity between the more mothering qualities of the Feminine, and the more heroic qualities of the Masculine, was just no longer adequate to explain what we were experiencing.

Something else was going on that was more complex than this.

If you look at this ancient Yin Yang symbol it is obvious that Yin and Yang are not just polar opposites. There is a point of light, Yang, within the dark Yin and a point of dark, Yin, within the light of Yang. This suggests that perhaps Yin and Yang are distinct and yet cross-pollinating energies.

Neither force is superior to the other; they coexist within and surround each other. The so-called "opposite" energies are in fact present and moving within each other all the time.[2] What we were encountering in our work with women was actually this dual nature of the Yin and Yang forces themselves. Each one had a more static and a more dynamic aspect.[3]

We called the more static aspect of each Yin and Yang force "Vessel" to represent the qualities of holding and containment. We named the more dynamic aspect "Flame" as a way to capture the active, outward, and fiery elements of this energy.

Instead of only two, we now recognized four separate Yin and Yang forces—each one representing polar opposites within the Masculine and Feminine.

1. **Vessel Yin**—Like a circle[4] this essence surrounds, contains, and gestates. Think of it as a kind of Yin Yin—a deeply Feminine Force.
2. **Flame Yang**—This essence with its forward movement and directional energy is like an arrow tracking toward its target. Think of it as a kind of Yang Yang—a deeply Masculine Force.
3. **Vessel Yang**—Like a cross this essence has the vertical reach of vision and horizontal stabilizing of structure. Think of this as a Yang essence with static Yin shading.
4. **Flame Yin**—This lights up as a kind of spiral force that takes things to

another level, outside the box, breaking through to something new. Here we have a Yin essence tinted with a dynamic Yang energy.

This expanded understanding of Yin and Yang was a breakthrough in creating The Mysterial Sequence. We weren't the only ones to see this, of course.[5] But seeing these four forces and their relationship to one another gave us very clear steps on the developmental pathway we were constructing.

Once we came to this more complete understanding of Masculine and Feminine forces, we realized that as we move from girlhood into womanhood we encounter each of these four Yin and Yang forces in a very specific order. We also saw that our families of origin, as well as our own inner predispositions and the cultural conditioning around us, determines the relationship we have with each of these four forces.

The real rocket power boost came, however, when we started to see how these four Yin and Yang forces seemed to line up with five primary **archetypes**. Putting all this together became the foundation of the archetypal source code of The Mysterial Sequence.

Engaging Your Archetypal Source Code

Existing in the unconscious, and being universal and innate (across all cultures and ages), the existence and influence of archetypes is detected through myths, symbols, rituals, images, dreams, and instincts. In fact, archetypes are probably constructed from instinctual patterns inherited genetically throughout the trajectory of our evolution as a species.[6]

At each successive stage of development throughout life there is a particular archetype or set of archetypes that comes online, around which the sense of self is then patterned. Though we may not always see or recognize their influence, archetypal energies are coded into the structure of our psyches as we develop.

We discovered that each of the four Yin and Yang forces align with one of five primary archetypes: *The Mother, The Hero, The Father, The Maiden,* and *The Crone*. And that they come online in our development from girlhood through to maturity, in that order.

Women's Archetypal Source Code

You'll see that the final archetype of *The Crone* brings together both Vessel and Flame Yin as well as having access to the Yang essences—an exciting and fully empowered integration that you'll learn more about later.

Yin–Yang Essence	Primary Archetype
Vessel Yin	The Mother
Flame Yang	The Hero
Vessel Yang	The Father
Flame Yin	The Maiden
Vessel and Flame Yin (Accessing Yang)	The Crone

Not only do these archetypes emerge sequentially in an individual woman's developmental unfolding, but our research also offered another fascinating insight.

Each of the archetypes also emerged in the same sequence in our collective consciousness at various turning points in history. They emerged organically and by necessity as an evolutionary response to the ever more challenging problems and opportunities of existence.

Remember when we discussed the waves of human development in Chapter One? Take a look now at this chart and notice the order in which these archetypes emerged and intersected with these waves.

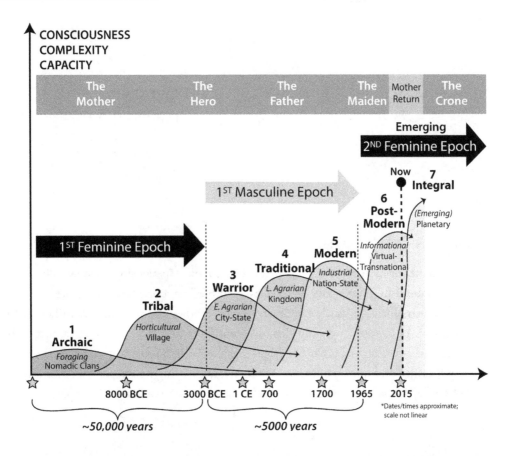

Putting It All Together—A Woman's Developmental Journey

Since The Mysterial Sequence takes you back over the developmental territory you went through from childhood into womanhood, let's begin then with a look at how these Yin and Yang forces and their archetypal allies come online as we mature.

Although the developmental process of every individual woman is remarkably complex and unique, at a very high level the following sequence is collectively shared.

The First Yin-Yang Polarity

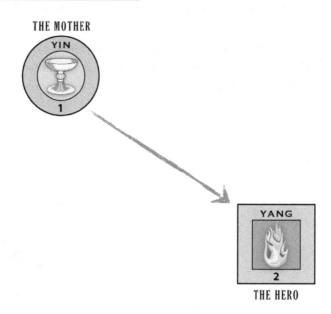

VESSEL YIN—THE MOTHER

We all begin in our mother's womb, connected to her and experiencing oneness. While boys feel an early need to differentiate themselves as "other," we don't because we are the same gender as our mothers. In fact, we are merged with mother and see ourselves in her as *The Mother* archetype engages. As young girls this is our first experience of the static aspect of the Feminine—what we call Vessel Yin. We begin engaging with this force through the experience of being breastfed and nurtured by our mother figures, playing house, playing "mommy" to our dolls or toy figures, and being contained by the protective structures of our parents.

At a collective level The Mother Archetype first emerged in consciousness in our most distant pre-historic hunting and foraging past: the time of Archaic culture.

FLAME YANG—THE HERO

Once more advanced motor skills and cognitive functions are established, the dynamic Masculine or Flame Yang archetype of *The Hero* begins to stir in the unconscious of our young-girl selves. At this point in the sequence there is a natural impulse for separation and differentiation away from the all-encompassing static nature of Vessel Yin. A new sense of autonomy emerges as we learn to do things on our own and experiment with our capacity for risk taking, focusing, goal setting, and action. Often this force shows itself through tomboy adventures, a passion for horses, setting and achieving academic goals, and an impulse to push away from our mother figures.

At the collective level The Hero archetype emerged when city-states and agriculture started to rise in the conquering, slave-taking time of *Warrior* culture.

The Second Yin-Yang Polarity

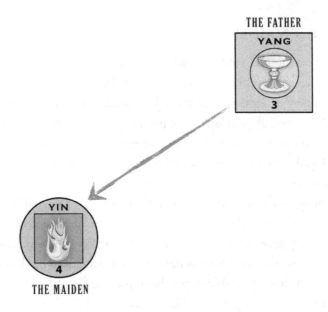

VESSEL YANG—THE FATHER

The next developmental move for women takes us to the second polarity to cultivate a Masculine Vessel Yang energy, a more static form of Yang. In the Masculine model of the hero's journey this movement from the first polarity to the second is the "fiery initiation" or "road of trials" that supposedly prepares us to participate within the cultural paradigm of success.

This essence manifests when we begin to build the structures of an adult life by making our place in the social order. For women this has often meant moving through the hierarchies of academia and/or working hard to gain entry into the primarily Masculine-dominated and often patriarchal structures of society.

The archetype at the center of Vessel Yang is *The Father*. When constellated in a healthy way, The Father empowers us to find our place in society, to be steadfast and patient, to establish theories of truth about the world, to create order and structure, and to learn how to work with the rules and systems in our lives. As this force gathers strength, we often enter into the structure of a committed relationship, set up homes, build our careers, have children, and create the solid foundations for building a successful life.

The Father archetype emerged in collective consciousness with the civilizing rise of monotheism, monarchy, and Traditional culture, eventually giving birth to *Modern* scientific culture.

FLAME YIN—THE MAIDEN

It can be both liberating and confusing when the dynamic Feminine Flame Yin impulse lights up in a woman at the other end of this second polarity. It can feel like betrayal to even consider the possibility of breaking free from the well-earned inner and outer structures of Vessel Yang. This is especially true given the predominantly patriarchal patterns that often still govern our worldview. We have come to understand that this Yin impulse is actually a naturally occurring, developmentally appropriate, transformative longing to shake things up and reinvent ourselves.

Unfortunately, without a road map and guidance, it can manifest destructively, compelling us obsessively to reject the world in which we have scarcely found our place. We might impulsively leave a job, a marriage, even our family, community, or country. Conversely, because the potential for loss of all we have worked so hard to achieve feels so frightening, we might just try to shut down the impulse and suffer in silence.

But rather than something to fear, this impulse toward the expression of our dynamic Yin essence is a beautiful evolutionary opening. It is arising inside us, not to destroy our lives or strand us in a dead end, but to open us up to a world that is way beyond anything we can now even imagine. This dynamic aspect of our Yin nature is calling us to shake things up: "Wake up, remember who you are!" We hear it, intensely, right in our bodies as it tries to get our attention often through illness, anxiety, or depression.

The archetypal energy igniting this new impulse is ***The Maiden.*** In its healthy expression it carries with it the transformative awakening of imagination and spontaneity. It is the playful, sensual and sexual, rebellious, inchoate and wild part of ourselves that welcomes change, awakens our joy, and liberates our passion.

The Maiden archetype emerged recently in collective consciousness with the social revolutions of the 1960s, the massively connected Information Age, and the rise of **Post-Modern** culture. No wonder we are feeling her so strongly!

The Third Yin-Yang Force

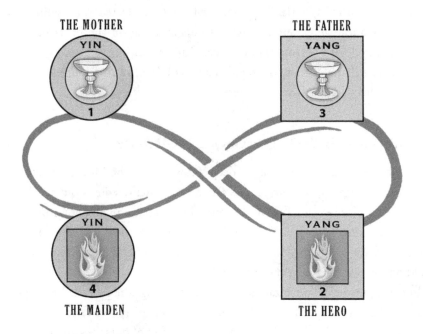

RETURN TO VESSEL YIN—THE MOTHER

Rather than jump to a new archetype, we have come to believe that the next stage of a woman's development is to return full circle back to The Mother. Only, this return visit looks very different from the first journey through this archetype. Having made it this far through all of the previous archetypal journeys, a new sense of self has begun to emerge. The next developmental move is to integrate this new consciousness into a consolidated sense of self that transcends and includes who we were before.

It is a hard-earned arrival when we make it back again to the Vessel Yin essence and The Mother archetype where we began our life journey. At this point there is a profound relaxation into the ground of being and the emergence of a deep care for others and the world around. We are no longer fused with The Mother energy or pushing away from it. And we now have access to all the other Yin and Yang forces, liberating the flow of our essence between the polarities as the image above illustrates.

There is little guidance in our culture to welcome this evolution of the self and even less to reorient us in the world following the deep changes this journey brings about. We are at the pioneering edge of evolution. Now that we have access to all of the Yin and Yang essences, with the right guidance over time, eventually a signal is sent to the next archetypal force within the psyche.

This step in The Mysterial Sequence is where we, collectively, are going now in the great arc of historical time—grounding and integrating all of the breakthroughs of the recent cultural cycle of Dynamic Yin essence. Our next task is to actually create the systems and policies that will allow the rapid changes of The Information Age to be installed sustainably in the infrastructures of society.

VESSEL AND FLAME YIN—THE CRONE LIGHTS UP

Once there has been time to soak in the deep Yin waters of The Mother, it is the final and often unacknowledged archetype of **The Crone** that finally comes online. As the third force of the Feminine beyond The Mother and The Maiden, this archetype brings together and synthesizes Vessel and Flame Yin. And because of this, she is also able to be a mediating force for Flame and Vessel Yang. She is like the Greek goddess Hekate in the days of old, holding the two torches at the crossroads.

In a woman's developmental path, the Crone brings the potential for truth telling, wisdom, synthesizing, fierceness, and compassion born of her suffering and experience. With this archetype available we know when to take care of ourselves and others, when to pulse forward with dynamic actions, when to slow down and build containing structures, and when to break those structures apart to allow new growth.

The Crone, or mystical wise woman, is the latest of the primary archetypes to fully emerge in human culture and consciousness. This powerful and complex energetic pattern has only recently shaped human awareness in recognizable numbers, and it could begin to

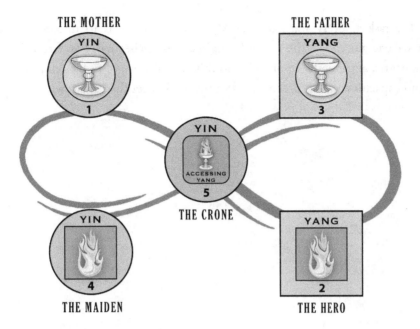

impact culture substantially within the next ten years. A simpler predecessor of The Crone was recognized in ancient times, often as a medicine woman or shaman. With the rise of Traditional and Modern cultures, that early Crone was demonized as a witch and brutally burned out of history.

The Pathway of The Mysterial Sequence

Now you have seen the map of a woman's developmental journey through the archetypes. Like us, perhaps you too have stumbled your way along in life, bumping into these Yin and Yang forces without much sense of what was happening. The cultural and family of origin norms tended to blunt the expression of our natural Yin and Yang essences, or exaggerate or distort them. Today we are awakening our capacity to *consciously* dance with these two great forces inside ourselves and in the larger world, for the first time in our 4.5 billion year history. No small feat!

To do this, we must now *deliberately* go back through the Sequence and liberate healthy access to each of the Yin and Yang forces.

This is the core of The Mysterial Sequence. We move from The Mother to The Hero, then from The Father to The Maiden, and back to The Mother before the final step forward to the Crone, the last gateway leading to the emergence of the Mysterial Woman.

The task at every stage of The Mysterial Sequence is to unblock the healthy archetypal energies so that the Yin and Yang essences can begin to flow freely through our bodies, hearts, and minds. In order to do this crucial work of unblocking the potential gifts and capacities of each archetype, we must now meet their shadows.

Chapter 3

UNBLOCKING THE CHANNEL—
Facing the Archetypal Shadows

There is a vitality, a life force, an energy, a quickening that is translated through you into action, and because there is only one of you in all of time, this expression is unique. And if you block it, it will never exist through any other medium, and be lost. The world will not have it.

It is not your business to determine how good it is, nor how valuable, nor how it compares with other expressions. It is your business to keep it yours, clearly and directly, to keep the channel open.

—Martha Graham

If you are like us, and the many other women we know and have worked with, then you too have probably noticed that the channel of your vitality, life force, and unique expression is not always open. So what blocks the flow? While there are aspects of your Yin and Yang nature that are conscious and integrated into your ego structure in healthy ways, there are also unconscious aspects that erupt in random ways. When they do, they sabotage the flow of your true self: they block the channel.

It was Carl Jung who first used the term **shadow** to describe these parts of the self that are hidden from conscious view and are not seen as an aspect of who you are.[1] As you learned that certain aspects of your nature were not acceptable to those around you, you disowned them. Since you looked to those people for love, safety, and belonging, you did what any wise child would do…you hid those aspects of yourself away by removing them from your conscious awareness. These parts of yourself, therefore, stopped developing and stayed frozen in time, never getting a chance to grow up. What should have been your shining (self-esteem, joy, wisdom etc.) became your shadows. And your gnarly bits too (fear, anger, shame, etc.) got disowned and stowed away down in the dark, only to erupt in unpredictable, self-sabotaging ways.

Perhaps a sibling was threatened by you being too extroverted or teased you for crying. Maybe your mother punished you for showing anger. Perhaps you were laughed at for wanting attention or acting proud of yourself or standing out in a peer group. Bit by bit, over those formative years, you quietly moved aspects of your core nature into the shadow bag, down in the dark cave of the unconscious.

Unfortunately, while these shadows became hidden and forgotten by your conscious mind, they did not go away. Quite the opposite! The longer they have remained split off and dissociated from your conscious awareness, the stronger they have become.

"Everyone carries a shadow," Jung wrote, "and the less it is embodied in the individual's conscious life, the blacker and denser it is."

You may have noticed that certain unpleasant situations seem to recur over and over—the unreliable partners, the late nights at the computer, repetitive conflicts, midnight ice cream, or not being recognized for your contributions. Shadow material acts like a powerful gravitational force in our psyches, trapping our life energy into unproductive and endless orbits around the same planets. These unhappy dramas will replay again and again until we interrupt their inexorable gravitational pull and boost ourselves into a different orbit, or perhaps even, a different universe.

Here's the tricky part of working with that shadow material: you cannot look directly at it. Why? Because it exists in your unconscious only. So, how do you see something that can't be seen? One powerful way is to work with archetypes: they are energetic patterns that bridge between the unconscious and the conscious mind.

Archetypal Shadows of The Mysterial Sequence

The Mysterial Sequence brings this understanding of archetypes and shadows together. As you move through the Sequence, the shadows are identified, experienced, and the Yin or Yang energies held there in the split-off parts become available. In essence you re-member yourself: you welcome all of yourself home.

As we worked with these archetypes more deeply, we found that each of the archetypal energies in The Mysterial Sequence has two distinct shadow expressions.[2] If we can get the love, safety, and belonging that we are looking for by over-identifying with one particular archetype, then this identification takes on an "active" shadow form. This then becomes a template pattern for our sense of self. We begin to merge our developing sense of identity with that archetype. This is a bit like plugging into a one-thousand-watt circuit. Once the ego becomes consumed by a powerful archetypal energy it is very difficult to unplug.

If, on the other hand, an archetype seems too threatening for us to have contact with it, then a "passive" shadow develops. In this case, the ego is constructed with a limited conscious relationship to this primal force. And, as we will see, it often gets projected out onto others.

We also discovered that at the core of each shadow expression of our archetypal sequence is an embodied *limiting belief* around which our identity has formed. As the shadows are cleared and the healthy archetype is cultivated a *liberating belief* that is more aligned with our Mysterial nature comes online.

The Activations and Initiations of The Mysterial Sequence

So now that you have all the building blocks of The Mysterial Sequence, let's go through an overview of what happens step by step. We will go into much more depth about each of the steps of the Sequence and how to work with clearing and cultivating the archetypes in Part II of the book.

As we showed you in the previous chapter, a woman's developmental journey takes us through five primary archetypes. The Mysterial Sequence takes us through this same developmental journey, step by step, clearing the shadows of each archetype so that the healthy capacities can be cultivated. Once this shadow clearing has been done and the capacities are developed we call it an Activation, as the healthy archetypal force becomes *activated* in the psyche. As soon as the archetypal energy has been activated it operates like a powerful magnet and over time will continue to draw more and more of your Yin or Yang essence into expression.

Every time you activate the Yin and Yang essences that are connected in an archetypal polarity, such as activating The Mother (Vessel Yin) and then the opposite energy of The Hero (Flame Yang), a quantum force kicks in that is greater than either of the individual essences themselves. And once you activate The Crone and an Inner Sacred Union takes place, the Mysterial Woman in her fullness begins to appear.

We call these quantum leaps **Initiations,** and we actually pause in The Mysterial Sequence each time this happens. These Initiations are a way of recognizing what you have left behind and integrating all the changes that have taken place so that you can step forward into the next phase of your Mysterial emergence.

There are actually *three* of these powerful Initiations that take place in The Mysterial Sequence:

FIRST INITIATION: **Empowered Radiant Presence** (Vessel Yin and Flame Yang)
SECOND INITIATION: **Joyful True Authority** (Vessel Yang and Flame Yin)
THIRD INITIATION: **Authentic Mysterial Emergence** (Vessel and Flame Yin and Yang + Sacred Union)

Don't worry about trying to remember all of this now. In Part II you will have a chance to immerse yourself deeply in all the elements of The Mysterial Sequence and the whole picture will naturally come into focus.

The Mysterial Sequence

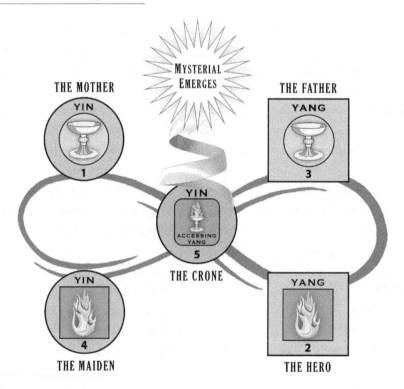

Archetypal Shadows and Beliefs

Now that you've been introduced to all the steps of the Sequence, let's meet the archetypal shadows and their limiting *and* liberating beliefs.

ACTIVATION 1: CULTIVATING THE MOTHER

Clearing The Devourer and The Neglector Shadows. Just like our development through the life cycle, we begin our Mysterial Sequence with cultivating The Mother. And the first step is clearing the shadows. For most of the women we have worked with their relationship to The Mother archetype is fragmented, outdated, and expressed in two primary shadows.

When you are over-identified with The Mother archetype, to the point that it becomes destructive, you are in the grips of an active shadow: **The Devourer**. This manifests as a tendency toward a kind of devouring, smothering, or overprotective way of being.

When you are under-identified, or unable to access The Mother archetype, then you are in the clutches of **The Neglector,** a passive shadow, which is experienced as a difficulty to receive, a kind of disembodied rigidity, and a tendency to neglect yourself and others.

Most of us will be able to relate to both poles of the shadow in different areas of our lives, though one of them usually tends to be more dominant as our more habitual way of being. For example, you could be The Neglector with your colleagues at work and with yourself but have Devourer tendencies with your children, or even your pets.

The embodied *limiting belief* that is a core driving force of both of these shadows is: *"I am not enough."*

This belief lies deep in the cellular memory not only of our personal lives and how we experience our worth, but also in our collective memory as women whose deep Yin value has been rejected for millennia.

When you liberate The Mother archetype from these shadows, Vessel Yin (static, Feminine) opens like a beautiful lotus flower and a quality of Radiant Presence naturally emerges. The *liberating belief* is: *"I am enough just as I am."*

This connects you with the deep ground of your being and drops you into an unshakeable sense of your own worth and sufficiency.

You embrace your body with tender compassion and nourish it with healthy food, adequate rest, and exercise. You honor your needs and take care of them as well as you do the needs of others. Now you really understand what it means to consciously hold a space in which something can move from conception through maturation to birth. When

Radiant Presence emerges you have an attractive quality that has nothing to do with any outer standards of beauty. People simply want to be around your fully embodied presence.

ACTIVATION 2: IGNITING THE HERO

Clearing The Dominator and The Capitulator Shadows. Each of us had our own early experiences of The Hero, first observing this archetype in action through our parents. These were not always good examples of a healthy Hero. Far too often the *limiting belief* of The Hero—*"I have to do, to be of value"*—was the internalized and unconscious mantra that arose in response to the conditioning from our family and continues to be a driving force in cultural models around the world. The Hypermasculine belief that it is only our "doing" that establishes our value leads us all into the shadows of The Hero.

The *active shadow* energy of The Hero manifests as **The Dominator**. When The Dominator is in charge, you are driven by an unconscious force that does not know when to stop! You will do whatever it takes to achieve goals, no matter what the cost to yourself or others. When the *passive shadow* of **The Capitulator** is in expression, you tend to give up, blame others for your inability to act, or rationalize with excuses when things get tough. The Capitulator rejects any connection with this powerful Hero energy and projects it onto others with both envy and resentment.

When the shadow energy is retrieved, the healthy Hero force becomes available. This liberating Flame Yang energy (dynamic Masculine), when properly contained, opens you into a whole new level of productivity, accomplishment, agency, and grounded mutuality in your relationships. When a compelling goal actually engages your heart, a mysterious internal drive turns on and fills you with the energy, confidence, discipline, and mental clarity you need to take appropriate risks and engage new ways of being and doing that align you with your intention.

You become able to pierce through complex issues and make difficult decisions in ways you hadn't before. In relationships, you become more able to know and value what you feel, sense, and think, while simultaneously being differentiated enough to be open to the experience of others.

With The Mother archetype forming the ground of your Feminine self-esteem, you can handle the fiery energy of The Hero and discover that right action comes naturally. When the embodied *liberating belief* of The Hero is operating—*"I am empowered to do what is mine to do"*— you know what is yours to do and what is not, and you are able to do it in a way that is powerful, sustainable, and effective.

You ignite ***Empowered Action.***

First Initiation: Empowered Radiant Presence—Uniting Vessel Yin and Flame Yang

The deep psychosomatic work of liberating the first Yin-Yang polarity is an enormous accomplishment. Once this channel is open it takes a period of time to flush out all the old ways of being and habits of behavior that were constructed over a lifetime. But with self-awareness and practice a new and very *liberating belief* of this Mother-Hero polarity fuels the engine of your inner operating system: *"I am enough just as I am and empowered to do what is mine to do."*

You rest now on the solid ground of being and know your value. You take care of yourself and others in equal measure. You source your actions with confidence, knowing when to pulse forward with goals and tasks and when to rest and reflect. You become the self-authoring force of your own life story.

ACTIVATION 3: ESTABLISHING THE FATHER

Clearing The Judge and The Outsider Shadows. Having completed the first two initiations that opened the Mother-Hero polarity, we move now to the second polarity and our Vessel Yang (static Masculine) nature. This shift takes us from the dynamic individualism of The Hero into the cultivation of the healthy Father archetype, establishing a sense of *True Authority* that is based on a solid platform of self-confidence.

The majority of our corporations and institutions and the concept of leadership itself were constructed around the paradigm of The Father. Indeed this worldview is the central archetype of the patriarchy. The Father knows best, and leads the hierarchy of power and control, shaping the rules of order that you need to obey if you are going to be taken care of and successful. This style of leadership was effective for many years and was simply the norm until only the last few decades when new organizational models started springing up to meet the challenges of today's constantly changing, interconnected global reality.

The *limiting belief* of The Father, *"I do not belong,"* has worked its way into women's psyches for generations. We tried hard to fit into a world that didn't seem to want us and shape-shifted ourselves in dangerous ways that undermined our own innate power and eclipsed our authentic expression.

With the *active shadow* of **The Judge** in control you become rigid, judgmental, overly structured, and rule-bound. To try to fit in and belong you align yourself with the powers that be, regardless of the cost. Identification with the *passive shadow* of **The Outsider** is characterized by an inability to create order or build systems and structures that could support the growth of your creative contribution in the world. You look for father figures to take care of you or to rebel against.

As you clear the shadows and establish a healthy relationship with The Father within, you develop the capacity for clear analysis, the creation of order inside and out. You are able to build reliable systems to provide a solid and enduring foundation for a life of substance and contribution. You honor the gifts and beauty of others and the world around you, recognizing that you are part of a diverse and interconnected ecosphere.

In the bedrock of your being, the *liberating belief*, *"I am at home in myself and naturally belong,"* profoundly changes the way in which you are able to show up in the world. The unshakeable True Authority that emerges from the connection to the deep ground of your own being becomes a signature of your expression.

ACTIVATION 4: LIBERATING THE MAIDEN

Clearing The Bohemian and The Puritan Shadows. Having built a stable foundation and healthy structures in your life with The Father, you are now able to engage the archetype of The Maiden and gain access to the wild, exciting, and sometimes-chaotic force of Flame Yin (dynamic Feminine). When balanced with the static nature of our True Authority at the opposite end of the polarity, this force gives us access to our ***Joyful Creativity***.

Yet for many women this is an elusive quest. We learned how to dial down our passion and unique creative expression in order to fit into a patriarchal world pattern. And now we feel trapped inside the structures that we worked so hard to build and which were supposed to bring us success and fulfillment. The *limiting belief*, *"I am not free to express myself fully,"* proved itself to be true far too often.

For some of us this repression is just too much and we dive into the *active shadow* of **The Bohemian**. While exciting in the moment, ultimately it leads to excessive forcing, distraction, thrill-seeking, and an inability to stay with the challenges of transformation and of life. For others, the fiery Feminine force of The Maiden seems way too dangerous and they align with the *passive shadow* of **The Puritan.** In the grip of this shadow there is a deep fear of change, a puritanical rigidity, insecurity, and a tendency to hold onto things far longer than you should.

As the split off shadow material becomes available to you, The Maiden archetype draws you into your deep intuition and the raw life energy that allows you to innovate and set off on bold adventures. You challenge your old ways of thinking and liberate yourself and others from unnecessary constrictions. You know how to go with the flow of life, and spontaneously shift directions when needed. Play becomes just as important as work and you stop taking yourself and life so seriously. Real intimacy opens up with others as you liberate your sexual and heart energy, easily drawing others into a dance of mutuality.

The *liberating belief*—*"I am free to express my true nature"*—gives you an unimaginable freedom to be yourself and to discover that Joyful Creativity is actually your birthright.

Second Initiation: Joyful True Authority—Uniting Vessel Yang and Flame Yin

With the second Yin-Yang polarity now open and connected to the first polarity there is a quantum shift in your experience. The *liberating belief—"I am at home in myself and naturally belong, free to express my true nature"*—opens up a whole new range of possibility.

Now you are able to confidently stand in your own true authority within society and yet you are not held hostage by the guiding structures of the patriarchal pattern. You can build the healthy structures of an adult life so that things can grow and build without cutting off your passionate life force. You can more systematically access your intuition to be innovative in grounded and productive ways. You are able to co-create with others in ways that you never imagined possible. You are simply more able to experience the joy of your unique expression making a difference in the world.

ACTIVATION 5: SUMMONING THE CRONE

Clearing The Hag and The Denier Shadows. This marks a significant shift point in The Mysterial Sequence. You have awakened The Mother archetype within so that you can count on your grounded *Radiant Presence* to sustain yourself and others in a field of love. You have brought your own Hero onto the field so that you are able to perform bold and *Empowered Actions*. This then awakened The Father archetype, enabling you to navigate the halls of power and build the inner and outer *True Authority* necessary to thrive there. You have reclaimed The Maiden and released your *Joyful Creativity*, reconnecting with your spontaneous, catalytic nature.

With the two Yin-Yang polarities now open there is a necessary transition from the dynamic energy of The Maiden back to the containing energy of The Mother archetype.

You return home again but with a very different and expanded sense of yourself and the world. This is a significant step forward in your life journey.

And it prepares you for the next big evolutionary leap ahead.

Now you are ready to invite the wise, shape-shifting part of yourself to come forward. When The Crone archetype enters the equation, the fullness of the Yin triad of Mother, Maiden, and Crone is complete. With this force you can now not only access the fullness of Yin, but also reach across the polarities to engage the Yang forces. You summon an *Alchemical Authenticity,* becoming the complex, synthesizing, catalytic woman so needed in the world today.

But this archetypal energy is like the new kid on the block and we don't really know what to do with it. Men and women alike have been afraid of the transformative power of The Crone and throughout history she was demonized and rejected time and time again. The *limiting belief* that has formed around this forgotten archetype is deep in the feminine psyche: *"I don't have enough knowledge, connections, or influence."*

When there is an over-identification with The Crone archetype the *active shadow* of **The Hag** takes over. You use your different ways of knowing to gather information as a source of ego-centered power, and then deliver your wisdom in a mean-spirited truth telling way. Underdevelopment of The Crone energy leads women into the *passive shadow* of **The Denier**. You doubt yourself constantly, feeling confused and powerless, deferring to everyone else to tell you the truth about what is going on.

When the light of your conscious awareness burns through these shadows the healthy Crone begins to gather strength and substance in your psyche. You can now hold seeming opposites without contradiction. What no longer serves you can be cut away with compassion, or allowed to dissolve. Seeing patterns in the chaos, you can pierce through confusion, drawing upon all sources of knowing whether conventional or not. Yet, you can also stay with the not knowing, the Mystery, if that is what is called for. You are a catalytic force, able to stand at the crossroads, synthesize complexity and bridge between extremely divergent people, worlds, and ideas so that something new and better can arise.

Deep in the foundation of your being the *liberating belief, "I am an evolving source of Wisdom, Love, and Power,"* resonates as true. This last initiation in the Sequence brings a great synthesizing force in the psyche that is now able to guide and direct the other archetypal forces—knowing when to be still and rest, when to pulse forward into action, when to build and structure, when to break apart and innovate, and when to turn up the heat and let things transform. You have an **Alchemical Authenticity** that makes you an agent of change simply by being yourself.

Third Initiation: Authentic Mysterial Emergence— Uniting Vessel and Flame Yin and Yang in Sacred Union

When The Crone is in place the fullness of the Yin forces begin to flow easily with the fullness of the Yang forces and an exquisite inner union takes place, giving birth with time to the fullness of your Mysterial nature.

With the barriers now removed and the channel open, the inner upgrade happens with intention, practice, and support. You begin to develop the integral capacities of a Mysterial woman who naturally leads. You will be able to explore The Way of the Mysterial Woman more fully in Part III of the book.

So that completes the Sequence. Now that you have taken a tour through the map of The Mysterial Sequence, let's take a look under the hood of the transformative vehicle that is going to take you on the journey.

Chapter Four

THE MYSTERIAL CHANGE PROCESS—
Technology of Transformation

Your task is not to seek love, but merely to seek and find all the barriers within yourself that you have built against it.

—Rumi

Throughout history there have been many ways and means for self-transformation. In today's postmodern, hyper-connected world those ways and means have multiplied into a vast and often perplexing smorgasbord of offers and methods. If you are reading this book, you've probably been to the buffet line a few times yourself.

Yet nature loves simplicity, and will choose the path of least resistance. In Chapter 1 we proposed that the Mysterial Woman had made an *elegant* upgrade—meaning that she has access to the most essential set of Feminine and Masculine capacities that could meet the challenges and opportunities of this time with grace and ease.

And this is only possible, as we described in Chapter 3, if we first reclaim the parts of ourselves that have slipped into the active and passive shadows of the archetypes— Shadow work.

Before you enter The Mysterial Sequence and liberate your healthy Yin and Yang energies, we want to introduce our core transformational "technology" that you will use to efficiently accomplish this archetypal shadow work: **The Mysterial Change Process.**

But first, you may be wondering why all this Shadow work is so crucial.

The shadows have a tremendous grip on our life experience, driving us relentlessly from the depths of the unconscious. Since they are mostly formed when we are young, they become built into the very fabric of our identity. Not only do they start to shape unconscious (and thus unquestioned) limiting beliefs about ourselves, they dramatically limit our behaviors and emotional responses to life. It's as if we are wearing blinders, yoked to a heavy wagon of compulsion moving along deeply rutted tracks of habit, urged ahead by the unseen driver's whip. We respond to life with conditioned, almost robotic reflexes that aren't in our best interest. And sometimes even harm those around us.

If left in shadow, these conditioned ways of being will remain so familiar, so habitual, and so dominant they have the power to hold us back. They are the unconscious reins and whips that yank us back to the same old patterns and make us feel discouraged and frustrated when it comes to trying to change. Such powerful forces far outstrip the well-intentioned but transient effects of a weekend workshop or a thirty-day self-improvement plan. When we are in the grip of these conditioned reflexes it can feel like lasting change is impossible.

To shift this and begin to liberate yourself from shadow reflexes and habits, you must do something that often seems counter-intuitive—the exact opposite of how most of us have been managing (i.e., denying) these shadow forces most of our lives. You must dive *down and in* to connect with the split off parts of yourself that are stored in the shadow corners of your unconscious.

This means you must turn *toward* the uncomfortable emotional feelings, the physical sensations, and the repetitive old stories that your mind keeps telling you are true. You must embrace and befriend the very monster you most want to flee. And you must do all this before you can come *up and out* into the more creative, liberated options for authentic action of the Mysterial Woman.

The Mysterial Change Process is a lifelong practice; a deep practice that you can learn to use until it is nearly a reflex.

Foundation—The Three Centers of Intelligence

The Mysterial Change Process is built upon three aspects of the self that are crucial for the alchemy of change: our thoughts, emotions, and body sensations. They each arise from what are now known as the *Three Centers of Intelligence*: The Head Center, The Heart Center, and The Hara Center (also known as the Gut or Body Center). "Hara" is a term used in eastern martial arts denoting the body's power center in the abdomen, located two-fingers' width below the navel. Here, we will use Hara to refer to "gut intelligence" as well as the distributed intelligence of the whole body.

The idea of three centers of intelligence has its origins in the ancient wisdom traditions. Today, neuroscience recognizes the Head, Heart, and Hara as three distinct "brains" because they are each dense with neurons and neurotransmitters.

Our feelings, thoughts, and movements are precisely timed electrical signals traveling through a chain of neurons or nerve fibers. It is like current moving through an electrical circuit. Myelin is a fatty insulation that wraps around these nerve fibers, increasing signal strength, speed, and accuracy.

"The more we fire a particular circuit," writes Daniel Coyle in *The Talent Code*, "the more myelin optimizes that circuit, and the stronger, faster, and more fluent our movements and thoughts become."[1]

When you learn to become consciously aware of your reactivity in the moment and deliberately choose different responses, even if they are awkward at first, you actually create new cognitive-emotional-somatic structures in the form of neural networks. This is what gives you new and more creative (less habitual) options for action. The scientific term for this is *neuroplasticity*, and there is a lot of evidence that our brains remain very capable of change throughout our lives. You really can teach an old dog new tricks!

Coyle's research on talent hotbeds revealed that it is the process of struggling with a new capacity—trying, coming up short, adjusting, trying again—which actually generates the most myelin and strengthens the new neural networks that generate high performance. He called this process *deep practice*.

For the last fifty years, women have had a mass experience of deep practice as they climbed the learning curve to play a shaping role in the existing Hypermasculine environments of our society. In fact, research on women's brain development shows how our brains have been changing as we have struggled with all of the twenty-first century demands and expectations: to be mothers, to hold down full time jobs, to come home and run households, to be attentive to our children and partners, to be fit and sexy, and to be active in the community.[2] All the while, we are doing this in an environment that is challenging us with the myriad ways that information is cascading into our bodies, hearts, and minds, to be perceived, sorted, remembered, and acted upon.

In order to upgrade our personal operating system and realize our wholeness as twenty-first century women, we must honor and cultivate this cornucopia of intelligence that is always available to us. We must develop and draw upon *all* of our ways of knowing. This expanded view of Head- Heart- Hara-intelligence helps us do that.

THE HEAD CENTER

When we speak of intelligence, most of us think of this center. When focused here we tend to filter the world through our mental faculties and the left hemisphere of the brain in particular.[3] Although the head brain is lateralized to varying degrees in certain functions, it is a highly complex system where both hemispheres of the brain still work together. Our left hemisphere gives us language and equips us to describe, categorize, judge, analyze, compare, and communicate. It helps us to know the rules, plan ahead, assess risks, and minimize fear. This is all extremely useful, but it is only half of the story.

In our dominantly left-brained Western culture the right brain has languished. We need to bring it back online in order to realize our full Mysterial nature.

For the right brain, no time exists other than the present moment, and it is alive with sensation. And it is in "the now" where we experience an unbroken sense of oneness with all things. This hemisphere is not concerned with distinctions or figuring things out. It is spontaneous, unlimited, imaginative, and connects us to the field of all possibilities.[4] Yes, a Mysterial woman has access to both hemispheres of the Head Center—at the same time.

THE HEART CENTER

The right hemisphere is a somatic ally of the Heart Center of intelligence. Today we are coming to realize that the heart is a highly complex, self-organized information-processing center that communicates with and influences the head brain via the nervous system, hormonal system, and other pathways.[5] The concept of a functional "heart brain" was introduced in 1991 by Dr. J. Andrew Armour, an early pioneer in neurocardiology, and expanded through research by organizations such as the Institute of HeartMath. Armour helped us to see that the heart has an intrinsic nervous system that is sufficiently sophisticated to qualify as a "little brain" in its own right. It actually contains an intricate network of several types of neurons, neurotransmitters, proteins, and support cells like those found in the head brain. This elaborate circuitry enables it to act independently, so that it can learn, remember, and even feel and sense.

Through the Heart Center we become aware of our needs for connection and approval and we know how to attune to others to make sure their needs are met as well. When we have developed emotional intelligence the capacities of compassion, empathy, and loving kindness are available. Yes, a Mysterial woman has full and easy access to this Heart Center.

THE HARA CENTER

And last but definitely not least, sitting beneath the Heart and the Head is the Hara Center of intelligence—our body knowledge. If we lead with this center we tend to filter the world through movement, physical sensation, and hunches. The enteric nervous system, which governs the gastrointestinal system, is the brain behind this center of intelligence. It is a web of neurons lining the gut and it contains more neurons than the spinal cord itself. It sends messages to the head brain more often than it receives them, and can function even if it is cut off from the Head Center brain. It is the source of "gut instinct" or the butterflies in the stomach that alert us to an opportunity or threat that the gut recognizes from subtle cues in our experience.

The body, it turns out, is not just something that carries around our almighty head. It is a vibrating source of engagement with the world that is constantly taking in and processing information on our behalf. Of course, to receive this input we have to be in our bodies and learn to trust what we sense. Yes, a Mysterial woman has access in every moment to this Hara Center.

CONDITIONED REFLEXES

The three centers of intelligence provide us a bounteous fountain of knowing when they are open, spontaneous and unconditioned. Research shows that our conditioned thoughts drive emotions, and emotions can invoke certain body sensations and have us take particular postures that slant our experience.[6]

For example, imagine that you are taking a graduate course from a professor who vaguely reminds you of a childhood bully. Maybe it is their voice or their arrogant bearing, or even the kinds of questions they ask. The mind thinks, "I'm in trouble here . . . I'm powerless!" The emotions of fear, shame, and submission start to take over, the body hunching down, as if in hiding, eyes cast toward the floor, shoulders curved inward in protection, feelings of anxiety rippling in the belly. In this state, you are probably not going to participate in the class discussion with your most sparkling ideas.

There is a kind of mutual causality going on. The body posture can actually drive a particular emotional state, which can then drive thoughts. For example, an ingrained habit of hunching the shoulders and dropping the head can induce a feeling of powerlessness.[7] Your view of the world literally becomes limited. (You are mostly looking at the limited possibilities of the floor!) This becomes a self-reinforcing pattern built into your musculature, and over a lifetime so habituated, automatic, and closed to outside influence that it is very difficult to change. We have to be very deliberate and willing to practice in order to change this dense triadic complex of Head, Heart, and Hara.

Putting It All Together—The Mysterial Change Process

Over the years we developed a step-by-step process to do the deep shadow work that would engage this full triadic pattern. We think of The Mysterial Change Process as a practical way that you can finally make a lasting shift from the *conditioned reflex* of your Habitual Way of Being to the *conscious response* of your Mysterial Way of Being.

From the diagram below, you can see that The Mysterial Change Process has two arcs. First we dive down and in, turning toward and metabolizing the shadows that we become aware of through the reactive or limiting thoughts, emotions, and body dispositions of our Habitual Way of Being. Next we return up and out, consciously replacing them with the liberating thoughts, emotions, and body dispositions of the Mysterial Way of Being.

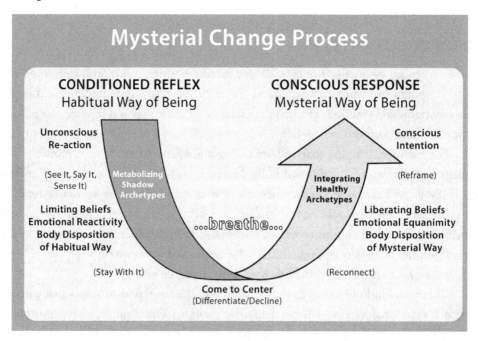

When you look at the diagram of The Mysterial Change Process you can see that the Mysterial Way of Being doesn't look that far away from the Habitual Way of Being. And isn't the straight line between two points the fastest? Couldn't you just jump right over to the Mysterial Way once you can imagine it and are aware that your current behavior isn't working? That is the mind's good idea. Indeed many of us have tried to make this leap using positive affirmations and skill-building programs without addressing the core limiting beliefs driving the pattern. After working with hundreds of women we know that this is not how deep and lasting developmental shifts occur.

Getting Started

The very first place to begin The Mysterial Change Process is developing enough self-awareness to notice when you are hijacked by your Habitual Way of Being. This takes significant self-observation, patience, and self-compassion because triggering happens rather fast. Your co-worker makes a thoughtless but minor remark about something in your work not being up to par, and it activates a deep wound related to your overly critical and punitive father, now internalized as The Judge shadow. Before you know it, your body is on high alert (fight, flight, or freeze), your emotions are in full force (fear, anger, grief, shame, etc.), and the stories your mind is telling you about the situation appear as absolute truth (and they almost always aren't).

The trauma train is all fueled up and pulls out of the station to charge along the same old neural track until it finally arrives at the same old destination with the same old unintended consequences. You are ready to fight for your life with a withering volley of criticism of your own! This is where the active and passive shadows of the five primary archetypes become helpful, as a way to observe yourself being grabbed in reactivity.

To emerge out of this habitual neural pathway we have to catch the reactivity earlier and earlier, and stop the runaway train by laying down some new tracks. Victor Frankl, neurologist, psychiatrist, and author of *In Search of Meaning*, the powerful book about his transformation as a Holocaust survivor, describes it this way: "Between stimulus and response there is a space. In that space is our power to choose our response. In our response lies our growth and our freedom."

When you are grabbed into reactivity, you must turn toward yourself with compassion and understanding so that you can come into more contact with what this structure is trying so hard to protect. It is from this tender place inside that you are making your way toward wholeness by deactivating the trauma in the body that is initiating the reactivity.

Step by step, by quieting the mind and staying close to the feelings and body sensations, you begin to move down into the valley of change, to befriend the very young part of yourself that has been held hostage inside of your habitual somatic responses. This old operating structure must be carefully and lovingly metabolized by first making it visible, and then by turning toward it with your full attention. Remember that this way of being has been holding a particular view of the world for you for a very long time. It is a view from the perspective of a young, vulnerable being that sees a world that must be appeased, feared, exploited, seduced, battled, controlled, tricked, or avoided in order to stay safe and secure. So step-by-step you will need to loosen its grip and reassure the hidden aspect of your deep, authentic self that it is safe to come out now.

Based on the work of Don Riso and Rick Hudson in *The Wisdom of the Enneagram,* Otto Scharmer's brilliant approach outlined in *Theory U: Leading From the Future as it Emerges,* and a variety of somatic experts, we have created a simple and yet very powerful process to go "down and in" toward the shadows of the archetypes.[8] As you go through the Five Activations of each stage of The Mysterial Sequence in Part II, you will find a customized and elaborated version of this process that engages the specific limiting and liberating beliefs of each archetype.

The main components of The Mysterial Change Process are:

1. Recognize when you are triggered into reactivity by one of the shadows.
2. Be willing to create a little distance between yourself and the pattern of reactivity. Take stock of what is going on at all levels—thoughts (Head), emotions (Heart), sensations/postures (Hara).
3. Move closer to your experience by relaxing the mind and as much as possible, letting go of the thoughts and stories. The mind will want to rush in with stories and explanations (drawn from the past) and the task here is to use your conscious will to stop the thoughts.
4. Bring your full presence to the sensations and feelings in the body, and the shape the body is taking, with kindness and compassion.
5. Let your breath interact with the felt sense in the body until the sensations and contractions diminish.
6. Let yourself come to center.
7. Now look out at the situation and see what actions or non-actions might be possible.

If you are not able to stop the reactivity train from leaving the station in the moment, all is not lost. The good news is that some time later in the day you can recreate the situation so that the emotional body state is re-activated. You can take yourself through The Mysterial Change Process after the fact. The brain does not actually know the difference between the experience in the moment and the re-experiencing of the situation in imagination.

With practice you will be able to do this process right in the moment when you are triggered into one of your shadow patterns.

Neural re-wiring is the result of deliberate practice over time. With The Mysterial Change Process, you have a practice that is portable in space and time and that will provide you the means to shift these formerly limiting situations.

You have the power to change. So let's begin.

PART II

Chapter 5

PREPARATION FOR THE
MYSTERIAL JOURNEY

*The real voyage of discovery consists not in seeking new landscapes,
but in having new eyes.*

—Marcel Proust

No serious traveler would embark on a journey to a new land without careful preparation. Entering into the activations of The Mysterial Sequence will begin to unravel millennia of patriarchal programming that is anchored deep in our cellular structure. We need to be very deliberate about creating the enabling conditions that will allow for the awakening of Proust's aptly described "new eyes."

Transformation literally means the crossing over (*trans*), to create a new form (*formation*). In simple English it means letting go of the way things are now so that something new can emerge. Easier said than done, as we all know. In fact, the psyche is constantly working to maintain a nice homeostatic balance, craving the stability of sameness, which makes it difficult to let go of the familiar, no matter how painful it might be.

How many women stay in relationships with men who hurt them in one way or another, ignoring the pleadings of family and friends urging them to leave? How many women suffer in jobs they hate with bosses who don't respect them? And how many women hate their bodies yet can't stop eating donuts or start working out? Millions. The answers cannot be found by just increasing our willpower, if it was that simple we would all be happy and healthy with the snap of our fingers.

As we guide you through this journey, we will turn toward our Habitual Ways of Being and head right into the place we do not consciously want to go: into the shadow territory of the unconscious where our deep inner resources are held hostage by our outdated beliefs about reality. And to do this wisely we will need to lay a little groundwork first.

Creating Enabling Conditions for Transformation

As you step onto the path of awakening your Mysterial nature you might want to find some allies to join you. Remember the "tend and befriend" oxytocin phenomenon discovered in women during times of emotional distress?[1] The transformative journey does have its stresses, and the support and encouragement of a learning partner or a circle of sisters who are in it with us can keep us going when we would have packed it in long ago, had we set out alone.

Before you step onto the path of The Mysterial Sequence we also encourage you to invest in a journal that is specifically dedicated to your transformation. It doesn't have to be expensive or fancy (although beauty is always inviting). It can simply be a spiral bound notebook. It could even be online. Whatever journal you choose, it should be easy to write in and feel safe and inviting to approach. You will see that we offer many journaling exercises throughout, and we have found that women enjoy having a special journal that documents their Mysterial emergence.

Now, with your Mysterial Journal close by, the preparations can begin.

There are five key tasks of preparation that will serve to both activate your innate Mysterial essence and provide containment on the journey itself. Each step will also begin to awaken the five archetypal energies that you will explore more fully in the Sequence.

1. **Awaken The Mother:** Embrace your Current Reality
2. **Awaken The Hero:** Ignite an Intention
3. **Awaken The Father:** Build Mysterial Leadership Practices
4. **Awaken The Maiden:** Welcome Resistance
5. **Awaken The Crone:** Create a Ritual Altar

AWAKEN THE MOTHER: EMBRACE YOUR CURRENT REALITY

The Mother archetype invites us to connect with the ground of our being in the here and now. It is often hard to face the reality of our lives the way that they are. We hope that by ignoring the suffering it will just go away. We get very good at distracting ourselves by staying busy, working 24-7, fixating on other people, daydreaming about the good times to come, complaining about what is missing, worrying about all the things we can't control, numbing out with TV, shopping, eating and drinking too much, or jumping into a new relationship—anything to keep us from feeling what we are feeling and knowing what we know deep down about what needs to change.

Of course, once you let yourself feel your actual experience it intensifies everything. This is, of course, why we don't want to do it—better to keep the devil we know than awaken the one that we don't know. Once you become fierce about feeling the truth of your current reality you will become uncomfortably aware of the ways your life is not working for you right now. And this will give you the incentive to do something about it. And sooner, rather than later.

Journal Inquiry for Awakening The Mother

Take some time to journal on the following questions. Go slowly and be as honest as you can. Let yourself keep feeling into "what is so" for you right now in your life.

- ✳ What aspects of your life—within and without, with others, and with the world around you—are working for you now?
- ✳ What might need to change if you were to step onto a path of growth?
- ✳ What are you afraid would happen if you awaken the Mysterial Woman within?

---

2. AWAKEN THE HERO: FOCUS YOUR INTENTION

The Hero brings you the focus and discipline to see what is out ahead of you. And this archetype also gives you the courage to envision a new image of the future, even if you have no idea how you will get there.

As you prepare for your journey through The Mysterial Sequence it is important that you identify what really matters to you. Why would you be willing to go "down and in" and disrupt your Habitual Ways of Being? What is at stake for you if you don't commit to envisioning what really matters?

If you have been armoring and insulating yourself from the call of your deep soul nature, the invitation to change your life may show up in the form of an accident, loss, illness, or twist of fate. As the father of psychoanalysis C. G. Jung said, "That which we do not make conscious emerges later as fate." Better that we listen earlier to the whispers of our soul's calling!

How do intentions work? Energy follows attention. Without thinking, planning, or controlling, your Hero's intention statement will begin to subtly reorient your attention, and imperceptibly shift your behaviors in alignment with that new reality, thus bringing it into form.

An intention is more than words on the page. It projects a multi-dimensional, multi-sensory vision or "image of the future." We need to be able to see, feel, touch, hear, smell, and taste our intention until the seed begins to grow in the field of all possibilities.

The potential future becomes much juicier because we open up access to all these ways of knowing. Once you set a focus of intention out ahead of you it also puts pressure on the shadow material in the unconscious that is blocking you from moving toward your dreams. While this can be uncomfortable, it is these deeply embodied limiting beliefs that we want to access and upgrade. Once you know where you want to go the engine of transformation starts revving up to take you there!

Journal Inquiry for Awakening The Hero

Take some time to journal on the following questions. Let yourself boldly imagine a new future even if you have no idea how you will get there.

* What are you longing to experience in your life right now? What is calling you forward?
* Why, or for the sake of *what,* would you be willing to welcome the process of transformation that would awaken your Mysterial nature?
* If you didn't need to know how you would do it, what is the life you could imagine living?

3. AWAKEN THE FATHER: BUILD MYSTERIAL LEADERSHIP PRACTICES

The Father archetype gives you the understanding that if you are going to awaken your Mysterial nature you will need to create structures in your life that support this intention. Mysterial Leadership Practices are designed to engage your body, heart, mind, and spirit to help you build a powerful container for the transformative process. Not only does each type of practice build "muscle," but the cross-training between them creates a synergy which accelerates the overall transformation.[2]

We can't emphasize enough the importance of having a direct connection with all levels of your being as you engage in this journey. The Mysterial Sequence guides you through an embodied change that stirs things up in the old structures. You will need to cultivate a deep connection with yourself on a daily basis in order to move through the activations. A set of Mysterial Leadership Practices become a way to do just that.

The following are a few examples of some specific practices that could help you forge a stronger connection in the core areas of body, heart, mind, and soul.

Body	Heart	Mind	Soul
Aerobic Exercise	Self-Compassion Practice	Reading	Meditation
Strength Training	Gratitude Practice	Group Discussions	Prayer
Yoga/Martial Arts	Journaling	Academic Study	Spiritual Community
Nutrition Consciousness	Soul date with yourself	Language Training	Reading

As we described in Chapter 4, by creating the conditions that encourage myelin to wrap around our nerve fibers, neural networks can actually be "re-engineered" to generate sustainable change. This is why a consistent set of practices is so essential. Myelination occurs with whatever we repeat. Let's say you have a tendency to distract yourself with Facebook, email, or housework when you're faced with working on your resume; then that's the neural circuitry you'll reinforce and strengthen.

On the other hand, your bandwidth literally increases as you engage in the healthier multimodal practices listed in the chart above. You can reinforce and strengthen new neural circuitry that supports you to make the changes you desire. It's not just inborn talent, but deep and targeted practice that leads to mastery of any kind.

Journal Inquiry for Awakening The Father

Take time to journal on the following questions.

* What practices (see the chart above for a guide) do you already have in place to support you in your journey?
* In which areas of your experience—physical, emotional, mental, or spiritual—do you need to bring in more structured practices?
* What are the steps you could take to do that?

4. AWAKEN THE MAIDEN: WELCOME RESISTANCE

The Maiden archetype brings the willingness to shake things up and disrupt the status quo. She is not afraid of change! Just as we can count on gravity to keep us here on Earth, we can count on resistance surfacing as soon as we are honest enough to be fierce with reality, bold enough to set a stretch intention, and committed enough to create a set of leadership practices. The gap between the two fundamental forces—the reality of where you are now and of where you dream to go—immediately creates the tension that surfaces resistance. And the moment you start to do something in the direction of your intention—like taking care of your body, starting to meditate, journaling, etc.—resistance will rear up like a slumbering dragon rudely awakened in her cave.

And even though you might feel like quitting as soon as this occurs the opposite is required. Resistance is not the thing you have to conquer in order to make changes, but rather it is a sign that the changes coming are directly challenging your ego's status quo. In that sense it is an early warning signal that you are moving in the right direction.

So we say, welcome resistance! Welcome discomfort!

In fact, once the forces of transformation are set in motion you can rest assured that the equal and opposite force of resistance will arise. A deep desire to change the current experience automatically activates the homeostasis-seeking function of the psyche. Resistance kicks in to make sure things don't destabilize.

We all have our habitual ways for the ego to respond when it feels under threat. The following steps allow us to engage resistance and not fight against it.

STEPS TO ENGAGE RESISTANCE

Let's say you plan to start meditating as a way to prepare for going through The Mysterial Sequence. You start out enthusiastically and decide to meditate twenty minutes every day of the week. Every time you try to sit down to do it you think of some crucial thing you have to do around the house.

* **Welcome** the resistance! It is an indication that you have ignited a compelling intention to carry what you long for into reality!

    This requires enough free awareness to notice that the idea to go and put in a load of laundry is a kind of resistance to settling down and being still. The act of noticing it is the moment of embrace.

* **Acknowledge** the belief, habit, or way of being that has helped to support the status quo and that is now being challenged. Clarify what issues, concerns, or beliefs need to be reframed in order to support making different choices.

    You recognize your father's voice in your head—how he used to tell you to "stop being so lazy" when you were just sitting quietly or daydreaming.

* **Center** in the face of resistance when you meet it—ground and settle your body. Bring awareness to your breath. Consciously reframe your concerns in the context of the intention *for the sake of which* you are inviting change.

    You sit down and close your eyes and do some deep breathing. You realize that you do not need to do your laundry right now and that the world will not fall apart if you sit still for twenty minutes.

* **Commit** to specific behavior changes in *incremental steps* that you can tolerate.

    You decide to just meditate three times a week while you are getting started.

* **Enlist** the support you need to effectively carry out your intended actions.

    You tell one of your friends about your plan and ask her to help hold you accountable to this practice, and that you will check in with her each week.

✳ **Celebrate** progress, *taking the time to register satisfaction*, with every step you make toward your ultimate goals.

You do something deeply nourishing to celebrate your accomplishment.

You can use this simple process to work directly with your resistance to any practice you are going to engage in as you lay the groundwork for this journey. Remember that resistance is not bad; it is just information that signals to you that you are going in the right direction!

Journal Practice—Awakening The Maiden

Take some time to journal on the following questions.

✳ What did you feel in your body as you imagined welcoming resistance?
✳ In what ways are you currently resisting the change that is already underway in your life?
✳ How have you resisted change in the past? What helps you to get through it?

5. AWAKEN THE CRONE: CREATE A RITUAL ALTAR

The Crone knows that ritual is a core language of an evolutionary woman.

Indeed ritual has the power to do the following:

✳ Connect us instantly to the Great Mystery—allowing us to bridge between the unconscious and conscious worlds.
✳ Engage all three centers of intelligence—bringing together the embodied intuitive knowing from the Hara, the emotional feelings from the Heart, and the mental ideas and images from the Head.
✳ Give us a focus to connect with others and send healing energy.
✳ Acknowledge the important rites of passage in our lives.
✳ Consciously celebrate with others our sacred times of the year and seasons of life.

❋ Help us access and channel powerful archetypal and spiritual energies, which begin to move once we open the gateways inside ourselves.

Ritual can help you with the unique *inside out* journey through The Mysterial Sequence. So much of what you must encounter and integrate is at invisible levels inside you. The ritual of creating and using an altar gives you a place in the *outer world* that represents your deepest *inner world* intentions. It is a very helpful way to anchor the invisible journey in form.

Your altar will become a home base or "true north" for you as you re-member yourself and do the deep work of navigating through the territory of the unconscious. As you spend time at your altar, setting it up and then working with it on a daily basis, it will begin to bring you comfort and become a kind of power place.

It is important that you explain to those with whom you live that this is your personal place—and that they are not to engage with it, rearrange it, or interfere with your altar. Creating your own place of power in a home you share with others may present some challenges. It is often our habit as women to tend and care for others at our expense. You may think or hear from others that you are being selfish if you request this for yourself or even feel guilty when you take the time to be with yourself in this very personal place. They might tell you it is weird and something witches and those in the occult world do. Remember that ritual and the use of altars for creative purposes is a very unfamiliar language in our culture. You are resurrecting this simple Feminine act of creating sacred space as a valid and powerful thing to do.

Steps for Creating an Altar Dedicated to your Mysterial Awakening

Step 1: Find the Perfect Place

Location, location, location. Take some time to find a place in your house that affords you some privacy and where you like the feel of the energy. That is not an airy-fairy idea. If you pay attention to the feelings and sensations in your body you will know where in your house you feel safe and a sense of well-being.

Ideally it is not in one of the more public places in your house, so that you are able to leave it set up for your daily practice. Find a place where there is not a lot of traffic or disturbance so that you feel a sense of tranquility when you are there. Often a small table in the corner of a room can work well, as it has a natural protection and built-in focal point.

(continued on next page)

One woman, who had two curious children and a small house, designated one shelf of her beautiful *en suite* bathroom cupboards as the place for her altar—a space that her children did not enter on a regular basis. Another woman put hers on a rolling table in a closet in her bedroom, and when she was ready to work with it she could simply open the door and roll it out. An empty basement nook became a sacred spot for another who loved the feeling of going 'down and in' to make contact with herself in the sacred setting she had created.

Step 2: Set Up your Space

Now that you have found the place for your altar, reflect on what you need to do to the area to make it feel special and beautiful to you. Take the time to engage with what we call the "Beauty Way." This is an invitation to awaken your senses to those elements that open you to the delicious nectar of your being. That is what beauty does when it captures your heart.

So, look around at the space you have chosen and ask yourself whether or not it relaxes or inspires you. Is the lighting soothing? Do you need to put a cloth over the table, or hang a tapestry behind it, or bring in a plant or hang a picture above it? What else would you need to do so that every time you come to this place the beauty of it ignites a fire in your soul?

Step 3: Choose your Symbols

Central to the practice of ritual and creating an altar is the use of symbols. Symbols have long been considered the language of the unconscious mind. And as such they are important in these practices that help us connect our conscious understanding with the great depths below. They point toward something that cannot fully be explained or understood through the tools we have available to our rational minds.

Reflect for a moment on an important symbol for you: a wedding ring, an old baby photo, a statue of Buddha, a stone picked up on an important trip, an eagle feather, an old sweatshirt your sister gave you, and so forth. Usually, even the very act of bringing the image of the symbol to mind activates something in the heart and the body. It awakens feelings and sensations that are outside of the domain of the mind and language itself.

Decide what symbols you would like to add to your altar that could represent your intention for awakening your Mysterial potential. Maybe it is a photo of your grandmother who always encouraged you to follow your dreams, or maybe a gift from a dear friend, or a statue of a goddess or other spiritual icon that immediately takes you into the sense of the sacred. You do not want to have a cluttered altar, but you do want it to be alive with symbols. You may want to consider adding a bell, or a Tibetan bowl that you will ring on your way in and out of your sessions. Incense is another wonderful way to evoke your full sensory awareness and help you shift your state of being.

We recommend that you always include a candle on your altar as a way to initiate and close the times that you engage with it. Often we like to add a small vase of fresh flowers to the altar—along with being a beautiful symbol of nature's creativity it is also a useful way to be sure that you are tending and caring for this sacred space in an ongoing way. When it truly becomes an outer symbol of yourself, you will notice a correlation between the times when your altar gets dusty and the flowers are dead and the juiciness of your own connection to yourself.

Step 4: Consecrate your Altar

Once you have set up your altar then you must consecrate it so that it shifts from being just a place in your house, closet, bathroom etc. to *your* sacred space. You ritually designate it as the point of connection between your inner world, outer world, and however you conceive of spirit or the Great Mystery. It is important that you are alone to do this and that you choose a time when you know you will not be rushed or interrupted. Center yourself by closing your eyes and taking a few slow deep breaths.

1. Light your candle with a simple prayer or invocation that connects you to something larger than yourself. Reflect upon your intention as you invite the sacred into your life through the activation of your altar.
2. Let your eyes take in the beautiful objects on your altar and let yourself feel what they ignite inside of you.
3. In whatever way seems natural to you ask that this altar become an outer symbol of your inner journey. You may want to invite any spiritual teachers or guides that you work with to be with you and bless your process.
4. When you have completed your time with your altar deliberately close the session by ringing your bell or bowl and blowing out your candle.

Step 5: Daily Practice

Once you have consecrated your altar as a sacred place you now bring it alive through your daily interaction with it. Like anything else, without your attention it will quickly

(continued on next page)

just become another table adorned with some objects. With regular engagement it can just as quickly become a place that starts to resonate with a nourishing quality of energy, which you will feel the moment you enter the space.

At the minimum we recommend a simple and regular (at least five days/week) ritual practice with your altar. Here is a sample morning practice:

1. Ground and center in front of your altar and prepare to enter into your sacred space.
2. Light your candle and set an intention for the day.
3. Engage in the discipline and structure of whatever practice you are doing today. It could be meditation, sending healing prayers to yourself and others, taking flower essences, etc.
4. Allow whatever practice you engage in to naturally and spontaneously touch your heart and body and let those feelings and sensations move in you.
5. When your time is complete blow out the candle and enter into your day.

The preparation is now complete. With all of the archetypes now gently awakened and your altar created you are almost ready. There is just one last thing we need to show you before you enter into The Mysterial Sequence. How the bones of an ancient Greek myth gave us the archetypal elements and the directional signposts for our journey of awakening.

Chapter 6

INITIATION—
Ancient Alchemy for Today's Woman

*And the day came when the risk to remain tight in a bud was
more painful than the risk it took to blossom.*

—Anais Nin

With the awakening of the archetypes in the last chapter, you are ready now to gather up the mythic forces for the life-changing initiatory experience of The Mysterial Sequence. Sadly, for the most part the concept of initiation has been lost in modern and post-modern Western culture. That has left us without a clear way to support women to cross over critical psychological and life thresholds into maturity. Until now.

The "recipes" or codes for these initiatory processes were often carried in myths that, to the conscious mind, may simply be fanciful stories. But the unconscious mind can recognize something deeper, namely, a call to grow.

In contemporary Western culture, the prevailing transformation myth is the Hero's Journey, and it seems that we are culturally wired to respond to its universally familiar plotline: *Separation from our old lives to answer the call toward a new future.* Then being tested on a road of trials with one's allies and enemies. This leads to metaphorically facing death, and finding something new within through rebirth and transformation. When transformation occurs, we return as the Hero. Joseph Campbell describes this powerful archetypal journey in *A Hero With a Thousand Faces.*

The Hero's Journey uplifts and inspires us and, in many ways, is our contemporary model for leadership development. It is also a fundamentally Masculine story of heroic challenge and response that does not address the healing of the deep wounding of the Feminine in ourselves and in the culture.[1]

We co-authors needed to find a guiding myth that could speak more directly to a woman's developmental path. We chose the ancient Greek myth of Kore/Persephone, with a basic plotline that has shown up across time and cultures, including the Sumerian Inanna and the Egyptian Isis myths.

Persephone's journey is a story of descent—going *down and in* before going up and out. In our translation, this means surrendering into one's deeply embodied experience, and into the depths of one's subconscious to liberate shadow material.

The DNA of this ancient classical myth holds the structure of a contemporary rite of passage. It will guide you over the threshold and into the activations of the archetypal source code of The Mysterial Sequence.

Although the myth is a story about outer characters, imagine that each one of them could represent a part of your own complex Yin and Yang nature. Pay attention to which people or events you feel the most connected with or repelled by as you follow the arc of Kore's journey. You may find in your reactions some clues to which of the five Mysterial archetypes might be the most compelling or challenging. Maiden, Mother, Crone, Hero, and Father are all in the story.

Settle into a quiet state of alert receptivity so that you can allow the power of this ancient myth to touch your heart and body as well as your mind. If this is not the ideal time, because distractions are claiming your attention, we recommend that you wait and schedule a better time. Take a few long deep breaths before you read and notice the sensations in your body. Feel the chair underneath you, your clothes against your skin, any tension or stress in your body. Prepare to welcome images, sensations, and feelings as deep archetypal fragments activate your soma and psyche.

Any myth that manages to survive for centuries, like this one, does so because it carries a powerful transmission within its bones. It is best if we approach it with respect and care. Ancient as it is, the Kore myth is also the beginning of our story as women and leaders today.

The Kore Myth—A Contemporary Initiation

It was a day like so many other days, with summer's abundance ripening into lush green leaves, vines, and flowers. Demeter, Goddess of the Harvest, wandered about the heavenly hillside while the maidens of Oceanus and her beloved daughter Kore gathered handfuls of purple crocuses, fragrant roses, royal blue irises, and sweet-smelling hyacinths. As Kore turned back toward her mother, excited to deliver her bouquet, her eyes fell upon the most exquisite flower she had ever seen. It was a narcissus and a hundred blooms sprang from its root. She knelt to savor its perfume, as sweet as the wide heaven above, as inviting as the fertile earth below.

The moment Kore stretched down to pluck this intoxicating flower the ground began to tremble. Suddenly, the earth split open into a gaping crevice and a golden chariot burst forth with Hades, God of the Underworld, astride. He had been watching this fair maiden in secret for many moons and had fallen deeply in love with her. But he well knew that her adoring mother Demeter would never willingly let her go. So, he had petitioned his brother Zeus, King of the Gods, who was also Kore's father, to release this innocent maiden to him. Zeus consented and Kore's fate was cast.

Hades whisked Kore away from the upper world and down into his own dark realms. As the earth closed behind them, muffling Kore's futile screams, his heart swelled with the promise of love. Hades had been swift, so swift that no one witnessed the abduction, save for Hekate, Goddess of the Crossroads, and Helios, God of the Sun.

But Demeter instantly felt her dear daughter's peril and began frantically searching for her. She searched for nine days, high and low, far and wide, but neither Gods nor mortals could help her. On the tenth day Hekate approached, carrying a torch, and said, "I saw nothing, but my ears heard the voice of he who stole your daughter away." Together they journeyed to find Helios, who, from his high perch, had seen it all. He told Demeter that Zeus had given Kore to Hades as his bride but sought to assuage her sorrow. "Among the Gods, Hades is a most suitable bridegroom," he told her.

Now that Demeter knew the truth, a terrible and savage grief consumed her heart. Driven by despair and anger, she fled Mt. Olympus to seek refuge in the cities of the human world, wandering the land disguised as a bereaved old woman. Broken-hearted and weary, she finally found shelter in Eleusis and collapsed beside the town well. As fate would have it the royal family passed by the well.

(continued on next page)

Queen Metaneria saw her and sensing her substance asked if she would be the nursemaid for her infant son Demaphoon. Demeter agreed and under her tending, the child began to grow beyond his humanness. Wishing to make him immortal, like her lost, beloved Kore, Demeter fed him ambrosia by day and placed him over the embers of the fire at night to burn off his mortality. One evening the Queen observed Demeter's secret fiery ritual and screamed out in terror. Demeter instantly shed her disguise and rose to her full stature, declaring herself as the Goddess and ordering that a temple be built in her honor. Once it was completed, she was finally able to surrender into the authentic mourning for the loss of her innocent daughter.

Meanwhile, deep down in the realm of the dead, Hades struggled to convince Kore of his love and the nobility of his actions. He confessed the plan her father had helped arrange and begged her to stay willingly, to become his wife and be Queen of the Underworld. Kore spurned his offer, longing to regain her world of innocence and beauty in the comfort of her mother's home.

Far above the darkness of this Underworld prison, Demeter continued to mourn, and neglecting her worldly duties as Goddess of the Grain and Growth the earth suffered turning into a barren wasteland.

As the famine intensified, the starving people prayed to Zeus with increasing desperation until he relented, realizing that if all humans died there would be no one left to worship him. Finally Zeus conceded and dispatched Hermes, his divine messenger, to order that Hades release Kore and escort her back to her mother, Demeter.

Hermes made haste to the underworld and gave Hades his instructions from Zeus—to return Kore to the upper world immediately. Kore was overwhelmed with joy. But as she celebrated her imminent return she couldn't deny feeling a flutter of regret, aware that her own deep, dark realm had just begun to open. Hades sensed this and offered her a parting gift—juicy, blood red pomegranate seeds. Kore recognized the genuineness of his offer and accepted, eating the seeds and gazing deeply into his eyes for the first time. Instantly, a jolt of energy entered her, and while she did not understand what it meant, she knew something powerful had just happened. She could feel her body alive with a new energy and vitality.

With Hermes as her guide, Kore bade farewell to Hades and returned to the land of her devoted mother. When they were reunited at Eleusis Demeter knew instantly that her daughter had changed.

"Did you consume any of the food of the dead while you were in the Underworld?" Demeter asked.

"Yes," Kore declared with pride, and told her mother how she had eaten the pomegranate seeds and about the new sense of womanhood she was experiencing.

Kore had tasted the fruit of life and death and there was no turning back. She would now be forever wedded to Hades and required to spend one third of every year with him in his home below. The other two-thirds she would spend tending to the Upper World with her mother Demeter. With this recognition, Kore assumed her destined role and the title of Queen Persephone.

And so it came to pass that Persephone traveled back and forth between the worlds every year, with Hekate as her wise guide. Each autumn Hades would greet her at the gates to his realm. Nourished by his deep and abiding care, she grew to love him deeply and to find her own true calling as midwife for the stream of new arrivals who descended to likewise be nurtured in the deep dark before being reborn into their new lives above. So it is that each year, when Persephone re-emerges as Goddess of the Spring, the earth bursts forth into fruitfulness once again. Seeds sprout, flowers bloom, babies are born, and crops fill the fields.

Over time, the wisdom, love, and power that Kore tasted in the juice of those first blood red pomegranate seeds fully transforms her from an innocent maiden with the potential for wholeness, into a full bodied Queen of both the upper and lower worlds. Persephone becomes a guide for others into the next phase of their lives and brings hope, harmony, depth, and fertility to all whom she touches.

And so it was written many years ago.[2] And remarkably it is still true today. Kore's transformation into Queen Persephone—heaven of above and below—required a descent, a deconstructing of her old identity, and it was only at this point that in the fertile ground of her being, the seeds of a new self could begin to take root. Over time these seeds matured and her full stature emerged.

For women to unblock the inner channel that will allow the next phase of our natural maturation to occur we have to be willing to be taken apart first. The old structures within are simply too narrow to hold the robust current of potential that wants to flow through us.

This is the dedication required for you to make deep inner shifts that can fundamentally change how you experience yourself, others, and the world. A weekend workshop can awaken you to the idea of change and even give you insights about the limiting patterns, but it takes going *down and in*—with practice—to transform those outdated Habitual

Ways of Being into more liberating structures. The Kore myth is a guiding story that suggests how we might do that.

Ancient Story—Modern Day Initiation

We believe that the bones of this myth provide a kind of structure today for a woman's initiation into wholeness. It contains all the elements for a contemporary woman's awakening to greater fulfillment, deeply satisfying relationships, and the ability to make a creative contribution in the world today.

In its time the myth spoke to the necessary separation of the daughter from the mother for her growth and development. And it took a kind of violent act to rip her from her innocence and thrust her into the ongoing cycle of maturation. It is interesting to note that in the earliest translations of the myth that come from the matriarchal times, Kore was not seized but rather chose to go down to the underworld to help those souls who were crossing over from life to death. It was understood in those earlier times that descent into the territory of the deep feminine was a natural gift of women.[3]

Our rendering of the myth is drawn from the patriarchal period when the seizure was added into the story because we live today still within the 5,000-year-old masculine story. Life does grab us and we do tumble down into the depths. The Mysterial Sequence offers us another way to consciously choose, as Kore did in the earlier version of the myth, to descend willingly and open ourselves to the alchemical heat of transformation.

Take a moment now to reflect on what touched or provoked you in the story. It may give you some clues about which of the five archetypal gateways, which we will explore in the following chapters, is likely to be the most catalytic for you. You may find some of these reflections helpful:

Which character in the story did you feel the most resonance with and why? Which character did you feel the least affinity with and why? Demeter (Mother), Kore/Persephone (Maiden), Hades (Hero), Zeus (Father), Hekate (Crone).

Where in the Kore story are you currently in your own life—innocence, tumbling down into the underworld, resisting change, opening to the transformation, returning from the dark night of the soul, sacred marriage within that leads to Queen of above and below?

There is a saying that when the student is ready the teacher appears. We could say then that when Hades appeared and grabbed Kore her soul was actually ripe for the change, even if her ego was not. Can you relate to situations in your life that pulled you against your will into a profound journey of transformation? And if, like Kore, you resisted life's inner or outer call for change did you suffer as deeply as she did?

If life circumstance calls you to the deep dark world below, into contact with the unconscious, disowned aspects of yourself, what might be different if you do not struggle, but rather open yourself to the forces of change? Or what might be different if you chose to go *down and in* before the big grab occurs?

Whether outer events in your life are telling you change is necessary or whether you can sense the inner brewing of a new way of being waiting to emerge, the pathway of The Mysterial Sequence offers you a guiding map.

Walk with us now through the five stages of this life-changing journey as it was experienced by ten different women, all composites of our actual students.

Chapter 7

THE ACTIVATION OF THE MOTHER—
Cultivating Radiant Presence

The myth of Kore-Persephone begins with the aching separation of young, unconscious Kore from her mother, Demeter. It concludes with Kore having transformed into conscious, mature Queen Persephone, returning to Demeter as a self-authoring woman, forever changed. As a guiding map for initiation, the myth signals to the unconscious that healing the mother-daughter split is where it all begins.

In this first Activation you will learn what it means to have more access to your Vessel Yin (static Feminine) essence through both clearing and cultivating The Mother archetype. It is also how you begin cultivating Radiant Presence.

Before you start into the content of the chapter we invite you to read the Invocation of The Mother aloud. We have found the vocalization to be an important part of the experience. Allow the words to touch your heart and awaken your soul.

Invocation of The Mother

Dear one, relax now into my embrace.
Let my peaceful darkness envelop you in its silken comforter,
inviting you to let go of your burdens.

Surrender and sink into my infinite ocean of love,
my liquid warm buoyancy.
In my eyes, you are perfect.
In my heart, you are enough just as you are.

Turn down and in to the exquisite vessel of your being
and there you will find me,
present in every cell of your body.

Feel how your suffering and your longing are welcome here
in my fertile womb.
Let the cycles of the moon guide you home to my hearth.

Rest into a natural great peace
in the transforming chalice of my Yin heart.

Turning on the Flow of Vessel Yin

The Mother is the most ancient and universally recognized of all archetypes, a pattern of nourishment and security in her ideal form. When out of balance, this pattern can swing toward devouring possessiveness or withering deprivation. Every person who has ever lived was birthed from a mother. For better or worse, it is the universal Mother pattern in our psyche that begins our lives. This is where we install our basic wiring for survival and connection, for giving and receiving. It is a deep *source code*.

Very deep indeed. Compared to The Hero, Father, Maiden, and Crone, The Mother's organizing template emerged in the first flickering of prehistoric consciousness. It can be challenging for modern women to connect with something so vital, yet so distant in human memory.

Most leadership programs overlook or deny the importance of building embodied, sensing, nurturing, connecting Mother capacity. The women's movement in the twentieth century was about breaking free from the limiting domestic roles of mother and wife, in order to participate in public or commercial life. Our biology—as the bearers of children—was no longer our destiny. The recent awakening of The Maiden energy from the depths of the millennia-old masculine paradigm was necessary. But we can now see that we don't need to reject or denigrate The Mother in order for The Maiden energy to thrive. Quite the opposite! It is essential that our move forward actually begins with a return to include developing embodied Mother capacities and a connection to the solid foundation of being.

Do you ever crave time to simply be? To feel the warm sun and fresh breeze on your skin with nowhere to go and nothing to do, to pause and take in the sights and scents of a beautiful garden or lush forest? To cook something utterly wonderful and delicious to share? To find a time out of time to snuggle with a loved one—child, lover, furry companion animal? In our world of abstract computer work, sterile office towers, and chemically based foods stripped of nutrition, women instinctively yearn for The Mother without quite knowing why.

When we are able to integrate the healthy inner Mother archetype, we begin to have more access to the life sustaining flow of Vessel Yin essence within ourselves. A vessel connotes a special, beautiful container for our deep feminine ground of being. Remember that Vessel Yin is the purely feminine expression of Yin, or Yin-Yin. It is the peaceful, containing, womblike aspect of Yin.

If you have struggled with negative, judgmental feelings toward yourself, found it virtually impossible to stay with a health and fitness regimen, been unable to feel honestly happy with yourself, then the flow of your Vessel Yin essence is likely down to a faint trickle. Turning up that flow gives you a healthy way of relating to/caring for your body and the body of our planet, and opening to the fullness of your senses and emotions. We need it for the unconditional love and empathic bonds that hold us together in mutual care and concern, and for the unassailable sense of being lovable and valuable simply for being who we are. Vessel Yin is the rich soil in which our *self-compassion* grows.

As we noted earlier, the world is only becoming more unstable, complex, and uncertain. Such challenges require that we first reclaim the fullness of our Vessel Yin nature. Not only does The Mother build our self-compassion and improve our health and resilience, she gives us the ability to contain, gestate, and nurture environments, teams, and projects so that they thrive and bear fruit.

Consider meetings, and how they are facilitated or "held." What do you notice about your experience when the facilitation of the time, space, and people is sloppy rather than thoughtful, life sapping rather than energizing, or toxic rather than creatively fertile?

Skillful holding includes being in tune with natural rhythms, and with the subtle undercurrents of what is in the room but isn't being said. It is recognizing that ideas and projects require periods of incubation and stillness, not just action, to be their most successful. It's futile to push before something is ready to be born, or to hold back when the baby is crowning.

The work of The Mother may be one of the most powerful life-changing experiences that you've ever embarked upon. It isn't always easy. But you can trust that your own inner Mother is deeply touched by your suffering, and knows instinctively what you need to begin to heal and restore. Following her call, however faint, to the sweet embrace of her Vessel Yin essence will help you to discover, develop, and integrate her four foundational capacities.

The Foundational Capacities of Radiant Presence

Every archetype in The Mysterial Sequence has four foundational capacities that are the focus for development in that particular Activation. The four capacities for The Mother are identified in the chart below: Self-Compassion, Sensuous Embodiment, Empathic Resonance, and Container Holding. To develop a "capacity" means that you have more muscle or bandwidth—more ways of being and doing that weren't available to you before.

Each of these capacities covers a specific quadrant, or territory of experience.[1] This ensures that all domains of life are efficiently covered. When combined, the capacities provide women undeniably potent results in their personal and professional lives.

The Mother

INTERIOR	EXTERIOR
My Inner Experience	**How I Show Up**
Capacity: SELF – COMPASSION	**Capacity: SENSUOUS EMBODIMENT**
To be compassionate with your own faults, struggles and personal failings. You extend kindness and nurturing to yourself, recognize your own humanity and are able to witness your negative thoughts and feelings as they are without suppressing them or believing them as truth.	To be present to your body and senses, interacting with your environment, registering pleasure or pain, empathy or revulsion, delight or fear. Using the perception of inner felt sense to recognize your state of being, attend to your basic needs, assess whether you are in balance or out of balance in your physiology.
Relating with Others	**Engaging the World**
Capacity: EMPATHIC RESONANCE	**Capacity: CONTAINER HOLDING**
To stay with your own inner experience (emotions, thoughts, sensations), while you also feel what it is like for another, such that the other feels "held" or "seen" in the energetic dynamic between you.	To consciously hold a space in which something can move from conception through the maturing of form to birth. Requires tolerating the natural rhythms of emotion and the building of excitement in your body without having to discharge it or move into action prematurely.

Quadrant labels: INDIVIDUAL, COLLECTIVE (left vertical); I, IT, WE, ITS (center).

The Promise of Radiant Presence

The process of this first archetypal Activation, though only one of five, delivers a benefit that is visible—a kind of radiance from the inside out. By liberating The Mother, you open a channel of connection between the three centers of intelligence: Head, Heart, and Hara/Body.

Many women are initially curious about our work because they know a graduate of a Mysterial Leadership course (typically a co-worker) they describe as having a glow, an inner light, a way about her that is powerful, poised, authentic, and attuned. They may have experienced her becoming a better leader as a result, but they couldn't always put their finger on what was different. She felt more present to them, and they in turn felt more comfortable and inspired in her presence.

"Whatever it is Rachel's got, I want some of it!" a prospective student exclaimed.

When the foundational capacities of Self-Compassion, Sensuous Embodiment, Empathic Resonance, and Container Holding are solidly built, Radiant Presence arises in the sweet spot of this fundamental reconnection with yourself.

Shadows of The Mother—The Neglector and The Devourer

Before you can have consistent access to Radiant Presence you must dive *down and in* to clear what is blocking your Vessel Yin essence. You must discover how you are unconsciously under-identified (The Neglector) and/or overidentified (The Devourer) with The Mother archetype in ways that have split off your natural mothering capacities and cast them into the shadow.

THE NEGLECTOR—PASSIVE SHADOW OF THE MOTHER

When The Neglector shadow is dominant, your Vessel Yin essence is like a thin, watery gruel that you accept in place of the nourishing nectar of The Mother.

Let's begin with a tour through the tendencies and behaviors that show up when you have distanced yourself from The Mother archetype and The Neglector shadow has shut you away in the attic. Notice if any of these strike a familiar chord in you.

CHARACTERISTICS OF THE NEGLECTOR

* You find it difficult to receive love and appreciation from others, often dismissing or denying it. You may not see much in yourself to like or love, and may experience self-loathing.
* You can't really name your own needs, wants, and desires clearly, and may experience a sense of futility in trying to meet those needs. Or, you may be convinced that as a grown woman you don't and shouldn't need much. You may get irritated when others seek to have their needs and desires met, labeling them as needy, self-centered, or greedy.
* You ignore your body's requirements for healthy food, rest, exercise, and general care, especially when busy. You may spend much of your time

detached from the inner felt sense of experience, withdrawn into the mind. Body signals that you recognize—like butterflies, racing heart, sweaty palms—are brushed aside or hidden.

✳ You find it difficult to simply be or be still. It feels wrong and lazy if you're not doing something every minute. You may be judgmental of others who take a more relaxed approach to life.

✳ You can only really relax or let go when you have worked really hard and have earned it.

✳ You are impatient with or baffled by other people's feelings or concerns, wishing they would "get over it" or "get a clue." It may be difficult for you to give your full attention to someone as you prefer to multitask, or you withdraw from connection when strong emotions are present.

✳ You may have a feeling of being un-mothered—alone in the world and left to fend for yourself.

✳ It doesn't come naturally to you to love and care for other beings, or the earth. It is a burden and responsibility, a checklist item. When you are busy, plants wither, and family and pets get cursory attention. You may feel disdain for stay-at-home mothers or women who demonstrate caring.

✳ You tend to drive projects to completion based on your plan, regardless of the fallout or what happens along the way. You may shift suddenly between activities and projects, feeling agitated or bored. You may dislike hosting events, family meals, or running meetings, mechanically organizing them in the sparest way possible. The venue makes little difference to you as long as it's functional.

✳ You have a linear approach to projects, events, and activities, diving right in and dispensing with formalities to move into action. Uninterrupted activity and continuous growth is what you expect. You often forget about breaks, and don't pay attention to the change of seasons or time of day. Every day is basically the same.

Sound familiar at all? Perhaps you can relate to some of these behaviors within yourself. When it comes to how you are with others, you might tend to swing in the opposite direction and into the clutches of The Devourer. We will get to that shadow tendency later.

CLEARING THE NEGLECTOR: KERRY'S JOURNEY

Kerry was forty-eight and still going strong after fifteen years of hard driving inside an iconic multinational software company. Highly competitive in everything she undertook, Kerry thrived on rising to challenges and showing what she could do, matching wits with some of the smartest people in her industry. While her subordinates generally liked Kerry and respected her accomplishments, they also experienced her insensitivity and ferocious drive when it came to meeting sales goals. She rarely took time off, and when she wasn't working she retreated to the sanctuary of her home to zone out on the couch. Not surprisingly, Kerry had been single for five years. Her last relationship with a physician had withered away from lack of attention.

Close to crossing the threshold into her fifties, even Kerry couldn't ignore the changes within her body signaling that menopause was upon her. Worrying that she couldn't keep going on as she had, and sensing a disturbing emptiness in her life, Kerry found her way to The Mysterial Leadership path.

ROOTS OF THE NEGLECTOR

Growing up in a small town in Idaho, Kerry had witnessed the dependency, despair, and limited options of her own mother, who had married young, quit college, and never started a career. "I ran from that world as if my life depended on it," Kerry grimly recollected, "nose down since junior high, straight A's, track star, and valedictorian." She added proudly, "Put myself through college selling computer hardware."

Kerry's mother had suffered from depression, and often stayed locked in her bedroom with the shades drawn, emotionally vacant and physically unreachable. Kerry learned at an early age to suppress her needs, or take care of them herself. Often women with The Neglector shadow had insufficient healthy mothering as a child, stunting the development of their own inner Mother function. Kerry compensated by over-relying on her Masculine capacities, driving herself and others to accomplish tough goals no matter what the cost.

The financial security that Kerry had acquired by running a highly profitable business division compensated for some of the early deprivation. But she worried that she couldn't keep going on as she had. "My body was just the lump on top of which my all important head sat. I treated that body like a workhorse that didn't merit proper feeding or rest."

Kerry was also driven by an urgent need to project an image to the outside world, a mask that others would reward and admire. She found it very difficult, in fact nearly impossible, to show up authentically.

Anything that hinted of failure or made Kerry appear less than successful in public was terrifying. This kept her in a frantic race to pile on the next achievement, never letting anything—especially other people or her own feelings and needs—get in the way of accomplishing the task at hand. Such a way of being required a monumental expense of life energy, energy that was not available for self-care, or the care for and connecting with others.

Kerry could be quite insensitive under performance pressure, and "disappear" when she was busy. Her problem wasn't so much that she was heartless, cold, or neglectful to others. She could actually swing to The Devourer pole on occasion, once devoting a significant period of her life to care for a dying friend at the expense of her own self-care. But Kerry was a Neglector to herself, a situation common to many women that we work with.

OBSERVING THE NEGLECTOR

Kerry's first step was to become aware of the ways that The Neglector shadow was driving her life. Through a daily Self-Observation exercise (at the end of the chapter), Kerry journaled about her mental, emotional, and bodily reactions to various situations, especially when she felt pressured to perform or look good. This was the first time she actually gave herself permission to take in the full reality of her life. The true cost of The Neglector—in terms of life fulfillment—was staring her in the face.

While cleaning the garage all day one Sunday without a break, Kerry became so fatigued that she fell off a ladder and sprained her ankle. This was a big wake-up call. Sitting glumly in the emergency room, Kerry could finally see how The Neglector had sabotaged her by blocking any physical sensations of tiredness, discomfort, or hunger. She thought of all the days when she was so intent on her work that she simply forgot to eat, or even to blink.

"I don't stop until my eyeballs burn so badly they feel like they're going to fall right out of my head," mused Kerry, rolling her eyes.

With The Neglector at the helm, your healthy life-supporting "self-mothering" instinct is dialed down. Turning off the signals from your body is a strategy for neglecting yourself in order to benefit something else. The problem with this distorted strategy is that you become so depleted that everyone loses.

Building Foundational Capacity

While turning toward your shadow aspects with compassion, you must simultaneously cultivate the healthy Mother within. This is most effectively accomplished by focusing on the four foundational capacities of The Mother: Self-Compassion, Sensuous Embodiment, Empathic Resonance, and Container Holding.

In Kerry's case, building the capacity for **Sensuous Embodiment** (Individual Exterior—How I Show Up) had to come first. She began slowly, with a practice of restorative yoga to help her consciously use stillness for the purpose of restoring her body. This was a significant advance from her tendency to overwork and then collapse on the couch, zombie-like, in front of the television.

Once the compulsion to override her bodily needs was somewhat tamed, Kerry signed up for a NIA class[2], or Neuromuscular Integrative Action. NIA is an intelligent blend of key aspects of yoga, martial arts, and dance that improves fitness, health, and flexibility with less stress on the body. NIA helped Kerry begin to move in her body in ways she hadn't in years, to feel the pleasure of Sensuous Embodiment while she strengthened. "That first NIA class was so intimidating," Kerry mused. "I felt like a total klutz, and I was sure that everyone else thought so too. But I stayed with it, and now I look forward to it every week!"

Sensuous Embodiment isn't just about moving physically in the body. It is about befriending the body as if it were a shy animal crouched at the edge of a forest. Our body intelligence is a vastly overlooked resource, particularly in leadership. It is through subtle signals transmitted by our body that we can learn to "sense the room" or receive intuitive impressions that help us make important decisions. Sensuous Embodiment gives us access to a sense of grounded presence in all that we do.

A tragedy of being deadened by The Neglector is how Sensuous Embodiment is flattened, grayed-out, and desiccated. This was certainly Kerry's experience. Not only was she deprived of an important source of knowing, but of the joy and juice of life itself.

Kerry, who loved hiking in the mountains and yet rarely did, took a day to walk one of her favorite trails in the Cascade Mountain Range for her Sensuous Embodiment Practice. Usually she would do this as a physical challenge and push herself beyond her limits. This time she walked slowly, taking in the rich smells of the damp forest floor, feeling the warm air on her skin, and her feet softly moving along the path. She heard bird songs and saw things along this trail that she had never noticed in the decade she had been hiking here. When she reached a mountain stream she sat down with her journal. From this new place of embodied presence a poem poured out of her, surprising even her with its simple beauty.

The second area of deep suffering for Kerry was around her emotional intelligence. Her heart was so sensitive that she had learned to block her emotions and constrain her capacity for **Empathic Resonance** (Collective Interior—Relating With Others) in order

Sensory Awakening Practice for *Sensuous Embodiment*

Open to life through your senses: go to a place in nature where you find yourself enlivened or nurtured. Spend at least an hour taking in the experience through your senses: touching, tasting, smelling, hearing, and seeing. Open the perceptive ability of your heart along with your other senses to enter into a relationship with your environment.

Notice how your body responds to the stimuli—pleasure, delight, joy, inspiration, and wonderment . . . Allow yourself to register the delight, take it in, just *be* and connect to the living nature of your being through your experience.

Reflection: At the end of your time of exploration through the senses, take fifteen minutes to do an automatic writing exercise, writing from your bodily experience. You might ask yourself questions regarding important decisions and then allow yourself to write whatever comes to mind.

to keep pressing forward to be successful. Empathic Resonance is the capacity to stay with your own inner experience (emotions, thoughts, sensations), while also feeling what it is like for another, such that the other feels "held" or "seen" in the energetic dynamic between you two.

This lack of capacity negatively impacted Kerry's effectiveness with her staff, and was a source of incompleteness in her personal life. "I know that I want a relationship. Not just companionship but a real soul mate, someone I can grow old with," declared Kerry. "It's such a painful area in my life, that I'm afraid to even let myself think about it."

With more capacity for Sensuous Embodiment to support her, Kerry began the critical work of thawing her own feeling realm—of being with her direct experience. She started to make contact with how she actually felt in the moment, to be open to the feeling nature of others, and allow that to inform wiser actions.

Thawing, however, has its discomforts. Kerry's long buried emotions began to surface. Over a couple of months, a backlog of tears flowed—more than she'd shed in the last decade. Floods of healthy feelings streamed through her frozen being, freeing up her rather stiff appearance with the lubrication of her emotional oiling can.

With more of her heart available, Kerry began a simple practice of being in openhearted presence with others. This helped strengthen her muscle for Empathic Resonance.

Open Hearted Presence Practice for *Empathic Resonance*

Build some time into your day, at least once per day, in which you are simply present and listening with an open heart to the challenges of a family member, friend, or colleague. You are not trying to fix anything; instead, you are compassionately with them, "holding space" as they express their suffering and immediate experience.

Listen with open attention. That means, if judgments or ideas for advice arise in your mind, just let them go. The practice is not about solving problems. It is about being with the other person, allowing them to feel your heart connection—your Empathic Resonance—even if it they are not conscious of it.

Beware of slipping into sympathy. Sympathy means that you are taking on another's pain as your own. That is not constructive for anyone. Empathy is about being with another, but staying connected to your own experience.

Reflection: At the end of the day or week, you can receive heightened benefit if you journal about your experience with Open Hearted Presence Practice.

1. How did this experience compare to how you usually engage with others' challenges?
2. What did you notice about yourself as you listened with open attention—your thoughts, feelings, body shapes, and sensations?
3. What did you notice about the person you were listening to? Did anything surprise you?

For Kerry, this practice felt extremely challenging at first, almost impossible. Kerry's Neglector was in full resistance, convinced that this kind of attention was time misspent when she could be solving their problem instead!

As her heart softened and her body became more available as a finely tuned instrument, Kerry's Empathic Resonance with others also increased. She realized that she had been fearful of the feelings that would arise in her when she made herself so available to another. The practice of Open Hearted Presence helped her learn when to prioritize simple connection with others in the moment over the millions of tasks that were always commanding her attention.

In time, Kerry began to experience the benefits of having access to her emotions and undefended connection with others. "I started to notice that my presentations were becoming more natural and easy—I was speaking about the same material, but I was more connected to the audience. And I could feel what was going on with everyone. People started giving me really great feedback about the meetings. "

Even with the strides she'd made with these practices, Kerry realized that it was still challenging for her to stay comfortable inside her own skin and not disconnect from her body or self when she was triggered. We encouraged Kerry to practice *Centering*. This highly portable practice simply requires a few seconds to consciously redirect attention so that you experience yourself in your body grounded to the earth and balanced in the space that surrounds you.

By *Centering*, you become fully present to yourself and others in the moment, more able to access all your channels for information: physical sensations, emotions, intuition, empathic connection, thoughts, and spiritual insight. This full spectrum of information, and the natural relaxation in the body, allows you to be more able to sense what is really going on, and what is the right thing to do (or not do) at any moment. It allows you to "be with what is" in the moment—a powerful place from which to take action.

Centering Practice[3]

Although we recommended this practice to Kerry to help her stay connected with herself and her experience, this is a valuable, foundational practice that can be applied to every Activation.

Centering is a way of bringing yourself into the present, opening to and aligning with your Mysterial self—body, mind, heart, and soul. Through centering, you become more relaxed and permeable to the wisdom of head, heart, and gut, growing the capacity to neutralize the effects of your reactivity and to source your actions from your deepest intentions.

When you center, bring your attention to the following four anchors in the body:

Ground: Begin by feeling your feet on the ground, using the sensations of contact with the earth to bring your attention into the present, into connection with your body and being.

Breath: Find your breath in the center of your body. Take full deep breaths so that your belly relaxes on the inhale; allow a long exhale to direct your attention and energy downward toward your Hara and through your body into the earth.

(continued on next page)

Gravity: As you exhale, allow your muscles to relax into gravity, letting the skeletal system do its job of holding you up. Release any tension you may be holding in your jaw, shoulders, back, and legs; soften your gaze. Through the exhale, feel your weight transfer through your feet, deepening your connection to the ground.

Shape: Check the alignment of your body in space along the dimensions of length, width, and depth—in doing this, you center yourself in the middle of the three- dimensional field in which you live and move. Feel the space in front of you, behind you, to the right, to the left, above, and below. Simply putting your attention to those places brings your energy there. As a double check you can ask yourself: Is the front of my field equal with the back? Is my vertical stature equal to my sense of ground? Am I balanced side to side?

Invoke a Quality: Ask yourself, "What would it be like if I had a little more Self-Compassion (or love, patience, courage, etc.) in my being?" Notice, through sensation, how your body naturally arranges itself in a way to make more room for the quality you invoke.

Centering became Kerry's constant ally, a way of "returning to herself" during times when she was caught up in her churn of thoughts and the mad dash to get things done. Even so, Kerry was not always able to catch The Neglector before it kicked into high gear in the moment. Therefore she also took time in the evening to go through **The Mysterial Change Process: The Deep Practice** (found at the end of this chapter). With time the traumatic body response became less intense and she was able to take herself through the process right in the midst of difficult situations.

As The Neglector relaxed its grip, Kerry was able to move more like a river flowing around rocks and logs, moving downstream with ease. She was not only more effective because she could meet her challenges with greater ease, she was also more enlivened. She no longer ended her days feeling exhausted, but rather she went to bed in a state of sweet satisfaction.

Shadows of The Mother: The Neglector and The Devourer

THE DEVOURER—ACTIVE SHADOW OF THE MOTHER

Not everyone starts out like Kerry with The Mother archetype at arms length. Over identification with the nurturing, caring archetypal energy of The Mother leads a woman into the active shadow of The Devourer. The ego literally experiences itself as the Great Mother, wanting to fuse with and possess all that is.

When The Devourer shadow is operating, the Vessel Yin essence is dense, heavy, and syrupy thick—a kind of possessive, sticky spider's web from which there is no escape.

CHARACTERISTICS OF THE DEVOURER

Let's take a tour through the tendencies and behaviors that show up when you have over identified with The Mother archetype, and the active shadow pattern of The Devourer emerges. Here are some of the signs that The Devourer has caught you in her web:

* You may have an exaggerated sense of being a sacrificing Good Mother, feeling superior to others in this way, and deserving of acknowledgment.
* You can react strongly when your loved ones do not include or inform you about the details of their daily living, or when you haven't been consulted for your opinion. You believe that you can't keep them (or you) safe without this knowledge and inclusion.
* Those around you complain you are smothering them with love, trying to live their lives for them and hampering their autonomy. This results in fusion with others and difficulty distinguishing between yourself and others. You may control them through a combination of over-giving followed by resentment if they don't reciprocate.
* You may often put your own needs and wants over those of others, demanding that they care for you and resenting them if they don't do that. (Because you believe that you deserve and/or have earned that care after all that you've given them.)
* You may have a tendency to devour your own inner impulses with addictions of one kind or another. You don't know when enough is enough.
* You may overdo physical connection, wanting to constantly hold and be held, to touch others in ways that may make them uncomfortable.

✳ It may be difficult for you to get your energy moving out into the world on your own behalf (for example, getting a career started), as your energy and attention is always directed toward others. This feels like a necessary sacrifice and a justifiable reason for not being more accomplished.

✳ You have a keen sense of what others are feeling and experiencing, often taking on the other person's emotional drama as if it were your own. You may use this knowledge in a manipulative way, building connection and anticipating their needs to serve your own ends.

✳ You relish creating the conditions for people and projects to grow and develop (for example, your children), but you don't know when to let them go. You may have a tendency to overdo and micromanage gatherings and events.

Did any of The Devourer tendencies seem like familiar territory? Notice if you are reminded of women in your family, friends, and co-workers or other women that you know. You can also be a Devourer to everyone around you, yet a Neglector toward yourself.

Typically, one shadow is dominant. However, many of us tend to swing wildly between the two from time to time, depending on circumstances, and are never quite able to land in the sweet spot of the healthy Mother.

CLEARING THE DEVOURER: RACHEL'S JOURNEY

Rachel, thirty-eight, was a devoted wife and mother of two young boys, who ran an impeccably tended home with the eye of a museum curator in a gracious, tree-lined neighborhood. She was the quintessential stage mother and soccer mom who held a fine arts degree from an Ivy League school. Rachel was brimming with talent and capability, much of it packed away like beautiful items in a hope chest, to be opened at a later day.

If you are inside any of Rachel's many social circles, she'll greet you with a warm enveloping hug that you can't help but melt into, and lingers just slightly too long. She'll make you feel like you're the most treasured person in the room. Person by person, Rachel works the room, weaving her web of connection, insuring that everyone's needs are met, and that the group is coming together in comfort and harmony. She agonizes over buying just the right gifts for every social occasion, and hosts many gatherings in her home. No social detail is too small to be ignored.

Despite her active life, Rachel felt creatively stifled and disappointed that she wasn't "giving more back." Her sense of self was almost entirely dependent on caring for others in order to receive their love in return. Her tendency to lose herself in the care of others left Rachel, time and again, on the sidelines in a powerless support position that she accepted on the surface and resented underneath.

ROOTS OF THE DEVOURER

Rachel had a complicated relationship with her own mother, a demanding and socially prominent hostess and beautifully attired patron of the arts. Since her college days, Rachel had been drawn to the mythical journey of Kore/Persephone. She resonated with Kore's fusion with her mother Demeter, and the transformation that occurred when Kore found her own path of individuation.

Rachel's father was a doctor and civic philanthropist who instilled in her the sense of responsibility for caring for one's community. "He cared so deeply about the health and well-being of the place where he lived, almost more than he cared for his family. He was incredibly generous and touched so many lives. I worry that I can't live up to his selfless example." Rachel had internalized the double whammy of her mother's need for attention and her father's altruism—a perfect storm for aligning with The Devourer.

At an early age she learned that to be loved in her family system she had to give. Self-sacrifice and the tendency to control others through her ability to know what they needed ensured that she would be indispensable. Relative to herself however this often meant that Rachel would swing over to The Neglector shadow, especially if she was consumed by a social project that required a great deal of relational tending. Her own needs and wants went way into the background—best not to even know what they were since to tend to them was a threat to her belonging. Yet beneath the surface a kind of resentment would begin to fester: nobody was taking her needs into account. Finally in some random moment the "good girl" would explode in anger and blame.

"I've always thought of myself as a really good person, very generous," Rachel confided. "In fact, I have a sense of pride about it. It was a total shock to consider that the source of my motivation for loving and giving wasn't entirely altruistic."

OBSERVING THE DEVOURER

As Rachel began to consistently self-observe and journal about her Devourer tendencies, she recognized the old truism: you can have too much of a good thing. What she believed was nurturing was actually smothering. In the grip of The Devourer, the deep limiting belief of "I am not enough" expressed itself through her desire to give and give with the unconscious intention to prove her value and worth by all that she offered.

Rachel finally saw how she constantly over-tended everyone she cared about—from children, pets, and spouse, to extended family, friends, employees, social groups, and the various organizations for which she volunteered. Her capacity for Self-Compassion was predictably low, as to be kind and nurturing to herself was incompatible with her focus on taking care of others.

It took a month of a daily reflection practice for Rachel to even begin to recognize how little time and attention she gave to her own inner world of thoughts, feelings, and sensations.

Morning Pages Practice for Self-Observation

This practice is another one that can be applied to identifying and clearing the shadows of every archetype. It is a way to enhance your power to witness yourself— a key component to The Mysterial Change Process.

Morning pages, based on the work of Julia Cameron,[4] are a stream of consciousness form of journaling that, with practice, leads to a stronger and clearer sense of self. They are a trail that you follow into your own inner landscape, where you have the potential to connect with the silent parts of yourself. Faithfully writing the morning pages will lead you to a connection with your source wisdom within.

The process itself is very simple: First thing in the morning find a comfortable place and write three pages (or for fifteen minutes, whichever comes first). This is a longhand, stream of consciousness writing. Some people may even want to do it in bed, given appropriate conditions. You really want to make sure you do morning pages before your mind gets a chance to gear up.

What is difficult, and will take practice, is giving yourself permission to feel everything that you are feeling and think everything that you are thinking in the moment. In other words, the inner censor needs to be silenced. To help with this, journaling is done on a pad of paper (not in a nice journal book). You do not correct spelling errors and you do not read over what you have written for at least the first eight weeks. This exercise is about process not product. After two months you may look back at the journal pages if you are interested in searching for patterns or themes.

There is no wrong way to do the morning pages . . . write whatever comes to mind . . . nothing is too petty, too silly, too stupid, or too weird to be included. "Oh here comes another day . . . I am tired as usual and don't really want to go for a run, but of course I will and I will feel better afterwards . . . that was a bizarre conversation last night with Matt . . . I wonder why I always feel stupid around him . . . blah, blah, blah . . ." Basically you are draining your heart and mind of anything that you would other-wise unconsciously be taking into your day.

In order to release yourself into the morning pages it is important that you know that nobody will read your morning pages except you. In order to be able to surrender fully to uncensored writing, you may need to speak to those close to you and ask them to destroy the pad of paper if something should happen to you. This may sound crazy, but you will find that your censor is very, very active and the op-portunity with the morning pages is to truly give yourself the gift of receiving all of your thoughts and feelings in the moment. As you do so, they have the chance to change . . . witnessing is a powerful and freeing force.

Reflections:
1. What have you noticed is different as you head into your day after doing Morning Pages?
2. What repeated patterns of thoughts, feelings and body sensations are you noticing?

After the first week of this practice Rachel noticed how hard it was to connect with her own feelings and thoughts and how hard she was on herself. With time she slowly began to open up the channel of communication and got connected to her authentic experience.

The Morning Pages were tremendously helpful, but getting The Devourer fully visible was not something that Rachel could do by simply observing herself. Others can see things about ourselves that we can't see—especially our shadow! Along with her growing capacity for self-awareness Rachel also needed the "container" of her relation-ships—the structure and environment where she comes together with others—to reflect her shadows back to her. By observing herself in these relationships, and listening to feedback, Rachel began to understand that she clung to people too tightly, cared too much about their approval, and that she had a need to control what was happening in order to feel safe. "I can see now why I'm not getting the results I want in my volunteer projects," she mused.

One container was a volunteer group of eight women friends. If the group wasn't happy, Rachel wasn't happy, and she took it upon herself to be constantly fixing, soothing, and reconciling. It was exhausting. With observation, feedback she invited from the group, and honest reflection, she recognized that until she fully metabolized The Devourer shadow, she could never land in an autonomous self that could satisfy her longing to make a difference in the world. She would not be able to hold her own ground in the midst of challenging or conflicting situations.

Rachel reflected on what was driving this behavior. "I realized that when a conflict comes up I experience an incredible amount of anxiety. I feel like I am a young girl and get panicky if I can't keep the peace. It feels like a primal survival instinct—the same as if a saber-toothed tiger just jumped out at me."

In fact, when the psychosomatic system is triggered around a deep area of trauma it does not know the difference between something life-threatening and something challenging. This is where the Deep Practice of The Mysterial Change Process (found at the end of this chapter) comes in—a powerful way to communicate with the embodied self that feels under threat.

Building Foundational Capacity

Rachel's incapacity for Self-Compassion was bound up in the belief that other people's needs were her needs. Whereas Kerry was driven by a deep unconscious belief that she needed to achieve and perform in order to receive love, Rachel believed that she needed to anticipate and fulfill other's needs, to shower others with love and compassion. To turn toward herself with that same love and compassion felt somehow wrong, even dangerous. In this parched desert devoid of the soothing waters of Self-Compassion Rachel's sense of a strong independent self could never take root and grow.

With encouragement she began to cultivate **Self-Compassion** (Individual Interior—My Inner Experience) through a simple daily Re-Mothering Practice.

Daily Re-Mothering Practice for *Self-Compassion*

This Re-Mothering practice helps you take on the individuated task of mothering yourself—the result of cultivating a healthy inner Mother archetype. You make space to listen to your feelings and respond to them; you listen to your body and respect its limits; you listen to your intuition; you welcome your creativity; you protect yourself and make decisions that support your well-being. Just as you would with a child, this process of inner mothering needs to be cultivated as a regular part of your daily experience.

To lay down the neural network of this growing inner Mother function, we invite you to engage in this daily practice.

As The Mother, ask the following question to your Being (the totality of your body, heart, mind, and spirit):

"What do you need and want today that will allow you to feel a sense of love, safety, well-being, and belonging?"

Ask the question and allow your Being to respond. You may be surprised by what she says, either through quiet inner words, feelings, intuitive impressions, or subtle energy moving in your body.

These do not need to be big events that require restructuring your day. The very act of engaging the inquiry begins to allow this Re-Mothering function to develop. Translating the desire into action may not be feasible immediately. Nevertheless, it is important that you follow through in some way with your Being's request.

Remember that as a wise Mother you might need to translate the desire into something that is doable. For example, if Being signals that it is longing for a day off to luxuriate in a spa and you know you need to work, you might suggest a compromise: a soak in your tub in the evening.

Examples of Being Desires

I need fifteen minutes of quiet time alone today.

I need my shoulders to be massaged.

I want to be with good friends and feel a deep sense of belonging.

I need a nap this afternoon followed by a cup of hot tea.

I want a hot bubble bath at the end of the day with soft music playing.

I need a hot sweaty workout.

I want to laugh and tickle my son.

(continued on next page)

I want to walk barefoot on the beach.

I want to prepare a great meal and share it with my family.

I want to go onto social media and share a story with my friends.

I want to work in my garden for a bit today.

Reflection: Your learning will accelerate if you take a few minutes to journal about your experiences.

1. What did your Being call you to do?
2. What change, if any, did you notice in yourself after you satisfied your Being Desire?
3. How might that affect how you approach tomorrow or the rest of the week?

Rachel also began a monthly "Soul Date" devoted to spending regular time on her own (about three hours a month) doing something that truly nourished her being. Some months it was a trip to the art museum followed by a glass of wine. Other times it was a walk on the beach, a trip to the zoo, some time alone with a good book.

"My monthly Soul Date was a breakthrough," Rachel confided. "To be able to take myself out for a couple of hours, treat myself the way I might a beloved friend—I realized how foreign it felt, how shriveled that muscle was. At first my Devourer was cringing in shame for spending that much time on myself when there were so many other people I could have been helping. Eventually I discovered that I am actually very good and worthy company!"

As she became capable of treating herself as a precious being she was also more understanding during times of struggle. Instead of just pushing herself through difficulties she used a simple somatic practice to first be with her actual experience of suffering.[5]

Holding her hand gently on her chest she would say to herself:

Rachel this is a moment of suffering. This is hard.
We all struggle in our lives—I am not alone.
May I hold myself with tenderness in this moment.
May I be kind to myself.

Then she would take a deep breath of healing Self-Compassion.

With her sharpening awareness of The Devourer's habits, her daily Re-Mothering practices, and her monthly Soul Date, Rachel's capacity for Self-Compassion skyrocketed.

Next, Rachel tackled the less obvious capacity of **Container Holding** (Collective Interior—Engaging the World). While the foundational capacity of Empathic Resonance deals with the invisible, inner connection with others, Container Holding refers to the way in which we tend and manage the outer structures, systems, and environments in which we live and work. It acknowledges The Creative Cycle,[6] that does not begin with Action, as we have been conditioned to believe, but with Stillness. With effective Container Holding you know that you must create the right conditions for beginning anything—relationship, work project, new life. And then from Stillness you are ready for Connection with the people and factors in the situation before Acting.

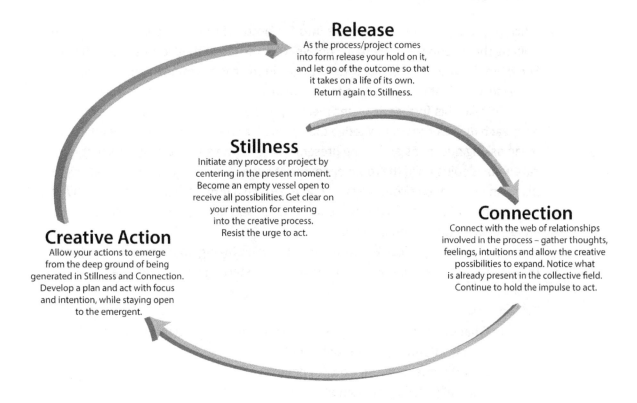

Release
As the process/project comes into form release your hold on it, and let go of the outcome so that it takes on a life of its own. Return again to Stillness.

Stillness
Initiate any process or project by centering in the present moment. Become an empty vessel open to receive all possibilities. Get clear on your intention for entering into the creative process. Resist the urge to act.

Connection
Connect with the web of relationships involved in the process – gather thoughts, feelings, intuitions and allow the creative possibilities to expand. Notice what is already present in the collective field. Continue to hold the impulse to act.

Creative Action
Allow your actions to emerge from the deep ground of being generated in Stillness and Connection. Develop a plan and act with focus and intention, while staying open to the emergent.

The Creative Cycle

Once Rachel began to master The Creative Cycle, the natural next step was to apply it with her teams in meetings. The female body is the ultimate model for containing the creative process. The darkness of the womb provides the environment in which growth and change take place and the miracle of life unfolds. This capacity to consciously hold a space in which something can move from conception through the maturing of form to birth is often underestimated in a world where more outward achieving action, and the quick shifting from one new thing to another, is rewarded.

Meeting Facilitation Practice for *Container Holding*

When preparing for a meeting, take into the account the setting in which you are holding the meeting. Is it the right container for the result that you want to achieve? For example, you might make little changes in the room arrangement, put flowers in a vase, or adjust the lighting to feel more inviting to participants.

To take this further, it might mean opening the meetings with a few words from each member to acknowledge their presence so that they feel included. It can mean asking questions and being present to the subtle emotional signals that indicate what is going on in the room beneath the surface. You might have a break every ninety minutes, and encourage everyone to stretch a little. It includes the sensitivity to rhythms and cycles of a project to know when something needs to incubate a bit more, or when fast action is called for.

And when a project is completed, it means taking some time to celebrate that—to savor the experience and let it go before starting something else.

Reflections:
1. What did you notice was possible in your meeting as a result of deliberately attending to the container?
2. How did it feel in your body to begin in Stillness and Connection instead of jumping into Action without the container being built?

Rachel was a master at creating a beautiful, supportive, inspiring container, and sensing what everyone needed. With her high need for control and tendency to over-manage, her work was to build more flexibility into her Container Holding. That is, to know when to let people and projects have their space, and to release them at the right time.

When Rachel learned The Creative Cycle, and built the capacity of Container Holding, it was a revelation. There was actually a productive way of thinking about the life cycle of a project that was in tune with nature—and with the Feminine.

Limiting Belief of The Mother: "I am not enough."

Shadow work can be difficult simply because it addresses that which can't be directly seen with the conscious mind. The Mysterial Sequence offers a shortcut by identifying the core Limiting Belief that is associated with each archetype. These Limiting Beliefs bedevil women's lives and limit their potential in varying degrees, regardless of their apparent success and accomplishment in the outer world.

At the root of clearing both the active Devourer shadow driving Rachel and the passive Neglector shadow driving Kerry, was the dismantling of the unconscious limiting beliefs of The Mother.

"I am not enough." Do you recognize this limiting belief in your life? Say the words, slowly and out loud to yourself. Notice how they land in you. What thoughts does this belief trigger? How does it make you feel? Do you notice any subtle sensations in your body as the words are expressed? These reflection questions provide valuable information about how you are habitually, unconsciously, and needlessly limiting your own potential.

Rachel saw clearly that her obsessive focus on taking care of others was a subtle way of making up for believing "I am not enough." She understood why she got so angry when affections were not returned in the way she expected—it felt as if her "not-enoughness" had been thrown back in her face.

Kerry recognized "I am not enough" as the root of her deepest suffering. Unless she received an accolade to validate some sense of worthiness, Kerry did not truly value herself. Kerry noticed that she often felt a sense of discomfort and even shame about herself, unable to shake the pervasive background feeling that she wasn't enough, and would never be enough no matter how much she achieved.

To shake this loose, both Rachel and Kerry continued to face their Mother shadow tendencies, to consciously observe and challenge the many ways they were telling themselves

"I am not enough." With time they both began to transform this often-unconscious "truth," into the liberating belief of the healthy Mother.

When the shadow of an archetype is cleared, and the healthy archetype becomes accessible, the Limiting Belief gives way to the Liberating Belief of that archetype.

The Liberating Belief of The Mother: "I am enough just as I am."

Now say these potent words slowly, and out loud to yourself. Notice how the words of this Liberating Belief land in you. Do you feel a subtle sense of relaxation, of relief? Do you feel more energized, more enlivened?

If not, or if you notice resistance, then it is likely that The Neglector or Devourer are at play. That's a reliable indication that more shadow work is needed!

To dislodge the limiting belief of The Mother, Rachel continued to unflinchingly face her overbearing Devourer tendencies, while Kerry worked on dismantling her Neglector. As the shadows slowly transformed in the light of consciousness, and the practices bore fruit, both Kerry and Rachel began to feel true acceptance of themselves, just the way they were. They had committed to a lifelong path of learning and continuous improvement. Something would always be pressing for change. But who they were at the core—that would be forever truly enough.

Finding Your Radiant Presence

What lit you up, or turned you off, in Kerry and Rachel's stories? Reactions either way can be signals from within that you resonate with the shadow behavior, or the essence that is seeking to emerge. Here's the important question: Do you sense it is time for you to work at this ground level of your Feminine nature? It does take some doing . . . or actually, being and thawing. Do you feel ready to create the space and time to welcome this unconditionally loving, accepting, nurturing, and emotionally attuned being who fully, and with all senses alive, inhabits the soft animal of your body?

Can you sense the one within you who is deeply embedded in the rhythms of earthly life? And because of this she has the patience to incubate something into form and maturity, even though the world is screaming for it to be born now. Can you feel yourself as a woman whose groundedness and clarity has a positive influence, inviting others to be their better selves? A woman who can care for herself, others, and the earth in a balanced way? A woman who exudes a **Radiant Presence**?

When the inner Mother awakens, a woman can speak in the multiple languages of Love. She can now begin to hear and understand the distant call of the Mysterial. There are more Initiations to undertake and languages to learn. But now she has some ground on which to plant her walking stick.

IMAGINE

Imagine a world where women are as comfortable in their bodies as they are with their dearest, oldest friend, and just as open to its advice.

Imagine a world where unconditional love is the air that we breathe, so essential to every moment of our existence that we can't imagine being without it.

Imagine a world where we are so present and open to our own and each other's experience that the entire globe comes into resonance like a great singing bowl, bringing us into collective ease and acceptance.

Imagine a world where nurture, center, stillness are as important as cheaper, better, faster.

Imagine a world where we all know we are an essential living part of the one great, sacred, alive body of Gaia.

Imagine a world where we know that we are always already enough.

Imagine this world and then imagine yourself shaping it.

Self-Observation Exercise for The Mother

The purpose of a Self-Observation exercise is to deepen your ability to become an objective observer of your own experience when The Mother shadows, The Neglector and The Devourer, make an appearance. It calls upon you to witness yourself in the moment, to intimately get to know those aspects of your way of being as they emerge in everyday situations.

As you become a better and better observer of your experience, you begin to see and discover things about the world inside and around you that would otherwise go unnoticed. You will in time clearly recognize when the shadows of The Mother take over.

This observation exercise does not include changing anything. It just means looking at things as they currently are now—just noticing and writing down what you observe.

Daily Exercise

In one or two situations during the day, simply notice the presence of The Neglector or The Devourer. One of them may arise when you are alone or interacting with others or when at home or at work.

1. What was happening when you noticed the shadow making an appearance?
2. What emotions did you feel?
3. What sensations were you aware of in your body?
4. What were your thoughts/stories about the situation?
5. What were you doing or not able to do?
6. When in the grip of the shadow, what were your habitual behaviors?

Weekly Reflection

At the end of the week, look over your reflections and summarize in your journal:

1. What consistent stories does The Neglector or The Devourer tell you about the way the world is and how you have to be in it?
2. What are your signature emotions?

3. What connections are you making with the shadows of The Mother and the felt sense and posture your body takes when one of them is present?

4. What are you learning about the way the shadows of The Neglector or The Devourer are structured to provide you love, safety, or a sense of belonging?

5. How is that working and/or not working for you now?

The Mysterial Change Process Deep Practice—The Mother

Recall from Chapter 4 the process of turning toward the reactivity in the body to enable you to transform the archetypal shadows into healthy capacities. Although the general process stays the same through all the activations of The Mysterial Sequence, each archetype works with different limiting and liberating beliefs.

In Deep Practice—The Mother, you will turn your attention toward seeing how The Mother shadows are helping to fuel the reactive patterns. In this practice, you will also start to come into contact with the suffering of the limiting belief of The Mother archetype, **"I am not enough,"** that is a driving force underneath The Devourer and The Neglector shadows. By engaging in Deep Practice, you will learn to turn toward this wounded, tender part of yourself and gradually build the capacity to stay with the embodied discomfort until the reactivity in the body has settled.

This is the powerful message that calls your disowned parts back into the wholeness of yourself, enabling you to invoke the liberating belief of The Mother: **"I am enough just as I am."** Eventually the painful story and protective strategies embedded in your habitual way of being will begin to ease and release, creating space for the arising of the healthy Mother archetype.

SEE IT—Recognize when you have been triggered and are in the grip of The Mother shadow. Notice the *state of mind* (thoughts, judgments, and stories), *emotional state* (feelings), and the *state of body* (sensations, contraction, shape) you find yourself in.

SAY IT—Name what is happening when you recognize the familiar reactions—the body, the emotions, the story, and the behaviors of The Devourer or The Neglector—overtaking you.

STOP IT—Decline the unproductive old stories or mental attitude of the shadow by telling yourself, "Stop!"

SENSE IT—Let go of the "story" or mental attitude for the moment. Bring your attention to the present by tuning into your sensation. Feel your feet on the ground, find your breath in the center of your body, sense the reactive places in your muscles and your core. Just let them be there with recognition, but not judgment; and with no requirement to change anything in the moment. From this place, turn toward the limiting belief of The Mother and say the limiting belief—**"I am not enough."**

NOTICE—Observe what happens when you drop this pebble into the pond of your being. As a compassionate and loving witness, simply be present with whatever arises. Allow yourself to softly touch into this tender place without trying to change or challenge what you find there.

DIFFERENTIATE—Ask yourself: Who would I be without this belief? Allow yourself to respond somatically (i.e., through body sensations and subtle postures) to this inquiry.

STAY WITH IT—Let your breath gently soften and settle places of contraction and tightening. Now call in the calm and nurturing energy of the inner Mother, differentiate from the shadow by inviting the liberating belief: **"I am enough just as I am."** Allow the energizing and grounding truth of these words to resonate through every cell of your body.

COME TO CENTER—As you begin to feel a release of the emotional feelings and sensations that have hijacked you, bring yourself to center. Find your grounding by feeling your feet on the ground and take full, deep breaths from the center of your body. As you exhale, allow your muscles to relax into gravity and find yourself centered in three-dimensional space so that you become more fully present and your energy is balanced between the front and back, the right and left, and above and below.

INVOKE THE MOTHER'S QUALITY OF SELF-COMPASSION—"What would it be like if I had a little more Self-Compassion in my being right now?"

CHOOSE ACTION—Take action or no action from this place of center. Remember to start with situations that have smaller charges and build from there so that you can get the full benefit of the practice.

Daily Practice

Select *one or two situations during the day* when you are aware that your Mother shadows are activated. Deliberately go through each step of the Deep Practice. If you were not able to stop the grab of The Mother shadows in the moment, take some time later in the day and recreate the situation so that the body state is activated and you are able to move through the process. Remember that the neural network can be shifted not only through experience in the moment, but also through recreating the situation using the imagination.

Reflections

Take ten to fifteen minutes to journal on the following:

1. What happened when you were able to let go of the thoughts and stay with the emotions and sensations in the body?
2. What happened when you touched into the embodied limiting belief—*I am not enough?* How do this belief and The Mother shadows influence the way you interact with others? What is possible and impossible when they are the driving force?
3. What was your experience when you brought in the liberating belief of The Mother—*I am enough just as I am?*
4. What, if anything, was different when you came to Center (i.e., the way you feel about yourself, how you interact with others, what actions are possible)?

Chapter 8

THE ACTIVATION OF THE HERO—
Igniting Empowered Action

L et's once again strike the archetypal tuning fork with an invocation to elicit a state and experience of the healthy Hero and invite this universally shared pattern to arise within your being.

As you read aloud this invocation let your body experience the energetic invitation of The Hero.

Invocation of The Hero

Fix your gaze on the Horizon
your mind is clear, laser focused
vibrating with readiness.

Feel the solid vessel of your being—
from which you can now launch yourself, with my help, into the world.
Let my flaming arrow of agency pierce your heart with the desire
to bring your unique gifts into a world that is so hungry for them!

Allow me to knight you upon each capable shoulder
with the potency of my golden sword, empowering and energizing you
to take creative action—sustainably!
Feel the current of my dynamic flame nature electrifying your being
with bold visions, goals, and plans.

I am here to help you consciously author your life.
In my eyes you are valuable beyond measure,
innately capable of doing what is yours to do.
Do not be afraid, for the sweet water of your Feminine Vessel
will keep my Flame nature in balance.

Ignite now the powerful fire of Doing
within the exquisite vessel of your Being,
and let your confidence soar like an eagle.
Awaken to me, and allow the hot coals of your creative impulse
to intensify into a steady flame,
casting your empowered radiant presence into actions
that light up the world!

Igniting the Flame of The Hero

There are myriad creative ways to make a contribution in the world if you are sourcing your actions from the deep ground and beauty of your being. Once you really land in the embodied experience of being enough (The Mother), a signal goes out to the other end of the polarity, and The Hero archetype naturally lights up. It's as if your Flame Yang essence is calling out to your Vessel Yin essence, "Hi honey, I'm finally home!" And your Masculine Hero self comes bursting through the door.

Flame Yang (dynamic Masculine) essence in its purest form opens the full force of our fiery Masculine nature. It gives us access to the energy and commitment we need to bring our deepest dreams and creative aspirations into form. When this Yang ally is suited up we have our own inner Warrior ready and waiting. We know how to set boundaries in ways that liberate us to find our deepest "Yes" and get our lives aligned with what has heart and meaning. We stop procrastinating and finally move forward on those creative projects that have been endlessly on the back burner. And we feel the full force of our becoming—connected now to the evolutionary impulse to develop ourselves to the next level of our potential.

For many years now, leadership programs for women have focused on developing The Hero, recognizing the need for this forward moving, action-oriented capacity; in other words, the need for agency. Courses on assertiveness training, empowerment, public speaking, and conflict management are all excellent ways to cultivate Hero behaviors. There are countless books written about how to fit into the male culture, how to become one of the boys, how to shape-shift ourselves to become successful. While many of these skills can be useful they are all being layered on like apps to an outdated inner operating system. And it isn't long before a woman becomes Hypermasculinized at the expense of her own well-being, and often that of others, and her system crashes.

In our approach we cultivate the healthy Hero archetype as the second Activation in The Mysterial Sequence after we have done the deep work of cultivating Vessel Yin. Without the grounding and containment of the healthy Mother archetype, the overly active Hero burns through our lives like a rampaging wildfire, rendering us barren, exhausted, and soulless. Or fearing this intense force, we can keep it at arms length, leaving its dangerous heat to others who become our heroes.

The Hero archetype has been well entrenched as an icon of success for millennia, and it is no surprise that men and women have tilted over into extreme versions of the Flame Yang essence. But once we do the deep healing work with The Mother, we are very ready to let go of the adrenalin-driven lifestyle and take care of ourselves. Depending on the way we have internalized this archetype, we are ready to either turn down the flame and rest or to turn it up and get out in the world. Either way, the balancing of the Flame Yang energy marks a huge step forward. As we do this transformative work we are redefining the Hero's Journey into one that is more congruent for women. We are leading the way for future generations and we are modeling the potential of **Empowered Action.**

The Foundational Capacities of Empowered Action

The Hero archetype is our ally. Consistent and healthy access to this fundamental force inside ourselves grows the capacities we need to succeed and make a positive difference in the world: Intention Holding, Rhythmic Drive, Mindful Differentiation, and Dynamic Manifestation.

The Hero

	INTERIOR	EXTERIOR
	My Inner Experience	How I Show Up
INDIVIDUAL	Capacity: **INTENTION HOLDING** To clarify and focus a vibrant and compelling image of a desired future way of being and acting. To consciously commit to engaging your body, heart, mind and soul in holding the vision as you move toward bringing this image into reality.	Capacity: **RHYTHMIC DRIVE** To modulate energy as it moves through your body in natural forward-moving pulsations, so that you are continually restoring your system. To pace yourself—cycling through a rhythm of stillness, connection, action and release for sustainable creativity.
	I	IT
	WE	ITS
COLLECTIVE	**Relating with Others** Capacity: **MINDFUL DIFFERENTIATION** To stay connected to your own thoughts, feelings and sensations while consciously remaining in mutuality with, and open to, the experience of others. To set boundaries that honor what is yours to do, needing no approval or permission to express your authentic self.	**Engaging the World** Capacity: **DYNAMIC MANIFESTATION** To take an idea from inception all the way through into form. To work through the necessary systems and structures to accomplish tasks and deliver goals in a consistent and reliable manner.

The Promise of Empowered Action

"Let the beauty we love, be what we do.
There are hundreds of ways to kneel and kiss the ground."

—Rumi

Think back to times in your life when you had a clear goal, one that engaged your heart. Do you remember how that naturally sparked a kind of inner will to accomplish it? An internal drive was activated, giving you the energy and confidence you needed to take risks and engage new ways of being and doing aligned with that intention. You became able to pierce through complex issues and make difficult decisions.

The Hero archetype helps us to focus a clear intention and direct our attention. As martial artist Wendy Palmer writes in her book, *The Intuitive Body*, "Energy tends to go where there is the most excitement, most clarity, most intensity. Energy follows attention. Wherever we focus our attention, our energy follows." The Hero energy helps you hold bold intentions and take the necessary risks to move toward them.

We tend to worry too much as women about whether or not we have the skills and capacity to do a job. That leads us to play it safe, working harder and harder yet never arriving at the destination of "enoughness." Facebook COO Sheryl Sandberg[1] suggests that "Women need to shift from thinking, 'I'm not ready to do that', to 'I want to do that—and I'll learn by doing it'."

This is pure Hero energy speaking!

This liberating Flame Yang energy opens you into a whole new level of productivity, accomplishment, and agency. Imagine being able to know and value what you feel, sense, and think, while being differentiated enough from others that you have the freedom to act on what is true for you while staying connected to others.

To be professionally successful in the world today, women have had to learn to harness this heroic capacity. Unfortunately the deep waters of Vessel Yin have not been accessible to all of them. There are a number of iconic women who demonstrate the fire of Flame Yang in expression. Think of the focus and drive that Hillary Clinton engages in her political career. Or Sheryl Sandberg, who applied herself with such discipline in various organizations before finally becoming COO of the rapidly expanding, largest online social media network. Think of IMF Managing Director Christine Lagarde, First Lady Michelle Obama, Burmese political opposition leader Aung San Suu Kyi, primatologist and UN Messenger of Peace Jane Goodall, and Oprah Winfrey. They all have drawn upon this archetypal energy to make a difference in the world.

There are countless unsung heroes as well. Like the young Nigerian woman who started her own beading business to send her children to school, or the brave woman in Laos who pulled herself out of prostitution and has dedicated her life to liberating other young girls. Closer to home, the American woman who raised three kids on her own, working two jobs while putting herself through nursing school!

We need the healthy Hero on board in order to brave the headwinds of countless challenges in our lives today. When the shadows have been cleared and the healthy archetype cultivated, we know what is ours to do and what is not, and we are able to do it in a way that is powerful, sustainable, and effective. We have cultivated **Empowered Action.**

Shadows of The Hero—The Dominator and The Capitulator

For most women The Hero is wounded and exhausted from the struggles of life. We must begin by tending to the shadow aspects as we nurse our Flame Yang force into good health. The two shadows of The Hero are **The Dominator** and **The Capitulator**. The Dominator is driven and controlling. A woman in the grip of this shadow will do whatever it takes to achieve goals, no matter what the cost. The Capitulator on the other hand gives up. When this shadow takes over, a woman rejects the fiery Hero energy and is stuck in a painful swamp of inertia.

We witness both shadows in action throughout today's world. The collective Dominator shadow created the atrocities of Darfur and the Congo, where rape and murder of women and children are calculated tools of conquest. It's in charge in the Amazon rainforest, where high-level corruption between corporations and governments fuels ecological devastation and the destitution of native inhabitants. The Dominator feels no relationship to any body, least of all Mother Earth or her most vulnerable beings.

The Capitulator collective shadow shows up in the gangs of child soldiers, stolen from their families. They seem to have no choice but to give in . . . and then become Dominators themselves. The Capitulator allows the mute acceptance and indefensible unwillingness to confront the epidemic of international sex trafficking.

Lest we relegate these shadows to less developed parts of the world, remember the financial meltdown of 2008. The Dominator didn't worry about how many families lost their homes and savings and what the theft of billions of middle-class dollars would mean for generations to come. Bigger, better, more, and mine were the driving forces of that collapse. The Dominator is present in the pride taken in the workaholic culture, where we boast about our "all-nighters" and being available 24-7 with our wired-in lives.

The Capitulator? She just sighs and says, "That's the way it is. I don't have any power to change it anyway." This creeping avoidance enables unobstructed influence peddling in Washington, health insurance refused because someone got cancer, insane wars that murder innocents . . . the list goes on.

To powerfully meet the challenges that these Hero shadows have created in the world requires that we ourselves face the ways the shadows have taken root in us so that we have access to the healthy Hero. Think of it this way: you have a legion of creative energy and action that is sitting idle on the sidelines as you make your way through the challenges of life. Imagine what might happen if you were able to harness that powerful Flame Yang energy!

THE DOMINATOR—ACTIVE SHADOW OF THE HERO

When the ego over identifies with the archetype of The Hero, The Dominator shadow is in expression. You are driven by an unconscious force that does not know when to stop. You will do whatever it takes to achieve goals, no matter what the cost.

A woman recalls how she grew up partially ignoring her deeply loving mother in favor of her dashing father. "I wanted to be my father's daughter and conquer the world just like him. He was constantly doing; when not at his desk he was building a barn, deck, guesthouse, endless projects. I grew up believing that if I was going to be successful like him then I must keep my own 'doing' switch turned on all the time. Even today I can hear his voice ringing inside my head whenever I sit down to be still or read. 'What are you doing wasting time? Aren't there things you could be doing?'"

This is an example of how what starts out in childhood as the healthy impulse to accomplish, can become The Dominator shadow.

CHARACTERISTICS OF THE DOMINATOR

Here are some signs that The Dominator is in the driver's seat.

* You work long and hard, driving yourself beyond healthy limits with an endless list of to-dos. You are proud of pulling "all-nighters" and being a Warrior woman.
* You measure your productivity against that of others in a way that keeps you in a competitive orientation.
* You push others as hard as you push yourself, often rolling over their natural rhythms with your demanding ways.

* You avoid intimacy and vulnerability in relationships by being sure you stay in control at all times.
* You do not know when enough is enough, both personally and interpersonally. This drives you to excess (alcohol, drugs, sex, food, work), and a kind of bullying of others who do not have your stamina.
* You devalue stillness and just "being" as a waste of time, and find it difficult to allow yourself or others to "do nothing."
* You believe you only deserve rest, relaxation, and fun after you have worked really hard and accomplished important tasks.
* You achieve results without taking the time to savor that success and return to stillness, moving quickly onto the next challenge.

These are just some of the ways in which your Hero nature splits off into The Dominator shadow. Do any of them sound familiar? Often it is easier to recognize shadows in others, so perhaps certain people came to mind as you read over the list.

CLEARING THE DOMINATOR: SANDRA'S JOURNEY

Sandra was forty-five and on the verge of collapse when we met her. Sandra was a chain-smoking, "take no prisoners" kind of manager and very successful at getting things done. She also saw herself as the ultimate champion for others and the causes she cared about. She would take any challenger to the mat who stood in the way of manifesting those things she believed in strongly. Anger often fueled her drive for power and control, and was central to her leadership style.

In the early days of her career, inside a very Masculine corporate environment, it worked well for her to be able to stand up to the strong men in her environment. They respected her swagger and her firm commanding ways. Yet as she progressed up the hierarchy of management, this style of leadership became more limiting. Her short temper and aggressive ways alienated her peers and made it challenging for her to be promoted past a certain level. Again and again she would be passed over for others with less line experience but more capacity to create productive, happy teams.

This is a pattern that we have observed with many women who learned to lead by becoming "one of the boys." For some of us, The Hero archetype became a powerful ally that supported us to get ahead professionally in the early stages of our careers, and then turned into The Dominator without us even consciously knowing it. Without a valued "vessel of being," a woman's natural and powerful Flame Yang energy has no container in which to burn. And the culture encourages that fiery energy of action and power over others. Over time The Hero will split off into the bullying shadow expression of The Dominator. For Sandra, the idea of taking care of her body, of slowing down, of receiving, of being willingly vulnerable, was an anathema to her very identity.

ROOTS OF THE DOMINATOR

Sandra was one of two daughters in a working class family where her father and mother worked hard to give the girls the opportunities they never had. This left no time in their busy lives for drama or hurt feelings. In fact, they called Sandra a "big crybaby" if she got emotional about anything at all. Life was wholly about getting things done and done well. Not surprisingly, Sandra set her sights on being successful so that her parents would be proud of her accomplishments. When a cousin received unfair treatment in the legal system as a juvenile, Sandra was determined to become a lawyer and advocate for those with no voice. She made many sacrifices over a long stretch of years to accomplish her goals. Her drive was phenomenal and took her all the way to a senior management position in a leading multinational corporation.

Relationships were always challenging for Sandra. They just seemed like too much work. Further, her experience as a younger woman taught her that if she showed her vulnerability, others would take advantage of her. Shortly after Sandra graduated from college she got pregnant with a high school boyfriend. Their marriage only lasted a few years and after it dissolved she assumed primary care for their young daughter Hannah. She hired good nannies, enrolled her in all the right schools, and hoped that this would take care of her growth and development. Sandra was too busy in her professional life to consider an alternative. The Neglector Shadow of The Mother was a natural ally for the steamrolling Dominator.

Oh yes, her flame burned hot and uncontrolled. The limitations of this way of being finally overwhelmed her when struggles at work overlapped with struggles at home with her daughter. Then the shock of demotion hit, just when Sandra was expecting to be promoted. Sandra finally realized there was a serious gap between how she saw herself and how others saw her. But it wasn't until she encountered her daughter's struggles at early puberty that Sandra realized she was not the role model that she wanted to be. Further, she had no idea how to become one. Hannah had become tough and driven just like her mother and pushed back every time Sandra would try to set a boundary with her. It was a powerful struggle between two strong-willed women. Her daughter was the one person whom Sandra had let into her heart, and the more she tried to keep her close through control the further away Hannah wanted to get. For the sake of Hannah's future Sandra knew she needed help.

OBSERVING THE DOMINATOR

At first Sandra approached even her growth process with the same kind of "let's get 'er done!" attitude. She wanted to find those shadows and slay them as fast as possible! With careful guidance, she softened and slowly began to shed her armor, piece by piece, and make contact for the first time in many years with the raw, tender, and vulnerable young girl hidden away behind her bold and assertive style.

As she began to heal The Neglector shadow of The Mother, the frozen river of her feelings thawed. A new and tender love for herself and empathy for others slowly began to bloom in her heart as she accepted herself just as she was. From this place of grounded connection to herself she was ready to move toward the shadow of The Dominator and build her capacity to make things happen in the world in a sustainable and interconnected way.

BUILDING FOUNDATIONAL CAPACITY

Under the sway of The Dominator Shadow, Sandra's Flame Yang energy was a destructive force in her relationship with her own body, and in her interpersonal relationships with others. The key to liberating her Flame Yang energy into a healthy Hero was to bring her well-developed capacity for agency and autonomy into constructive relationship with her capacity for embodiment and connection. Developing the capacity of **Rhythmic Drive** (Individual Exterior—How I Show Up) rather than overdrive became her goal.

She realized that she needed to find ways to build connection with herself and others during the press of her demanding days. She recognized that she did not always need to discharge the intense driving energy in her body through conflict and learned how to align with the natural rhythms of her body. She began to cycle through doing and resting, maintaining a steady relationship with the flow of her energy.[2]

Sandra set her phone alarm to go off every ninety minutes during workdays so she could take ten-minute rest periods where she left her desk and moved her body, listened to music, or ate a healthy snack. She even became an advocate for twenty-minute power naps in the afternoon and was proud to be known around the office as the "Nap Nazi" as she tried to enroll everyone else in the practice. It didn't take long before she found that she was no longer exhausted at the end of the day. Her chronic frustration eased and, along with experiencing more joy in her days, she also became significantly more productive.

Recent brain research is challenging our workaholic culture with evidence that time for the brain to be idle is essential for our physical health and our actual productivity levels. Science is catching up with the experience many of us have had where our best ideas

Pacing Your Day Practice for *Rhythmic Drive*

Choose a day when you have the freedom in your schedule to experiment with this rhythm.

* ✳ When you begin your work set an alarm for ninety minutes. Allow yourself to drop fully into the cycle of work until the alarm goes off.
* ✳ Take a ten-to-twenty-minute break.
* ✳ During your break stand up and move around to shift your attention from whatever it had been focused on before. Go for a walk around the block, put on music and dance, take a power nap, do a little sketching, spend time in your garden, take your dog for a walk . . . etc.

Reflections:
1. What did you notice about the quality of your energy and attention during the day and at night following this practice?
2. What did you notice about your moods and emotional waves?

drop in out of nowhere during a shower, a workout, sitting staring out the window at the birds, or walking in the forest.[3]

As Sandra broke out of the "full steam ahead" approach to her days something new started to happen inside. There was actually space now for her to imagine a life other than the one that she had brought into reality through force and hard work. Images of the possibility of a life that was more fulfilled, connected, and creative began to float through her mind. She was ready to develop the capacity of **Intention Holding** (Individual Interior— My Inner Experience) to focus and energize a positive image of her future. This had to be clear and compelling enough to provide inspiration that could compete with the years of habitual sabotaging patterns, and yet still be doable.

When The Dominator is in charge, we often set intentions that are way too far beyond our capacity and push ourselves until we get there. It doesn't matter that we, and the others working with us, are exhausted and alienated—we completed the task! If The Capitulator is in the driver's seat then we tend to never get past the roundabout of inertia, afraid to stretch ourselves in an intention because we do not know how we will actually get there. We bury our dreams and close down our hopes until we can see a glimpse of how we could accomplish them. This approach doesn't allow for the "friendly universe" to participate with us in surprising ways.

When the healthy Hero comes online, we are willing to take a risk and stretch into an intention way out ahead of ourselves. Sandra set a bold intention that was a big stretch from her current experience, and began each morning by bringing it into her mind, heart, and body: "I am consciously committed to being deeply connected with my soul, moving through my day in an easy rhythm, staying present in the moment and connected to others with an open heart."

It took some time before she could really feel this physically, emotionally, and mentally. Once that occurred, however, it became an irresistible pull forward that she counted on to get her through the tough times.

Conscious Intention Practice for *Intention Holding*

Allow yourself to imagine a way of being/doing in your life that you do not currently have access to and yet deeply long to experience. It could be in your living situation, relationships, work life, creative life, etc. You do not need to know how you will get there from here. You only need to be willing to hold the intention by energizing it in your body, mind, heart and soul.

Keep the following things in mind as you write your statement:

* Write it in the positive (not the absence of something you don't like).
* Write it in the present tense as though it has already been accomplished.
* Keep it short enough that you can call it to mind easily.
* Begin with the words, "I am . . . "

Examples:

I am developing a relationship with myself through knowing the needs of my heart, mind, body, and soul, and meeting those needs.

I am living more fully from my heart so that I may flow through my days with grace, ease, and authentic connection with others.

Once you have written the statement say it aloud to yourself and see if it evokes positive and strong emotions in your body. See if each and every word reso-

nates for you as you speak them aloud (you will feel something like a subtle vibra-
tion or lift of energy). If not, tweak your statement until it all resonates.

Accessing the emotional charge in your body around your future intention is
what turns on the engine and activates the field of all potentiality.

Begin each day by energizing your Intention Statement through saying it out
loud and allowing it to resonate in your body, heart, and mind. See yourself living
into your Intention.

Be willing to be surprised by what begins to unfold.

Reflections:
1. What, if anything, do you notice is deepening around the connection
   you have with this image of your desired future?
2. What little glimpses are emerging of this new way of being in your life?

After several months of holding her clear intention, Sandra was surprised when one
day as she said it aloud to herself she realized that she was actually beginning to live it. "I
startled myself one day when I said my intention aloud," Sandra exclaimed, "and realized
that it was no longer out in the future. I *was* living from my heart, connected to others,
and more successful than ever at work. But the greatest validation was in my relationship
with my daughter. As I got off the treadmill of work and spent more time with her, showed
her more of my feelings, and became more vulnerable, *she* actually began to soften. At
least, I am no longer seen as the enemy."

Without the bully persona obscuring her essence it wasn't long before those in her
organization recognized her natural leadership abilities and opportunities began to open
up again. The healthy Hero had lifted her over a major threshold in the trajectory of her
career and her life!

Shadows of The Hero—The Dominator and The Capitulator

THE CAPITULATOR—PASSIVE SHADOW OF THE HERO

Not all women we have worked with grew up with a desire to follow the Hero's Journey.
Flame Yang energy was just too terrifying for them. They learned how to get love by
not forcing their independent will into the world. Instead, they repressed their emerging

capacity for agency and autonomy, often becoming Daddy's little girl or hiding behind mommy's skirts. As one woman described it, "I was one of five children. My father was an angry alcoholic who worked hard all day and drank hard all night. When I stayed under the radar things seemed to go okay. If I tried to do something for myself he would yell at me for being selfish and not thinking of the rest of the family. I was afraid of him and afraid of ever being like him, so I just shut down my own inner fire."

Although you might choose to turn off the connection to your Flame Yang energy, it does not go away. Quite the opposite! This powerful Yang force continues to look for ways to express itself and ends up in all sorts of compensatory behaviors, as you will read below.

CHARACTERISTICS OF THE CAPITULATOR

Here are some signals that you are in the back seat of your life.

* You let others blaze a trail for you to follow, intimidated by what you assume it would take to actually initiate creative action on your own.
* You find it difficult to set goals and stay focused to achieve them, often leaving projects when the hard work of manifestation really begins.
* You are as afraid of success as you are of failure, and tend to talk about your "great ideas" or dreams, but never take steps to do anything about them.
* You prefer to just fade into the background when things get challenging and not rock the boat or add fuel to the fire with your perspective or ideas.
* You don't trust what you think, sense, and feel or that your contribution will make a difference.
* You experience a kind of exhaustion and paralysis when you even think about doing something that will upset the status quo.
* In the presence of powerful others you withdraw or shut down.
* You may have occasional bursts of creative action, but these usually fade away leaving you drained and discouraged.
* You get impatient when desired results aren't immediately forthcoming.
* You procrastinate and blame others or your circumstances for not being able to get things done or create the life you want.
* You give your power away to others, projecting your strengths onto

them, and then secretly resenting them for their abilities (which you don't believe you have on your own).

❋ You do not believe that you can create the life you want and just accept whatever comes your way.

❋ You crave the approval of others and need their acceptance before acting.

Women will tend to have one dominant shadow but often swing unpredictably into the other one under stress. One familiar pattern is the classic hard driving workaholic Dominator, doing whatever it takes to get ahead in the corporation during the week who then swings over to The Capitulator on the weekends, giving away her power to her husband/partner and children.

Or, a strong Capitulator may passively support an abusive boss all week and then erupt into unpredictable bursts of energy, for instance, cleaning her house in a Dominator frenzy, or working all day and night to complete a work project at the expense of her health. She might then swing back to the lethargy of The Capitulator when challenges arise and look for her Hero to rescue her.

Most women today experience this split, both individually and in the collectives of which we are a part. It is an inevitable reality of growing up in a world without adequate modeling and guidance to integrate these energies. But once we start to reel in The Hero from the shadows, unimaginable futures become possible.

CLEARING THE CAPITULATOR: GABRIELLA'S JOURNEY

Unlike Sandra, the fire of Flame Yang was terrifying for Gabriella. Like other similar women she did everything she could to avoid contact with it. When and if she caught fire for a moment, it was usually in service to someone else's vision and goal. Over time her initial skill at staying under the radar turned into an attitude of "I'm nobody special." She increasingly directed her creative energy and attention toward others. She would become so accommodating and self-effacing in social settings—in order to avoid the risk of alienating others—that she began to disappear.

The wake-up call came for her when she realized that as harmonious and comfortable as her life was, she did not feel happy. Her children, both at home and when at school, were expressing a joy in life that was completely missing for her. She felt like a wet blanket was draped over her creative fire, and even if she lit a spark for a moment it would soon go out. The Capitulator had taken over but underneath this shadow her healthy Hero energy called out in a small voice that finally she turned toward.

ROOTS OF THE CAPITULATOR

Gabriella, forty, was the oldest daughter in a first generation Hispanic family. Her parents embodied the traditional roles of men and women within that cultural paradigm. She learned early on that the males in her family had the power. She followed her mother's example and accepted the role of making them happy. When she was ten years old, her father suffered an injury on the worksite of his construction job. He lost some of his mobility and fell into a deep depression. Her ultra machismo uncle stepped in to help out with the family. He was the ultimate Dominator and went to great lengths to let everyone know that he was in charge. The only way to avoid his angry tirades was to be passive and do exactly what he said without question.

The Capitulator shadow often links arms with someone else's Dominator. But this is not a friendly connection. Underneath, deep distrust and wounds fester, arising from the fearful impact of uncontrolled shadow Flame Yang in expression. Such women have often experienced or witnessed firsthand the abusive power of The Dominator and have chosen to "go along" to "get along."

When Gabriella was young she found it easy to forget herself and morph into whatever she felt others expected of her. This strategy had worked well for a time, bringing her the love and attention she needed during that phase of her life. As soon as she could, she enrolled in college, aiming to become a teacher, a profession that was respected by her family. Given the challenges of her own childhood, she had a special interest in creating environments where young children could thrive. She met and married a man she had fallen deeply in love with, had two children, and poured whatever energy was left at the end of each long school day into care for her family.

At home and at work she struggled to ask for anything for herself. The word, "No," was almost impossible to say when someone asked her to do something. She became a motherly servant for her two children, her husband, her fellow teachers, her students, and her family. No wonder she was exhausted and soul dead. Over time, she began to harbor deep feelings of resentment and discontent. These feelings confused her. "Why am I not content with my life?" she anguished. "I have everything that my family dreamed for me—a good job, a husband, and two healthy children. Why do I want more and why can't I seem to do anything about it? What is wrong with me?"

OBSERVING THE CAPITULATOR

In contrast to Sandra, Gabriella was very familiar with The Mother archetype and over-identified with it to such an extent that The Devourer shadow dominated most of her life decisions. "I just truly never thought about myself or my needs, and if my husband, children, family, or students ever needed me I wouldn't hesitate to give up my own desires." Through deep work with clearing the shadows and cultivating The Mother archetype, Gabriella learned to find her way into her own body, heart, mind and soul. This was like entering a new and unexplored country. She slowly began to learn the language of her unique needs, desires and passions and to accept that they had as much value as the needs of others.

Once Gabriella understood that the impulse she was experiencing to know herself and find more meaning and alignment in her life was a natural step forward in her developmental journey, something began to relax inside. Perhaps she wasn't crazy after all.

This awareness made it possible for her to begin to track The Capitulator shadow, noticing what conditions seemed to activate it and drain away The Hero's drive to move forward. "Once I had an understanding of what to look for, I began to notice when I would drop a wet blanket over my Hero energy. In conversations at work and at home, as soon as someone said something different than what I was thinking or saying, or wanted me to do something I didn't want to do, my body would sag in the chair and I would feel all my vitality drain away. I would go silent and become compliant or disappear into the woodwork. It was like someone just pulled a plug on my energy."

Building Foundational Capacity

Using **Deep Practice—The Hero** (found at the end of this chapter) Gabriella learned how to tolerate in her body the charge of her own conviction and risk setting clear boundaries with others that would allow her to differentiate from her fusion with them. This powerful somatic practice actually rewires the body so that it recognizes the force of Flame Yang energy as healthy, to be channeled and expressed effectively. As Gabriella shared, "It was deeply empowering for me to feel the energy in my body when I would say 'no' and act in a way that was *for me, not against others*. I realize now that I was hooked up inside to believe that if I did something for myself I would hurt others, so I just always said 'yes,' and went along." The Hero was beginning to take up residence!

The capacity of **Mindful Differentiation** (Collective Interior—Relating With Others) requires us to practice skillful boundary setting. Boundary Setting requires that you draw on your healthy Inner Hero. Without this inner function we will either create boundaries that are too rigid and do not allow intimacy, or we will have no boundaries and allow others to trample all over us.

One of the ways we establish boundaries for ourselves is by saying "no," or declining. A decline is a promise not to put our attention in a certain place. Many of us have trouble saying no to things that we are really not committed to or that take our attention away from what we care about. This can lead to feeling overcommitted, resentful, or as though life is out of control. We may even resign ourselves to never having what it is we want.

Many of us have also set boundaries relative to others that are too strong and do not allow for intimacy and connection. We may be overly protective of our time and energy, of our need to be "good," or perhaps so task-driven that we forget the human impact.

Boundary Setting Practice for *Mindful Differentiation*

Reflect on which boundaries in your life right now might need to be made clearer and healthier in order to facilitate your movement toward your Intention. Observe the choices that you are making—what you say yes to, and what you say no to—that either support or compromise your intentions. Examine the various places that boundaries can be made or broken. Notice the promises you are making, the conversations you are in, the spaces you need to create or protect for yourself. What are the stories, assumptions, and self-talk you are listening to around boundaries?

1. Select an important boundary that needs to be made clearer and healthier *inside yourself* in order to move toward your Intention. Take at least one action to make it healthier. Examples:

   ✴ I will set a boundary with myself around hours worked. For two nights during the workweek I will not do work after I return home.
   ✴ I will set a boundary with myself around numbing out with my husband in front of the television, so that I can loosen the boundary around intimacy and open up to deeper ways to be together.

2. Select an important boundary that needs to be made clearer and healthier *with another* in order to facilitate your movement toward your Intention. Take at least one action to make it healthier. Examples:

   ✳ I will set a boundary with my family so that they know I do not want to be disturbed during my morning practice time. I will reassure them that this is *for me*, not *against them*.
   ✳ I will set a boundary with my boss around taking on anything that she asks me to do. I will give myself permission to say, "No," and take the time to discern what is mine to do.

Note: Remember the ripple effect when you take a stand for yourself . . . sometimes the waters can be a bit choppy. Your choice to take a stand for yourself is not about being against others, but being for you! "This is for me . . . not against you."

Reflections:
   1. In what ways did you notice resistance showing up to this practice in the way of thoughts, feelings, or body reactions? What do you think you might be afraid of?
   2. When you did find the courage to set a boundary, what did you notice that your 'no' made more space for in your life?

Gabriella started to work with Boundary Setting close to home with her husband Dan. "I have always just said 'Yes' to what my husband wants. It was easier than rocking the boat and I was afraid of his anger. When he asked me at the last minute to take care of our son Ryan on the night that I had a meditation class, and I was able to say 'No', I surprised him and myself," she reflected. "He got ready to fight and bully me but I simply said that I would not listen to his verbal tirade and if he wanted to discuss it further I would help him come up with another solution, but that I would not be yelled at nor would I just capitulate and stay home. He sulked off into the other room but eventually returned, and we were able to discuss an alternative solution that allowed us both to meet our needs, and our son to be well tended. I was so proud of myself that I literally skipped the whole way to my class."

As Gabriella worked systematically with the liberation of her powerful Flame Yang essence she grew to welcome the fiery nature of her being and finally found the courage to leave her teaching job and join with some friends to start her own company. She grew beyond her default pattern of fusion with others and was able to not only speak up with her ideas but also not collapse in conflict situations. Her predisposition to endlessly think about things and never take action began to shift as her inner Hero ally carried her ideas into the foundational capacity of **Dynamic Manifestation** (Collective Exterior—Engaging The World). Once she had felt the fulfillment of accomplishing small steps in the direction of her larger vision she began to trust the fire of the Hero inside herself.

She learned to *stay with* the positive and new feelings of accomplishment in her body and exaggerate those so that she could begin to get more comfortable with the energy associated with The Hero's agency. We know from recent brain studies that the brain is programmed to notice and record those negative or unpleasant things that happen to us and downplay the positive.[4] It is called a "negativity bias"—a survival mechanism based in the amygdala that is set to respond to perceived danger. This worked well when we were in the jungles with life-threatening wild animals, but the same fear mechanism today can keep us oriented toward those things that don't go well. And as neuroscientists say, "Neurons that fire together wire together."

In the past, Gabriella had fear of conflict and discomfort that kept her scanning for things that might go wrong. She would have an uncomfortable encounter as she tried to manifest her new ideas, and even if there were positive things that happened she would focus on the difficulties and get discouraged. Breaking this habit took practice. She learned to allow the embodied experience of satisfaction from accomplishing just a small task to last ten to twenty seconds more each time she followed through with new actions.

Glass Half-Full Practice for *Dynamic Manifestation*

To manifest most of our intentions we need to engage with a complex world of systems and structures. It is important to be able to break down a large goal into smaller steps that allow us to move forward in a balanced and yet dynamic way. We need to celebrate the completion of the small steps that lead to our destination.

Reflect on the Intention that you set earlier and find a small step toward this that you can actually accomplish in a relatively short period of time and commit to doing it.

Write it down in a clear statement: "I will do . . . by (*insert date*)." Make this a stretch, but doable.

When you have completed the step, stay with the feeling of accomplishment in your body. Orient your attention to what you have completed and not what is left to complete.

Enjoy the feelings and sensations in your body. Stay with them at least ten seconds longer than you normally would do. This creates new neural pathways that help you recognize and appreciate your accomplishments. "The longer that something is held in the awareness and the more emotionally stimulating it is, the more neurons that fire and thus wire together and the stronger the trace in memory."[5]

Reflections:
1. What did you notice occurring in your body when you stayed with the feelings connected with accomplishing a task?
2. What difference does it make when you break down a larger goal into smaller steps that you can act on easily?

With time and practice Gabriella generated the circuitry required for action and autonomy. Her fear that The Hero energy would become The Dominator and take over her life and ruin her relationships proved to be quite wrong. In fact, she found that the more she expressed her own needs and wants in her relationships, the more she was able to have deep intimacy and authentic connection with her husband, children, family, and colleagues.

Limiting Belief of The Hero: "I have to *do* to be of value."

In the deep realms of the unconscious the limiting belief of The Hero drives us in ways that we are mostly unaware of. Take a moment now and consider these questions: Do you recognize this limiting belief in your life? Say the words of the limiting belief slowly and out loud to yourself. Notice how they land in you. Do you recognize how this has lived as truth inside you? What thoughts does this belief trigger? How does it make you feel? Do you notice any subtle sensations in your body as the words are expressed?

These reflection questions provide valuable information about how you are habitually, unconsciously, and needlessly limiting your own potential.

Deep in the unconscious of both Sandra and Gabriella this belief lived as truth. Sandra learned early on that she needed to not just *do* a lot but to also be the one who did more than others and had the control. At first the family system she grew up in, and then the corporate culture, rewarded this behavior and reinforced the belief. Her Dominator way of being was applauded until she reached the point in her life and career where only *doing* at the expense of *being* was no longer working.

For Gabriella this deep belief constantly eroded any sense of confidence she began to build. She never seemed to be able to do things the way others could, and when deadlines would press in or someone would disagree with her she would simply give in to The Capitulator—it just wasn't worth the fight. And this defeat would reinforce her sense of being a failure and not being of value. A vicious and life draining circle.

When the shadow is metabolized and the healthy Hero emerges, a liberating belief takes root and gives us a very different relationship to the fiery Yang force.

Liberating Belief of The Hero: "I am empowered to do what is mine to do."

Now say these potent words slowly, and out loud, to yourself. Notice how the words of this liberating belief land in you. Do you feel a subtle sense of relaxation, of relief? Do you feel more energized, more enlivened?

What if it was not your job to *do* everything all the time? What if by deeply connecting to the sufficiency of your being (through the work with The Mother) and by activating the healthy Hero you simply know what is yours to do?

When Sandra lived into this new belief she didn't do as much as before, and what she did do she did in a way that aligned with the rhythms of her body. A kind of effortless effort replaced her bulldozer approach to life. It was a huge paradigm shift for her when she could find as much joy and fulfillment in a quiet evening at home with friends as she could in winning an important court case. Before Gabriella cultivated The Hero, she was hesitant to take action. Now she began to do more and learned to love the feeling of excitement in her body when she would take an idea into creative expression. She found that there was far more that was actually hers to do than she had ever imagined.

Igniting Empowered Action

When The Hero is ignited deeply in your psyche and soma, you have the energy, confidence, and enthusiasm to plant the seeds of your creative essence in the fertile ground of the world. We all have something unique to contribute, and it is when we have cultivated **Empowered Action** that we can experience what Frederick Buechner[6] is pointing toward: "The place God calls you to is the place where your deep gladness and the world's deep hunger meet."

You are not afraid to set bold intentions and you have the inner discipline to move steadily toward them. You know how to pace yourself so that you use your energy and that of others wisely and sustainably. You are discerning about what is yours to do and are able to leave the rest to others—or perhaps it didn't need to be done at all in the first place!

Can you see yourself stepping forward with boldness and a new willingness to take risks . . . for the sake of your dreams? Can you imagine doing that in a way that honors your being and the embodied pleasure and needs of your soul?

The Hero sounds the trumpet and calls us forth to follow our dreams into manifestation. It is time for us to align with a healthy expression of this primal Yang force and chart a new course for "becoming," on our own terms as women.

IMAGINE

Imagine a world where The Hero is alive and well in women and we have full access to the exquisite piercing energy of Flame Yang. Where we are able to bring our deepest dreams and visions into reality in a way that is congruent with all of who we are and is in mutuality with others.

Imagine a world where women source their actions from a connection to the deep well of their being.

Imagine a world where women become advocates, activists, and change agents who have the focused intention and commitment required to show up and make a positive difference.

Imagine a world where women are not afraid to take risks and boldly step into new ways of being and doing that are aligned with their goodness, beauty, and truth.

Imagine this world and then imagine yourself shaping it!

Self-Observation Exercise for The Hero

The purpose of this Self-Observation exercise is to deepen your ability to become an objective observer of your own experience when The Hero shadows make an appearance. It calls upon you to witness yourself in the moment, to intimately get to know those aspects of your Habitual Way of Being as they emerge in everyday situations.

As you become a better and better observer of your experience, you begin to see and discover things about the world inside and around you that would otherwise go unnoticed. You will in time clearly recognize when the shadows of The Hero take over.

This observation exercise does not include changing anything. It just means looking at things as they currently are now . . . just noticing and writing down what you observe.

Daily Exercise

In one or two situations during the day, simply notice the presence of The Dominator or The Capitulator. It may arise when you are alone or interacting with others, at home or at work.

1. What was happening when you noticed the shadow making an appearance?
2. What emotions did you feel?
3. What sensations were you aware of in your body?
4. What were your thoughts/stories about the situation?
5. What were you doing or not able to do?

Weekly Reflection

At the end of the week, look over your reflections and summarize:

1. What consistent stories do The Dominator and The Capitulator tell you about the way the world is and how you have to be in it?
2. What are your signature emotions?
3. What connections are you making about the shadows of The Hero and the felt-sense and posture your body takes when one of them is present?

4. What are you learning about the way the shadows of The Dominator and The Capitulator are structured to provide you love, safety or a sense of belonging?
5. How is that working and/or not working for you now?

Take some time to observe The Dominator or The Capitulator in yourself without any attempting to shift anything. Give yourself space to really see how they operate (maybe take a few days to a week). Then move into the Deep Practice.

Mysterial Change Process
Deep Practice—The Hero

The core technology for metabolizing the shadows of The Hero is the same structure as for The Mother. You must first have enough free awareness to notice when you are triggered and the shadow expressions of The Hero erupt out of the unconscious. With practice you will actually be able to use The Mysterial Change Process in the moment but to begin with you will likely need to remove yourself from the triggering situation and take yourself through the cycle.

SEE IT—Recognize when you have been triggered and are in the grips of The Hero shadow. Notice the *state of mind* (thoughts, judgments, and stories), *emotional state* (feelings), and the *state of body* (sensations, contraction, and shape) you find yourself in.

SAY IT—Name what is happening when you recognize the familiar reactivity—the body, the emotions, the story, and the behaviors of The Dominator or The Capitulator —overtaking you.

STOP IT—Decline the unproductive old stories or mental attitude of the shadow by telling yourself, "Stop!"

SENSE IT—Let go of the "story" or mental attitude for the moment. Bring your attention to the present by tuning into your sensation. Feel your feet on the ground, find your breath in the center of your body, sense the reactive places in your muscles and your core. Just let them be there with recognition, but not judgment; and with no requirement to change anything in the moment. From this place, turn toward the limiting belief of The Hero and say: *I have to do to be of value.*

NOTICE—Observe what happens when you drop this pebble into the pond of your being. As a compassionate and loving witness, simply be present with whatever arises. Allow yourself to softly touch into this tender place without trying to change or challenge what you find there.

DIFFERENTIATE—Ask yourself: Who would I be without this belief? Allow yourself to respond somatically (i.e., through body sensations and subtle postures) to this inquiry.

STAY WITH IT—Let your breath gently soften and settle places of contraction and tightening. Now call in the fiery and motivating energy of the inner Hero and differentiate from the shadow by inviting the liberating belief: *I am empowered to do what is mine to do.* Allow the energizing and grounding truth of these words to resonate through every cell of your body.

COME TO CENTER—As you begin to feel a release of the emotional feelings and sensations that have hijacked you, bring yourself to center. Find your grounding by feeling your feet on the ground and taking full, deep breaths from the center of your body. As you exhale, allow your muscles to relax into gravity and find yourself centered in three-dimensional space so that you become more fully present and your energy is balanced between the front and back, the right and left, and above and below.

INVOKE THE HERO'S QUALITY OF COURAGE—What would it be like if I had a little more Courage in my being right now?"

CHOOSE ACTION—Take action or no action from this place of center. Remember to start with situations that have smaller charges and build from there so that you can get the full benefit of the practice.

Daily Practice

Select *one or two situations during the day* when you are aware that your Hero shadows are activated. Deliberately go through each step of the somatic awareness process. If you were not able to stop the grab of The Hero shadows in the moment, take some time later in the day and recreate the situation so that the body state is activated and you are able to move through the process. Remember that the neural network can be shifted not only through experience in the moment, but also through recreating the situation using the imagination.

Reflections

Take ten to fifteen minutes to journal on the following:

1. What happened when you were able to let go of the thoughts and stay with the emotions and sensations in the body?
2. What happened when you touched into the embodied limiting belief—*I have to do to be of value?* How does this belief and The Hero shadows influence the way you interact with others? What is possible and not possible when they are the driving force?
3. What was your experience when you brought in the liberating belief of The Hero—*I am empowered to do what is mine to do?*
4. What, if anything, was different when you came to Center (i.e., the way you feel about yourself, how you interact with others, what actions are possible now)?

Chapter 9

EMPOWERED RADIANT PRESENCE INITIATION—
Uniting The Mother and The Hero

Having now stretched ourselves across opposite poles of Yin and Yang to generate an alchemical force, we stand at the threshold of the first Initiation of The Mysterial Sequence.

When the healthy Mother and the healthy Hero archetypes are both fully activated, an important transformation—a higher order synthesis of The Mother's quality of Radiant Presence and The Hero's quality of Empowered Action—naturally occurs within a woman. The meta-quality of *Empowered Radiant Presence* arises, suffusing a woman's way of being and doing. This is the true fruit of inner initiation.

Able now to source her doing from the healthy ground of her being, a woman's very presence uplifts those around her and encourages their best performance. She embodies both the kindness of The Mother and the courage of The Hero. She inspires trust, respect, and cooperation simply by being who she really is. Others are attracted to the natural inner glow of a woman who acts purposefully in the world while deeply grounded in her own sufficiency.

It can be completely counter-intuitive for a modern career woman to expect that deepening into the nourishing, embodied embrace of the loving Mother archetype will lead to empowerment. Yet it's true. Others who long for the subtle Yin appeal of Radiant

Presence might find the fire of the Yang Hero a bit jarring. Yet for those who make the leap, this initiation marks an important step toward showing up as a powerful woman who is truly and fully herself.

How does this happen? The Mother and The Hero are not simply distinct transformative archetypes. They have a dynamic between them that forms a natural system.[1] The Vessel Yin Mother and The Flame Yang Hero are, in their essence, polar opposites. When they come together a third synthesizing force engages and the alchemy of initiation occurs.

The Limiting and Liberating Beliefs of The Mother-Hero Polarity

In shadow, these natural Yin and Yang conspirators are magnetically drawn together to form an unholy inner alliance. In other words, The Mother and Hero shadows actually collude with each other, addictively feeding their respective dysfunctional patterns and holding each other in place.

You can actually feel the collusion as these limiting beliefs come together: *I am not enough* and, *I have to do to be of value.* Together they create a self-reinforcing system fiercely resistant to change.

When the limiting belief of this polarity is driving our behavior, we do not trust the innate preciousness of our very Being. We have to keep compensating, proving our worth over and over, unconsciously accepting being "less than." For some, this means aggressively seeking power over others, fearful that it is the only way to accommodate for these lacks. For others this may be an overwhelming compulsion to always anticipate and serve other's needs in order to prove one's own worth.

The clearing and cultivating work of the first two activations de-couples the shadows of the polarity. This allows for a combined Liberating Belief to be enacted: *I am enough just as I am, and do what is mine to do.* The old limiting beliefs lose their energy and charge, fading into the background like a painful but long forgotten love.

As you claim your innate sufficiency, a fresh, bright world of possibility fills your sails because you know just what you need to do. You achieve your goals in a way that is satisfying to you and beneficial for the whole.

Empowered Radiant Presence Emerging in Women

This Initiation represents the fruits of two powerful descents into the unconscious. The first we experienced through the Vessel Yin gluttony of Rachel and the Vessel Yin starvation of Kerry. The second we experienced through the polar opposite Flame Yang overdrive of Sandra and the Flame Yang deficit of Gabriella. How did Empowered Radiant Presence start to show up in these women you met in earlier chapters?

KERRY: THE MOTHER ARCHETYPE, NEGLECTOR SHADOW

You were introduced to Kerry as a single, workaholic senior manager at a major software corporation. For Kerry, The Neglector made sure that she didn't devote any energy to nurturing and caring for herself because she had too little access to the nourishing nectar of Vessel Yin.

The Neglector played perfectly into the hands of its diametric opposite, The Dominator. With precious little safe containment of Vessel Yin, and fueled by an unrestricted fire hose of Flame Yang, Kerry had no problem driving herself and others into the ground to accomplish her goals. With little ability to empathically tune into others, or the patience for container holding, she had no external governing mechanism to staunch The Dominator's rampage.

After completing the Activation of The Mother, Kerry's co-workers began to notice that something about her was quite dramatically changing and softening. By the time Kerry had finished the Activation of The Hero, they could clearly identify the difference, especially in meetings. Her uptight, demanding, every-minute-at-the-grindstone manner relaxed, and Kerry appeared more approachable and inviting.

Even though she wasn't pushing and driving things forward in the same way, paradoxically more seemed to get done. It was easier to bring up new ideas and discuss challenges constructively. Everyone on her team felt more motivated and energized. In fact, Kerry was looking so fresh and vibrant that a rumor was circulating that she had gotten some discreet "enhancements," but nobody knew for sure. It was no surprise to anyone when, after several years solo, she began showing up at company gatherings with a significant other.

"What I realized," sighed Kerry, "is that I was making things harder than they needed to be. I thought I had to keep pushing the rock up the hill like Sisyphus or something horrible would happen. But once I was able to lighten up, take a breath, and look around, I found that there were so many easier ways to make things happen—and that others were there to share the load!"

RACHEL: THE MOTHER ARCHETYPE, DEVOURER SHADOW

Rachel was an Ivy League educated full-time mom who wanted to bring her gifts to the world, but was so entangled with taking care of family and friends that she couldn't even make time for a hobby. For Rachel, The Devourer's over-attention to others coupled perfectly with The Capitulator's inability to take a stand for herself and make her mark in the world. Even at home, she was constantly capitulating to the demands of her family. With no access to Flame Yang, and mired in a sticky swamp of excess Vessel Yin, it was almost impossible for her form an intention and move forward to achieve goals on her own behalf.

Rachel began to find herself drawn beyond her comfortable home by a startup non-profit dedicated to saving the Amazon rainforests. With a clear direction to constructively channel her immense love and care out into the world, she was able to set clear boundaries with her family so that both career and home were well tended. She was surprised at how quickly she was able to dust off her business and management skills, and became an indispensible member of the new organization.

And even though her time was filled with more responsibilities outside the home, Rachel found it somehow easier to focus and discipline herself. She lost weight, got into her best shape in years, and spontaneously began working in her neglected art room again.

"I always thought it was more time that I needed to get back into my art," Rachel mused, "but that wasn't it at all. Once I had connected to what I really came to do in the world, the artistic expression just wanted to come through me—I almost couldn't stop it!"

SANDRA: THE HERO ARCHETYPE, DOMINATOR SHADOW

Sandra was a tough, combative corporate lawyer and single mom whose interpersonal troubles were affecting her ability to be promoted. Sandra's "take no prisoners," warrior-woman approach to leadership went hand in glove with The Dominator's oppressive, unsustainable drive to achieve. With almost no access to the empathic and embodied ground of Vessel Yin, and burning far too hot with Flame Yang, the tracks of Sandra's Sherman tank were on the backs of her colleagues, and ultimately ran down her own career. Sandra was so addicted to this imbalanced energy that she was unable to moderate her behavior, even though she had been warned it could be a career killer. She couldn't envision an outcome worth having if it meant "playing nice."

Before she had experienced any of the activations, Sandra greeted us at her very first retreat with bluster and bravado. "I don't believe in any of this feminine crap!" she declared, insinuating that her manager had pressured her to take the program. As Sandra began to relax in the nurturing environment of the Vessel Yin Mother retreat container, surrounded by the comforting beauty of nature, she tearfully revealed a deeper reason for entering into the program: to heal the relationship with her daughter and become a better role model for her.

"I don't want her to turn out like me—but I don't know any other way!" she sobbed.

Sandra was incredibly relieved when her heart finally started to thaw and her sensual body awakened after she worked through the activation of The Mother. She began to soften and finally turned toward her long-neglected self. Even her colleagues started noticing that something seemed different.

But it was after the work of The Hero activation that those around Sandra recognized an unquestionable transformation had taken place. As Empowered Radiant Presence arose within her, Sandra resolved the deep conflict in her heart between being a "Feminine woman" and a loving mother while also maintaining her power and accomplishments. In fact, as her legendary drive became modulated and sustainable, and as her relationships became less charged with conflict, everything in her life began to move more easily. Goals were achieved without the collateral damage. Co-workers began to trust and include her, feeling comfortable in her presence. Sandra's sense of well-being and acceptance of herself rose. As her confidence in her Yin energy began to grow, she introduced some colorful clothing to a wardrobe that had mostly consisted of Masculine dark suits. One of the surprising gifts of this transformation for Sandra was that she started making women friends.

There came a day when Sandra realized she was finally becoming the role model she always wanted to be for her daughter. And her daughter took notice—offering encouraging words of approval to her mother. Her daughter even told Sandra that she felt more connected to her now than she ever had before.

"I realized," Sandra mused, "that the friction factor in my life was incredibly high— and it was entirely caused by me!" Sandra had been forcing her power instead of being a radiant force of empowerment. "I was making all my relationships harder and more painful than they needed to be—with my co-workers and direct reports, with my daughter, even with my own body. I didn't realize what I was missing. My life is so filled with blessings these days. I am even more determined to give something back!"

GABRIELLA: THE HERO ARCHETYPE, CAPITULATOR SHADOW

Gabriella was a first generation Latina, and a devoted wife, mother, and teacher who had trouble setting boundaries and putting her ideas forward. When the over-tending Devourer shadow hooked up with the accommodating, fuzzy-boundaried Capitulator, Gabriella literally had no awareness of her own needs, desires, or even a sense of her own self. It was second nature to train all her attention on others, surrendering to everyone else's agenda, like an empty canoe drifting downstream with the current.

After the activation of the healthy Mother, Gabriella began to notice some changes even though she hadn't yet lit the Yang flame. As the quality of Radiant Presence emerged in her, Gabriella felt more appreciation and compassion for herself, and started getting a sense of her own needs and desires. "I got clear that I really want to focus professionally on creating healthy environments for children to thrive," she said. "It's wonderful to be able to do that for my son, but think what can happen if I train others to do this all over the country!"

Soon other teachers and colleagues were attracted to her passionate ideas, and she didn't have to bend over backward to get their attention. This recognition seemed to catalyze a desire to make her vision for starting an educational consulting firm become a reality. The Hero activation was profound for Gabriella. "I discovered, ironically, that by focusing my energy and attention toward goals that I felt passionate about, it made many good things possible for others. I didn't have to over-give, or give in so much." Gabriella leaned in, now feeling more than enough and empowered to do what was hers to do. She was thoroughly delighted when her new company landed its first big consulting contract with a K-6 educational nonprofit she had long admired.

As the meta-quality of Empowered Radiant Presence lit Gabriella up, her company began to hum along and the client base grew. With all this new business, Gabriella had to be even more self-disciplined and firm with her boundaries at home. Her son starting becoming more self-reliant, not so inclined to run to Gabriella for everything. Her husband Dan's respect for her grew as she began bringing in more income and asserting herself in a positive way. When the company outgrew Gabriella's home office and moved to an office in town, he started helping out more around the house, taking more responsibility for his partnership in the home.

"I always felt that I was a good mother and wife," said Gabriella, "but it seemed to require enormous sacrifice. Now I feel that I can be so much more myself—and so much more for everyone around me. We're all getting more of what we need and want, and I feel truly accomplished in a way I never expected."

Making it Real—The Ten Mysterial Leadership Competencies of Empowered Radiant Presence

Completing the first Yin-Yang Initiation, and experiencing the emergence of the meta-quality of Empowered Radiant Presence is just the beginning—even if you decided not to move any further through The Mysterial Sequence. What it actually means is that you have made contact with the Mysterial pattern within and your essence is starting to flow more freely and in time your Mysterial capacity will grow.

As the combined eight Foundational Capacities become consistently available, they support us to develop ten specific embodied competencies in a practical way in our lives. In other words, the four foundational capacities of The Mother (Self-Compassion, Sensuous Embodiment, Empathic Resonance, and Container Holding) and The Hero (Intention Holding, Rhythmic Drive, Mindful Differentiation, and Dynamic Manifestation) provide the raw material for new competencies to come online as you show up in your world as an emerging Mysterial.

In essence, using the Kore myth as a metaphor, it is the translation of our "descent" work into "upper world" work.

Capacity versus Competency

Before we define these competencies, let's look more closely at what competency means. A **capacity** is the ability to use our life energy in a particular way, and is the result of the deep transformative work. It reflects our way of being. A **competency** takes the capacity into the next practical step. It is a specific muscle that we build to help us achieve our goals, a more conscious, connected, and creative way of acting in the world.

To build competency means that we have to practice, practice, practice in our lives in specific areas of challenge. We must try out new behaviors and not be afraid of the awkward phase. Now that we have new inner capacities to draw on, building these outer competencies is actually possible.

Embodied means that we have developed an "unconscious competence." That is, we can naturally draw on that competence, without thinking or worrying, as it is needed in the moment. However, it does not necessarily mean that we have ultimate mastery in this area. Just as a doctor newly graduating from medical school has been certified to embody sufficient capacity to practice medicine, we know that she will continue to embody more competencies through additional residency and experience with patients.

In this same manner, our Mysterial Way of Being will continue to deepen and grow, and our competency, wisdom, and mastery will build as we live more consciously in our day-to-day lives.

The Mysterial Competencies of Empowered Radiant Presence

We have found that these new competencies develop in three interdependent domains: **Living, Loving, and Leading (LLL)**. Looking at the chart you'll see that each of the LLL domains includes and transcends the last, with an ever-expanding embrace of reality: stretching from a healthy embrace of one's Self (Living), to include a healthy embrace of Other (Loving), to a healthy embrace of the World (Leading).

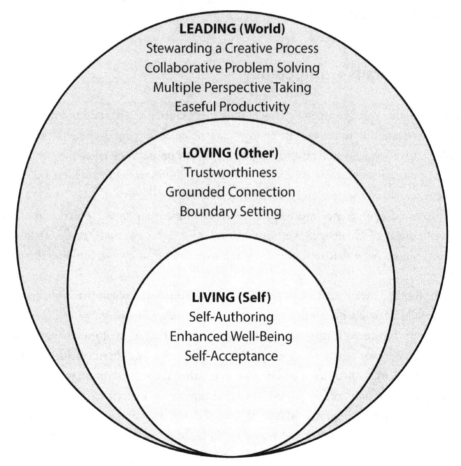

**Mysterial Competencies
Empowered Radiant Presence**

LEADING (World)
Stewarding a Creative Process
Collaborative Problem Solving
Multiple Perspective Taking
Easeful Productivity

LOVING (Other)
Trustworthiness
Grounded Connection
Boundary Setting

LIVING (Self)
Self-Authoring
Enhanced Well-Being
Self-Acceptance

LIVING: Self-Acceptance, Enhanced Well-Being, Self-Authoring
LOVING: Boundary Setting, Grounded Connection, Trustworthiness
LEADING: Easeful Productivity, Multiple Perspective Taking, Stewarding a Creative Process, and Collaborative Problem Solving

These competencies, arising from our Mysterial capacities, give us ways of being and acting that are actually a match for the demands of our lives.

IN THE DOMAIN OF LIVING:

Self-Acceptance: Ability to access an unwavering belief in your own worth and sufficiency, aware of your strengths and weaknesses you authentically bring your full self to any situation.

Enhanced Well-Being: Ability to care for yourself, nourishing your body, heart, mind, and soul so that you have the energy and presence to powerfully engage the world.

Self-Authoring: Ability to align with what is deeply meaningful and choose the actions necessary to manifest a life that is congruent with who you are.

IN THE DOMAIN OF LOVING:

Boundary Setting: Ability to know what you are saying YES to in your life, which allows you to clearly say NO to those requests and situations that are not aligned with your clear intentions.

Grounded Connection: Ability to access information using your emotional and social intelligence in order to stay connected to your direct experience while also being open to the experience of others, enabling powerful partnering.

Trustworthiness: Ability to be congruent between your inner experience and outer expression, so that you are authentic and reliable, inspiring trust and commitment in others.

IN THE DOMAIN OF LEADING:

> **Easeful Productivity:** Ability to set clear intentions and effectively and efficiently engage your energy to accomplish tasks and activities, with ease and flow.

> **Multiple Perspective Taking:** Ability to source and process information from yourself, others and the environment, enabling you to see situations from multiple points of view and to bring a fresh and creative perspective to challenging issues.

> **Collaborative Problem Solving:** Ability to be open and curious with others, flexing and flowing in order to generate greater synergy and innovative solutions.

> **Stewarding a Creative Process:** Ability to understand the structure and timing of the creative process so that you know when to act decisively and when to let factors ripen for the best possible outcome in the situation.

Taking the Next Step—
Empowered Radiant Presence to The Father

Completing the first two Yin and Yang activations of The Mother and The Hero polarity is a significant developmental milestone in how a woman lives, loves, and leads. For many women, the expression of Empowered Radiant Presence is so deeply satisfying that they don't feel the need to go any further. Perhaps for the first time in their lives, they are experiencing the inner harmony and outer congruence that comes when healthy Yin and Yang essences begin to dance together. And practicing to strengthen and refine the Ten Mysterial Leadership competencies of Empowered Radiant Presence might be quite enough.

But for others, their appetite for what is next has been deliciously whetted. After an appropriate period of integration, they are ready for the work of the second Yin-Yang polarity: The Vessel Yang Father and The Flame Yin Maiden.

Whether you are moving onto the next activations of the Mysterial Sequence or not it is wise to pause here at the time of initiation to allow for integration. We highly recommend that you engage the following triad of support during this time:

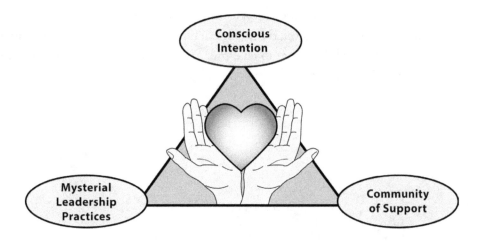

Conscious Intention: Having a clear and compelling Conscious Intention—something that you care deeply about manifesting in your life—is an important counter balance to the forces of your habitual way of being that still want hold you in the status quo. Take some time to revisit the Intention you set during the preparation phase and see if it still is relevant or if a new Intention for this integration phase is more appropriate.

Mysterial Leadership Practices: Practices that engage the body, heart, mind, and soul are a powerful way to keep you in constant connection with yourself while you are growing into a Mysterial woman. Once these structures become a part of your day you will never want to be without them. See Chapter 5—#3 Awaken The Father—for a starter set of Practices.

Community of Support: A resonant community of friends and family who are encouraging your newly emerging self is the third leg of this supportive structure. Finding others who share your worldview and with whom you can continue to deepen into your Mysterial self is critical. Sometimes the path of change can be very lonely, and while we do have to do our own work we do not have to do it alone. Find the communities where you can flourish—places where other awakening Mysterial women are gathering.

The Next Call Forward

With the channel of the first polarity open, your Mysterial essence will naturally begin to move more fluidly through you, expanding your worldview and your options for creative action. Now that you are resting into a deeper sense of sufficiency and are able to act in the world with more focus and power, the stability and structuring influence of The Father archetype calls you forward. You want to take your sovereign seat and stand in your own true authority. The Father awaits you.

Chapter 10

THE ACTIVATION OF THE FATHER—
Establishing True Authority

After a time of reveling in the open channel between The Mother and The Hero polarity, the call of The Father archetype happens naturally. With the liberating belief of Empowered Radiant Presence—*I am enough just as I am and empowered to do what is mine to do*—you have become more self-authoring and are creating a life that is much more aligned with who you are. Let's turn now toward The Father archetype that helps us create order and structure in our lives so that we can bring our gifts into the world sustainably. Here we confidently land on the solid ground of own true authority and stop pretending to be someone we are not. We know that our presence and contribution on the planet matters and we are ready to take our sovereign seat.

As you read this Invocation aloud, let your body and Being rest in the caring stability of The Father.

Invocation of The Father

Blessed One,
I honor your very existence
which is unique in all of time.
Know that your life is purposeful, guided by higher forces,
and that you are an essential part of the beautiful web of life.

I fortify your heart,
clarify your mind,
and give you strength to stand for what you believe
and uphold what you care about.
I protect you, that you may protect what is precious.
My mantle of integrity and justice
rests naturally upon your deserving shoulders.

With me you have the intelligence, confidence, and discernment
to bring order to chaos.
To see what is truly important
to choose what is best for the whole.

Together we are held by structures,
and stand upon solid foundations
like mountains, sturdy and unshakeable.
So that your great work on this earth endures
and you can gladly announce your place in the family of things.

Turning on the Flow of Vessel Yang

The Father is the second most universally recognized archetype after The Mother, and in its healthy expression is a pattern that gives us the ability to be organized, create systems and structures, and helps us successfully join and bond with groups. It is this Father pattern that ensures that our lives hum along like a well-oiled machine, that we do our fair share, and that we honor those who are making a difference.

Not every person has a father figure in their life, but everyone learns early on (sometimes the hard way) that there are rules and pecking orders. It is with the universal Father pattern that we install our basic wiring in childhood through adolescence for respecting rules and limits, for routines and structure, for rational thought, and for being productive "good" members of society.

With a healthy inner Father, an adult woman has the self-discipline and steadfastness to build, step-by-step, the structures and reliable systems that will ensure that the things she cares about can endure and grow. The Father is essential to making a positive difference in the world.

Drawing upon a developed sense of accountability, a woman can follow through on all that she is responsible for. She can rationally discriminate and create logical hierarchies and systems of order that instill her leadership with staying power. Honoring others for who they are and their unique contributions becomes natural. A new level of confidence emerges, grounded in both her inner assurance and her outer capabilities.

When out of balance, The Father can push us to be rigid, judgmental, controlling, and unfair. Or, with little access to the archetype we can be disorganized and uncertain in taking our place, finding ways to distance ourselves from the unwelcome expectations of the collective.

When the healthy Father archetype fully activates, we have clearer and more direct access to the methodical, coherent, immutable flow of Vessel Yang within ourselves. Contrast that to the Vessel Yin of the Mother, which is stillness, womb-like containment, and deep embodiment—the Feminine ground of our healthy being.

What is a vessel in the Masculine sense? It connotes stability and security. Using the metaphor of a great ship, a vessel provides the structures and systems to maintain a well-managed life, a holding place for the dynamic engines that speed us across the water. Vessel Yang is actually a Feminine expression of Yang, a Yin-Yang. It is the calm, composed, enduring, protective, and trustworthy aspect of Yang.

The Father is alive and well in many leadership models and training programs, particularly the traditional ones. Analytical thinking, managing hierarchies, decision trees for strategies to reach a goal, protocols and standard operating procedures, making plans, managing finances, even writing software code are very much his orderly province. These tasks and duties are often related to classical "management."

You will also likely recognize this archetype on the home front. Do you ever wish you could just take a day off, or a month, to get the garage cleaned, your files reorganized, and basically put your life in order? Have you ever felt that things would be easier if everyone just "did what they were supposed to?" Have the tantrums of a toddler ever made you fantasize about sending him or her off to school early? The Father is lighting up that part of you that seeks order, stability, and organization. If you feel compelled to show up in a suit or other "work" clothes at your job or vocation, then you're feeling the influence of the conforming Father who seeks to fit in.

Was there ever time when you felt a reverence in your soul for a higher power? The Father archetype activates that part of us that reaches above, seeking transcendence of this earthly world. It also reaches into the inner space of the mind, into the rarified world of ideas, formulas, and abstractions.

Have you ever considered starting a business or nonprofit of your own? Many women today long to create a career that is more family-friendly and flexible. Others are simply done with the glass ceiling and want to see what they can do in the world. We may think this requires Hero drive and intention—and that is true. But no less important is a healthy inner Father who motivates us to build the strong infrastructure that any business needs. And instills the self-confidence to take on that huge challenge.

The inner Father also supplies the discipline and patience to do the research, make a plan, prioritize, follow budgets, and stay with them when you want to throw in the towel. The Father pattern feeds the desire and confidence to create something of quality that can actually support us over the long haul.

If your inner Mother and Hero are reasonably healthy, you will have the sustainable energy and vision to get something initiated. It is the work of The Father that can build it into a stable success through all the ups and downs, and ensure an enduring legacy.

The Foundational Capacities of True Authority

According to many cultural forecasters, our fast-moving world is headed for even more chaos. We need the stabilizing, measured influence of The Father like never before, even at the most mundane level. Having the wherewithal to shop and get dinner on the table day after day, to set curfews for a rebellious teenager, pay taxes on time, attend lackluster

PTA meetings, save for retirement—the inner Father isn't exactly the life of the party. But without the important capacities of Self-Confidence, Creating Order, Honoring and Upholding, and Building Reliable Systems he brings, there might be no party at all!

The Father

INTERIOR	EXTERIOR
My Inner Experience	**How I Show Up**
Capacity: SELF-CONFIDENCE	**Capacity: CREATING ORDER**
To believe in yourself and trust your ability to express your unique gifts in life. You trust that your life has a higher, guiding purpose. This allows you to be realistic about situations and remain positive and accepting of yourself, even when things don't go the way you expected, or the way others might want.	To create hierarchies of value in all areas of your life so that you know what to prioritize and where to direct your energy. You systematize knowledge and organize things to bring coherence and beauty into your life. You are steadfast through the chaos of change to allow a new order to organically emerge.
Relating with Others	**Engaging the World**
Capacity: HONORING & UPHOLDING	**Capacity: BUILDING RELIABLE SYSTEMS**
To deeply value and respect others and the world around you, and stand up for them when challenged. You are benevolent toward others, recognizing their unique gifts and contributions, and freely communicating your appreciation in both private and public ways.	To create the structures and systems in your life to provide more stability and sustainability. You are able to bring together diverse elements into a more complex whole that gives you an enduring and reliable foundation from which to move in the world.

INDIVIDUAL

COLLECTIVE

I | IT

WE | ITS

The Promise of True Authority

When the foundational capacities of **Self-Confidence, Creating Order, Honoring & Upholding, and Building Reliable Systems** solidly anchor in a woman with Empowered Radiant Presence, the emergent quality of *True Authority* arises. This imparts within her an unshakeable claim to her rightful place in society. She can now systematically access her life force energy to think and act in productive, enduring ways on a scale that garners respect and standing in her relationships, organization, community, and the world.

Over the last fifty years, women have climbed history's steepest learning curve in order to adapt to a culture shaped by back-to-back Yang eras. The transformation of this third Activation completes this healthy adaptation, so that women can begin to access this archetypal force on their own terms and can create change that lasts.

Consider the world figures we discussed in The Hero. While The Hero archetype gave them the ability to pierce the world with focused, dynamic, and balanced action, it didn't give them the ability to persevere beyond that initial achievement day after day, with confidence and discipline. That combination is what enabled those world figures to build something from the initial creative spark to enduringly serve the world.

Aung San Suu Kyi's impact on the democracy movement in Myanmar (Burma) took more than heroically standing up to the military leaders. It called from her a steadfast commitment to her ideals in the face of tremendous discomfort and difficulty. In November 2010, after fifteen years of house arrest, she was finally set free. Aung San Suu Kyi's expression of True Authority gave her and the followers she inspired the fortitude to stay the course in the midst of uncertainty so that their movement could finally take root and grow.

Similarly, in 2011 The Nobel Prize Committee equally honored Ellen Johnson Sirleaf, Africa's first democratically elected female president; Leymah Gbowee who mobilized women divided along ethnic and religious lines to end the war in Liberia and ensure women's participation in elections; and Tawakkul Karman for her leading part in the struggle for women's rights and for democracy and peace in Yemen. They were recognized, "for their non-violent struggle for the safety of women and for women's rights to full participation in peace-building work." When a woman establishes her **True Authority** on a significant scale, the world bows in "Namaste."

Shadows of The Father—The Judge and The Outsider

While The Father in his natural element stands tall and reaches above toward the heavens, establishing True Authority calls us to another descent. You must once again dive *down and in*, this time to clear what is blocking your Vessel Yang essence. You must discover how you are unconsciously under-identified (The Outsider) and/or over identified (The Judge) with The Father archetype in ways that have split off your natural ordering and structuring capacities into the shadow.

After the deep nourishment of The Mother, and the excitement of The Hero, activating The Father might seem rather mundane by comparison. Keep in mind how shadow traps us into unpleasant habits over and over. The Father has a lot to do with how we bring organization, routine, and standards into our lives, and "fit in" with the group. Having too much or too little of this essence can really bind us into a rigid, joyless existence of subservience to authority and rules, or leave us frustrated, scattered and alienated from the center of things. And we're not much fun to be with either.

THE JUDGE—ACTIVE SHADOW OF THE FATHER

Because The Father is a key part of the dominant cultural paradigm today, both shadows are very much alive in our collective experience. Throughout the modern world the collective shadow Judge mercilessly persecutes innocent and inspired women, echoing Roman tribunals martyring early Christians and Inquisitors burning so-called witches. In the pre-Modern world, sanctioned genital mutilation of girls—which dampens sexual pleasure—is happening as you read. In some countries, cruel death sentences (stoning) and torture (flogging) are being meted out to women who appear to upset the restrictive moral codes of theocratic Traditional societies. In these societies men are superior to women by law—religious law—the word of God The Father.

In the western world women still comprise a relatively small percentage of leadership roles in politics, government, business, and institutions. There is still a strong bias in education toward rational intelligence as more relevant than emotional, social, or spiritual ways of knowing. Many conservative church hierarchies still do not have women leaders and have pushed state lawmakers in the US to pass more than fifty measures in the first half of 2011, restricting abortion and undermining family planning. The Yang "old boys network" remains alive and well, riddled throughout all our political and financial institutions.

CHARACTERISTICS OF THE JUDGE

Let's take a tour through the tendencies and behaviors that show up when you have over identified with The Father archetype, and the active shadow pattern of The Judge emerges. Here are some of the signs that The Judge is at his bench.

* You are rigid and controlling most of the time, demanding that others follow your rules and beliefs.
* You micromanage everybody around you, unable to trust others to come up with their own creative ways to get results.
* You see yourself as better than others (some might call that self-righteous and arrogant).
* You notice what isn't working, or what standards aren't being met, and you are very critical of those who do not "fit in."
* You are overly bureaucratic, insisting that you and others strictly follow the rules even if this diminishes overall effectiveness.
* You find it hard to flex and flow with changing conditions. You resist change and the disruption of the status quo.
* You are convinced that you know the Truth, and work hard to convince others to believe your truth.
* You are brittle and detached from your heart and the lusciousness of your soul.
* You overvalue your rational mind and disregard your emotions and your embodied knowing.
* You punish yourself and others when perfection is not attained.
* You do not take criticism well and punish those who do not agree with you.
* You are not able to honor others, either putting down their talents, hopes, and dreams or withholding blessing by ignoring them.

Any rings of familiarity? Or, did anyone you know come to mind? Being in the grip of The Judge can seem like a prison sentence for you and for those around you, with standards and rules that are virtually impossible for anyone to live up to. Growing up with a parent who has been captured by The Judge can encourage some of us to flee to the opposite pole, The Outsider.

CLEARING THE JUDGE: MEG'S JOURNEY

At thirty-nine years old, married with one son, Meg had the potential but not the desire to become a celebrity in her quiet western community. She had married young and enjoyed a stable marriage with a supportive husband. Her loyalty to her family, organization, and community helped build her family's small manufacturing business into a respected, prosperous mid-sized corporation.

As the child of an alcoholic, Meg knew that life could be insecure. Controlling her environment and becoming a successful CEO helped her feel safe. Her exceptional caution and care—always looking out for what might go wrong—helped her navigate the Great Recession without any layoffs. Her concern with planetary destruction led her to implement sustainability processes at the company, a move that was beginning to garner some national attention.

The loyalty that all this engendered helped make up for her often rigid, critical, micromanaging leadership style. Imagining the worst scenario about everyone and every situation, her mistrusting accusations and contradictory resistance to change were hard on those around her, draining her own inner resources as well. She was always at the mercy of the debilitating fear and doubt that constantly ran through her daily experiences.

ROOTS OF THE JUDGE

Meg's father had been a minister and a closet alcoholic. Her grandfather, the company founder, had survived the traumas of the Great Depression and fierce battle in World War II. After his return, the family life he established and the manufacturing company he founded were militaristically regimented and rule-bound. Everyone in the family was expected to work for the company, and everyone was expected to tow the line in all aspects of life.

Her father, a more sensitive soul, had not wanted to work for the family company. He chose instead to go into the ministry, one of the few alternative paths available to him. Meg realized that her father had been suffering inside for a long time, medicating his pain. In the community he was accepted as a role model, but at home after a few drinks, Meg saw a different side. The harsh judgments and punishments he meted out were really a reflection of the judgments he held against himself. Fearing his unpredictable angry outbursts and abusive punishments for minor (and sometimes imagined) transgressions, Meg became highly vigilant, endlessly scanning her environment for danger.

Keeping the home in perfect order and everyone else in line was one way that Meg could find security for herself and protect her siblings as well as her mother, who had long been in denial about her husband's dark side. In some ways, Meg took on a Father role in the family to make up for her father's disappearance into drink. True to form, she was an exceptionally hard and committed worker who graduated from college already knowing that she would return to her community and join the family company, now run by her uncle.

Given Meg's deep-seated self-doubt, it was very important for her to fit in and please others in hierarchies of authority.

"I wanted approval, from my father and then my teachers and then my husband and then my uncle, the boss," Meg recalled. "And the bar got higher and higher. The standards I set for myself were always just out of reach. I believed that if I could just make it up that next rung on the ladder I would finally 'arrive'—and I would be safe and accepted. But it never happened. Even after being named CEO there was always another step to go, some way in which I never seemed to get high enough."

The active shadow of The Judge has been strongly encouraged in our corporate environments. Often the two Yang active shadows collude, as The Dominator becomes an aggressive advocate and enforcer of The Judge's policies and regulations. The movie *Avatar* is a great example of how The Dominator's brute force and The Father's technological systems merged to nearly conquer and subjugate an instinctual, heart-centered culture.

Women learned that hitching The Hero's Dominator shadow together with The Father's Judge helped us excel and ascend the hierarchy of power. With The Judge at the bench we buckled down to learn the rules of the Patriarchy so that we could position ourselves on the inside of the power structure. This meant that we often became inflexible and controlling workaholics ourselves. This proved confusing to women in the mid 1990s when, in response to dramatic shifts in the market place, rigid bureaucracies crumbled as a more collaborative, empowered management approach created successful companies that were nimble and flexible in nature. After working so hard to earn their way into positions of influence, women were often the most resistant to letting go of the old power structures.

What finally drew Meg to seek help with leadership development was the inner conflict she felt. She knew that to be successful she would need to create a more collaborative and nimble culture in her company, but she was afraid to let go and trust others. From Human Resource surveys she knew that people didn't really like working for her, which made her feel a bit paranoid. And her debilitating self-doubt made every decision agonizing.

OBSERVING THE JUDGE

For most of her adult life, family, friends, colleagues, and bosses had advised Meg that she worried too much and was too hard on herself. The overly structured and harsh ways of relating to herself and her embodied needs were taking their toll in anxiety, and a brittleness of being that was aging her prematurely. Meg would need to begin her healing with The Mother archetype, reclaiming her own Self-Compassion from the shadow of The Neglector. With time and tenderness she learned to connect to the inner life within her body and quiet her mind. Remarkably, whenever she did this her self-doubt and confusion dropped away.

With a deeper connection to her own inner guidance, The Dominator shadow of The Hero was also less likely to take over, running her and others into the ground. The practice of Rhythmic Drive was particularly powerful as she learned to pace herself throughout the day. She began to trust that she didn't need to do everything, just what was hers to do, and to delegate the rest.

Now she was ready to let in the cost of The Judge and his harsh ways at work. At home her own son was drifting further into a rudderless and risky Goth lifestyle, in open rebellion against her over-controlling and mistrustful ways. A vicious cycle was underway in her family dynamic and she knew she needed to break it. She needed to find the inner authority of the all-loving Father within, who recognized and valued her being and accepted her without needing constant perfection.

When women over identify with The Father archetype and activate The Judge shadow, it becomes such an intrinsic part of their identity that it feels like defeat and betrayal to give it up. The very nature of The Judge makes it hard to let go. Even though they may have recognized the suffering and limitations of this way of being, they are often simply unable to release the powerful grip of this toxic shadow.

At the advice of a friend she met at a public speaking practice group for executives, Meg participated in one of our programs. The group experience within the learning cohort of her program provided a place where she could actually witness the consequences of The Judge in relative safety. With feedback from her circle of sisters she began to observe more clearly her mistrusting, critical persona. With the distinctions of the shadow archetypes, Meg recognized when The Judge would start banging down his gavel and take over her interactions with others. She could now recognize the shadow in full force.

Building Foundational Capacity

While taking on shadow aspects with strength and steadfastness, you must simultaneously cultivate the healthy Father within. This is most effectively accomplished by focusing on the four foundational capacities of The Father: Self-Confidence, Creating Order, Honoring and Upholding, and Building Reliable Systems.

In Meg's case, building some capacity for **Self-Confidence** (Individual Interior— My Inner Experience) was foundational to anchoring the healthy Father pattern. This was a tall order given that she always felt that something bad was about to happen. A "committee" in her head seemed to be shouting out all the things that could go wrong, and she could not get past the pervasive sense of self-doubt. There seemed to be no reliable ground underneath her feet anywhere.

At the advice of her leadership coach, Meg began to work in parallel with a therapist who was also skilled in trauma work. Meg's high level of vigilance and the incessant, shaming voice of her inner critic pointed to a degree of trauma in her being that required professional care.

It's helpful to remember that The Judge is an agent of the Patriarchy. Besides delivering his withering judgments, his voice also tells us that the soft animal needs of our bodies are irrelevant and that our non-rational ways of knowing cannot be trusted. This was certainly true for Meg who had all but disowned her feelings and the tender vulnerabilities of her heart.

"I really thought that my feelings would mislead me from making the right decision" she recalled. "If I wanted to succeed I just had to shut them down, follow the rules and do things right. It felt dangerous for me to do otherwise. I was so judgmental of people who showed their feelings, seeing this as weak, risky, and self-centered. Slowly, and I do mean slowly, I started to open up to my feelings and trust that I could share them with others."

The first time Meg let herself cry in the group it was a powerful moment for everyone. "Not only did I survive, I felt stronger and more connected to others afterwards. And I have started to realize that my feelings can actually help me assess things more accurately. That's a big deal for someone who second-guesses herself as much as I do."

Meg began a simple practice called Three Good Things, which not only helped her build Self-Confidence, it made her feel happier, and lightened up her rather pessimistic view of the world. Sometimes small, simple practices done with consistency can make a big difference.

As she began to gain more trust in the world and in herself, Meg knew that she needed to work on the interpersonal capacity of **Honoring and Upholding**

The "Three Good Things" Practice for *Self-Confidence*[1]

Every morning, start your day by writing down three good things that happened the day before, and also write about why they happened. What positive contribution did you make toward these good things?

They can be small things such as, "my friend Linda surprised me with a hazelnut latte in the morning," or red letter events such as, "I'm going to be an auntie!" As you write out your vignette, clearly envision and describe the event. Elaborate on the positive emotions you felt, invoking them again.

Let go of the tendency to attribute these things completely to others, or to luck. Recognize and celebrate that you had a hand in this beneficial outcome. This is an important part of the practice.

At the end of the week, review your week's worth of three good things and your contribution to them. Journal for a few minutes on that, and notice any patterns that arise. Over time you will notice that your life is overflowing with blessings great and small, and that you are at the heart of creating them.

Reflections:
1. After you did the practice what did you notice occurred in your body and emotions?
2. How has the practice affected the lens through which you look at the world?

(Collective Interior—Relating With Others). As the chief executive of her company, she recognized that she had a vital public role in honoring those who deserved recognition, and upholding the values and ethics important to the organization. With The Judge shadow, she had been so overtaken with doubt, mistrust, and criticisms that she had failed to perform this fundamental executive duty of The Father.

To help remedy that, Meg began a nightly Gratitude practice as a way to build her healthy Father capacity for Honoring and Upholding. It may seem similar to the Three Good Things practice, but it has important differences: focusing on the heart and sending the blessing outward.

Nightly Gratitude Practice for *Honoring and Upholding*[2]

Gratitude practice helps you shift into a positive emotional state before ending the day, and amplifies what is affirmative and joyful in your life. This heart opening practice connects you to others, and has been shown though scientific research[3] to benefit health and well-being within as little as a month. Please do this practice every night before going to sleep.

* Lie comfortably in bed, eyes closed, preferably in the "corpse" position (flat on your back, head comfortably on a pillow, arms at your side, feet falling apart).
* Take a few deep breaths, and begin to focus on your heart center. Feel it warm and begin to glow.
* Scan back over your day and select three occurrences for which you feel gratitude and appreciation to someone for something they did, said, etc. Bring these to mind, one by one. As you relive them, connect to your heart, and feel the joy, love, gratitude, and other positive emotions that these blessings invoke in you.
* Extend your heart blessing to the people who were involved in these moments. In your mind's eye, see them receiving this warm golden ray of light of blessing from your heart to their heart.
* Feel the glow in your own heart swell and grow larger with each blessing—your gratefulness becomes your "Great Fullness." Sweet dreams!

Then at least once a week, actually reach out to someone and extend your blessing/recognition. This could be in person, on social media, commenting on a blog, etc. You might extend kind words of recognition to someone on the street you don't even know, if you see them doing something you appreciate.

Reflections:
1. What have you noticed about the quality of your experience following the practice?
2. How has the practice impacted your experience of Self-Confidence and connection with others?

At first, Meg felt awkward and a bit anxious when she actually extended her blessings in person. But the warm responses she received were so heartening that she felt emboldened to continue. After a few weeks of practicing, Meg was sleeping better, and her generalized anxiety seemed to be diminishing. At meetings she began noticing the positive things that her employees were doing, particularly if they were demonstrating company values. Genuine gratitude began to well up in her spontaneously. Meg's world was becoming safer, brighter, and more loving—a place she didn't feel so compelled to control.

She began to feel a deeper sense of gratitude even for her alienated son. In the light of her authentic blessings and gratitude toward him, the strain between them began to relax. The healthy inner Father had truly anchored a solid foundation within Meg.

Shadows of The Father—The Judge and The Outsider

THE OUTSIDER—PASSIVE SHADOW OF THE FATHER

Next we shall swing to the opposite Father archetype shadow, from active to passive. Under-identification with the ordering, systematizing, structuring, "fitting in" archetypal energy of The Father leads a woman into the passive shadow of The Outsider.

When The Judge shadow is operating, your Vessel Yang essence is hardened, stiff, and unyielding—an uncomfortable corset that binds you into an idealized form from the past that can never change.

When The Outsider is operating, your Vessel Yang essence is flimsy and unreliable, a poorly constructed foundation and scaffolding that cannot bear your weight, causing you to collapse and crumble when faced with the challenges of life.

For some women, the domineering energy of The Father was not something they wanted to get close to. They chose instead a kind of complacency and disempowerment, even alienation, by staying outside of the systems and structures of authority. As one student said, "My father was an academic and only valued what could be rationally and scientifically proven. I rebelled against him when I was younger and that reinforced the feeling that I didn't belong, that I was a failure. I rejected any structures and lived the life of the bohemian artist. But I could never take a stand for my art and bring it into the world."

CHARACTERISTICS OF THE OUTSIDER

Let's take a tour through the tendencies and behaviors that show up when you have under-identified with The Father archetype, and the passive shadow pattern of The Outsider emerges. Here are some of the signs that The Outsider is headed for the hills.

* You feel disempowered and unable to build solid structures in your life, often sabotaging yourself when success or recognition seems imminent.
* You have little self-confidence and are insecure around powerful people.
* You dissociate easily, retreating into your head when things become challenging.
* You have a hard time disciplining yourself to stay with those things that matter to you but are challenging.
* You chafe under systems and structures that require you to work with external authority.
* You feel alienated from the mainstream and its responsibilities, and withdraw to your own world and clan.
* You tend to be envious of the strengths of others, comparing yourself and falling short.
* You resist bringing order to your life and live in chaos and disorganization. You are often confused by systems for accounting and finance, technology, productivity, and so forth.
* Although you try, you just can't seem to get projects past the startup stage.
* You are afraid to show up fully in your life and be seen for who you really are.

Did any of these Outsider characteristics ring true for you? Our Outsider tendencies may show up in some of our roles but not others. A physician, for example, may have learned to put The Father in overdrive, becoming the uptight and hypercritical Judge at the hospital who then collapses into a disordered and withdrawn Outsider at home.

With the active shadow of The Judge so present in our cultural zeitgeist, you can be sure that the passive shadow of The Outsider is lurking nearby. The Outsider is present when members of a society look the other way while the "other" is eliminated through genocide (which is still occurring in the twenty-first century). In many parts of the world, severe dress codes for women, house imprisonment, and restriction from education restrict women from developing their voice in society, keeping them outside. Terrorist sects of all stripes from Al-Qaeda and ISIS to white supremacist militias express The Outsider in their extreme alienation from society. They don't want to fit into the global family. In fact, they deliberately position themselves as enemies of the mainstream, ironically seeking to unilaterally impose the rigid rules and codes of The Judge.

Millions of us today isolate and alienate ourselves from our bodies, from others, and from nature by living in a virtual reality: texting rather than talking, watching rather than doing, numb to sensation unless it is killing us. Even the desire to transcend mundane lives to follow a spiritual path can be motivated by alienation. The collective Outsider shadow is also evident when we isolate ourselves from others who have less, or those of different social classes, by gathering in elite clubs and using exclusive gated communities to further distance ourselves from the messiness and danger of the "rabble."

CLEARING THE OUTSIDER: KIM'S JOURNEY

Kim, forty-seven, was a highly intellectual, second generation Asian American who, contrary to family expectations, had remained single and childless. She lived on a small northwest island filled with many nature-oriented artists and "creatives" exploring alternative lifestyles.

Valuing her personal freedom, Kim had been reasonably secure and content for over a decade working on contract as a senior researcher and writer inside a large ad agency. At night, rather than socialize with her colleagues (a ritual she found more exhausting than fun), she scurried home to her island sanctuary. There she could happily hole up with a book and a take-out vegan dinner from the local food co-op.

Kim loved the experience of losing herself in research, exploring the intricate network of pathways to gather information, and the solitary process of shaping words into content. Her work product had always been excellent. It came as a shock when the agency declined to renew her contract: she was simply told that the company was cutting back on personnel. A colleague informed her confidentially that managers will champion certain individuals they favor, and while Kim was good, she just hadn't stood out or fit in enough to get their backing.

Kim lived in a simple cottage that got little use save her small office and well-stocked library, which was cluttered with piles of paper, sticky notes, books, and images ripped out of magazines. She tended to hang on to things forever, as if gathering it for a nest. Now she faced the daunting task of finding new work and launching herself out in the world.

Kim also began to question her hyper-mental and cloistered approach to life. In this phase of involuntary exile, the time alone felt more disturbing than nourishing. "It started to really dawn on me in a profound way," mused Kim, "that I had been living life almost entirely in my mind . . . My work kept me involved with what was trendy and fascinating, what people in our society are wanting and doing and making—yet I was not a part of that world!"

Kim was a lesbian, something she'd kept quiet about because her family did not approve. She had dated some, but tended to let relationships fizzle out. That, coupled with her general introversion, made it hard for her to meet potential partners and cultivate a long-term relationship. "I looked into the future and saw more of the same . . . sitting here in front of a computer screen, alone. It scared me. I really do want someone to share my life with." Shaking her head in resignation, Kim sighed, "I'll just have to get myself out there."

ROOTS OF THE OUTSIDER

Kim had always been something of an enigma to her tight-knit, conservative Korean-American family. Her father had been a highly respected physical chemist at a national laboratory. At home he was very much the stern Judge, enforcing strict rules and harshly criticizing any minor deviance from his traditional values. Her grandfather and his family had endured horrendous suffering and displacement during World War II. Some of her family who survived were captured and taken away as forced laborers by the Japanese. They suffered the experience of being Outsiders in the worst way.

Her grandfather managed to immigrate to the US, but life was still hardscrabble. Her father had almost no childhood, working long hours for the family restaurant whenever he wasn't at school. A university scholarship was his ticket out, and he applied tremendous self-discipline to make it all the way through for a PhD. No wonder he was in overdrive with The Judge archetype!

Though Kim earned family approval with her high grades, she distanced herself the moment she graduated from university, heading to the West Coast. She had always needed enough space and time to keep from being overwhelmed by the demands of her father and the world, and to be able to stand back and analyze everything going on.

Kim's strategy for staying on her father's good side had been to hide away in her room, which her dutiful mother kept in order. There, she was able to indulge her intellectual fascinations with subjects that her father would not approve. The conservative values of the Korean Christian church her family attended secretly grated on Kim's emerging feminism. She chafed at the weekly obligations expected of congregation members, and of the clannish Korean community in general. She just couldn't wait to get out.

OBSERVING THE OUTSIDER

Before Kim could tackle The Outsider she needed first to come into relationship with her own sense of negative self-worth and her difficulty setting goals and being visible for her accomplishments. The Neglector and The Capitulator alliance of the Mother-Hero polarity kept her trapped inside her mind and unable to express herself in a way that was visible to others.

As she cleared The Neglector shadow and cultivated the Mother capacity of Embodiment, she went through a challenging thawing process, encountering deep layers of grief and fear. Although it was uncomfortable at first, Kim started to feel herself coming alive through this process. When she realized that contact with her deep emotional experience was one of the primary reasons that she kept herself withdrawn in her head, she was ready to explore the benefits of connecting more fully with her body, heart, and soul.

Now that there was some ground underneath her feet, The Capitulator transformed into the healthy Hero energy of Intention Holding and Dynamic Manifestation on her own behalf. Kim knew that the first thing she had to do was get her professional life in order and start networking for new contacts. She would have to update her resume, and start from scratch with networking systems such as LinkedIn. Creating a website would also be a good idea if she could figure out how to do that. Her personal files had gone so long without any maintenance that she couldn't even find her old résumé, much less update it. Now it was time for The Father.

The urgency of the job search shone a spotlight on the fact that Kim needed to create some new structures in her life, and put together systems that could help launch and sustain her freelance career. Giving up was not an option. With a clear incentive to heal the shadow of her inner Father, she was ready to be seen and valued, to liberate her capacity to show up in the world with her tremendous gifts.

Kim related to The Father archetype via the passive pole—a rejection of The Father. The Outsider was an easy ally of The Capitulator shadow of The Hero, and they teamed up to effectively disable her leadership abilities. As she tracked this specific shadow dynamic she quickly became able to identify just how her Yang saboteur operated.

During a group service project designed to support the women in her leadership program to develop the Yin and Yang capacities to build deeply collaborative, high performance teams, Kim began the process in her usual withdrawn way. She initially opted to do "research" for the group, hiding out in her Outsider shadow. Someone else would take care of the group, and she would quietly go off and do her part, mostly on her own.

As Kim explained, "It was much easier to just let this pattern stay unconscious, and I had some really good excuses for not taking leadership. But once I could see The Outsider shadow—and got feedback from others—it was obvious how I was giving my power and authority away by distancing myself. I was not stepping up and taking responsibility, and so I hadn't grown as a leader. I was staying small."

Once Kim could detect The Outsider in her group interactions, she began to notice that this shadow was shaping her frayed connection with her family, and also encouraging her to avoid the responsibility of a committed relationship.

Building Foundational Capacity

Kim's incapacity for creating order at home was bound up in her rejection of the Father ways that she had quietly endured as a child. Chores like cleaning her room when she'd rather be lost in a book felt painful. To create order, choices have to be made, and limits set. That felt like a loss to Kim, until she began to observe how much she was losing by not having it. Order also requires a commitment to ongoing maintenance; it is going against entropy, or the natural tendency for things in life to become more disordered over time.

Clutter Clearing Practice for *Creating Order*

At the end of every week, go into the space that is most connected to the intention you set in The Hero activation. Notice your feelings and thoughts as you encounter the disorder.

Resolve to clear one thing that will support you in your move toward your intention. For example, organizing and logging the daily expense receipts sitting on your desk, if your intention is to make your business financially stronger.

After finishing, notice if you are drawn to do another task (though you do not have to). Allow it to pull you forward rather than pushing yourself. Let yourself enjoy the feeling of being motivated and energized toward this routine.[4]

Reflection: Take a few minutes to journal after you complete that one task.

1. Do you notice any difference in your thoughts and feelings?
2. What got liberated inside?
3. Were you drawn to do another task?
4. How did you feel afterward?

Kim began **Creating Order** (Individual Exterior—How I Show Up) in her office, by hiring an organizing consultant. Once she had things sorted out and a system in place, she continued to build her habit for maintaining the order through a simple weekly practice of clutter clearing. This process doesn't simply teach the mechanical activity of clearing clutter; it works to transform the negative feelings that create the resistance.

After practicing clutter clearing for a few days, Kim noticed that she felt lighter and more motivated to follow through on her intention. In fact, she actually started looking forward to the little "buzz" it was generating. And once Kim had some order in her life, she had space to start **Building Reliable Systems** (Collective Exterior—Engaging the World) that would support her intention of landing contract work that would meet her financial and vocational fulfillment needs.

For women whose Outsider shadow is in power, there is tremendous benefit in building the systems that will actually make your life easier in the long run. At first it may seem challenging—The Outsider loves to throw up a smokescreen—but if you stay with it the structures themselves will actually allow for more ease and creativity.

Meta-View Practice for *Building Reliable Systems*

First do an assessment. Imagine you are helicoptering over your life.

What systems do I have in place to support the different domains of my life? How healthy and reliable are they? How are they enabling or restricting me from reaching these intentions?

* My alignment with my purpose and values
* My soul/spiritual life
* My psychological life
* Lifelong learning
* My physical health and well-being
* My vocational skills and accomplishment
* Intimacy, partnership, and family relationships
* My connection to community and tribe
* Supportive and productive home and work environments
* Financial health

(continued on next page)

Once a week, identify a system that needs some shoring up, or needs to be built from scratch. Answer the following questions in your journal:

* What am I desiring to build or fix?
* What constrains me from having this system fully in place and healthy?
* What feelings and concerns does it bring up that stop me from moving forward?
* Each day: What is one small step I can take in the direction to support the system that I desire to build or fix?
* How do I feel once I've done that? (If you feel either overwhelmed or bored, then the step was either too big or too small. Adjust as needed until you find the right pace.)
* Do the steps until they are complete. Take time to celebrate the completion. Notice how that feels in your body.
* Go on to the next system.

Always remember to celebrate when you complete a system. Do something for yourself that you really enjoy, such as going out to dinner at your favorite place, or going to your favorite yoga class. Be explicit about why you are doing this. The fiery Hero will encourage you to move right on to the next thing. It takes The Father to pause for a bit to celebrate, honor yourself, and anchor positive feelings together with the completion of that task.

Reflections:
1. How did resistance to this practice show up and how did you move through it?
2. What did you notice changed in your experience (sense of Self-Confidence and authority) as a result of this practice?

The Father brings us the capacity to systematically tackle our challenges, staying with them until they are resolved. In time, Kim was able to get her professional identity and networking underway with a website and was promoting herself through social media. She surprised even herself by how natural it was for her to connect with others through the various social media sites. And she organized her home systems to create more order and beauty so that she would feel comfortable welcoming a new relationship into her life.

The Limiting Belief of The Father: "I do not belong."

At the root of clearing both the active Judge shadow driving Meg, and the passive Outsider shadow driving Kim was the dismantling of the unconscious limiting belief of The Father.

"I do not belong." Do you recognize this limiting belief in your life? Say the words, slowly and out loud to yourself. Notice how they land in you. What additional thoughts does this belief trigger? How does it make you feel? Do you notice any subtle sensations in your body as the words are expressed? These reflection questions provide valuable information about how you are habitually, unconsciously, and needlessly limiting your own potential.

Meg recognized that "I do not belong" was wired into The Judge with her deep-seated fear of life and her constant need to mistrust and find fault. She had always sought the safety of warm groups or family bonds. The fear of not belonging is deeply buried in the human psyche, going back to very early days when being cast out of the group meant certain death. Each vulnerable baby re-experiences this, because to be abandoned by a parent, to not belong, is also certain death. To belong is fundamental to our survival.

Kim recognized that this limiting belief of "I do not belong" had been fundamental to her Outsider way of being up until now. The deep assumption that she didn't belong kept her distanced and withdrawn as a means of self-protection. What would life be like, she wondered, if it weren't true?

The Liberating Belief of The Father: "I am at home in myself and naturally belong."

To dislodge the limiting belief of The Father, Meg continued to squarely face her Judge tendencies, while Kim worked on dismantling her Outsider. Using The Mysterial Change Process, Meg learned how to be still and calm enough to allow the healthy Father to do his job in his steady way rather than let herself be hijacked by the overprotective, exaggerated Judge. Kim learned to recognize when she needed to call upon her healthy inner Father, and how to engage his responsible capacities rather than flee the challenge.

As both women worked to clear the shadows and cultivate healthy Father capacities, the Liberating Belief—**"I am at home in myself and naturally belong"**—began to be a natural part of their experience. Old habits of mistrust and alienation faded into the background.

Finding Your True Authority

Could you recognize yourself in either of Meg or Kim's encounters with The Father archetype? Did you sense the benevolence of this archetype that is seeking to make contact with you? Can you feel the possibility of a new quality of confidence in yourself and your unique gifts? What would change if your authority was drawn from the substance of your true essence, rather than based on fitting into an outdated patriarchal system?

Your own Mysterial nature is inviting The Father to take his loving seat in your consciousness. He will support you to take a stand for what matters to you and create the systems and structures that empower them to flourish. As Henri David Thoreau said, *"If you have built castles in the air, your work need not be lost; that is where they should be. Now put the foundations under them."*

The presence of The Father within gives us the Self-Confidence to own our genius and take responsibility for putting foundations under our castles.

As Meg began to release the trauma from her body, and her Self-Confidence and optimism grew, life took on a new vibrancy. Instead of being chained in the prison of criticalness and hyper-responsibility she began to relax and respond to the call of her life purpose.

Once Kim had identified The Outsider, she could no longer just drift along unconsciously, waiting for someone else to make things happen. As her habits for creating order around her became second nature, and her new systems started to function, she was able to pick up the thread of her destiny, and build her professional identity step-by-step.

With The Outsider on the run and her career back on track, Kim decided to try some new ways of having fun. She enrolled in a ballroom dancing course. It required her to leave her sanctuary, to commit and follow through each week to engage in an activity that previously she could never imagine doing. The active, dynamic nature of ballroom dancing allowed her to build upon The Hero capacity for Rhythmic Drive, while at the same time engaging The Father through the strong, elegant forms and systems of dances and dance sequences.

And sure enough, through the ballroom dancing community Kim "met someone," a dentist with a busy practice and a loving heart, also ready to make room in her life for a co-creative partnership. Challenges were no longer something to run away from, because Kim was on fire with the possibilities for success, and was standing firmly on the solid ground of her own **True Authority**.

As Meg's relationship with her employees improved, the culture of the company became more honoring and mutually respectful. The entire organization began to take on a lightness and an optimism that began to translate into her brand.

IMAGINE

Imagine a world where women have a natural sense of self-confidence and value their unique contributions while also honoring the contributions of others.

Imagine a world where women are able to transcend the experience of being servants to anachronistic patriarchal values. A world where we know we belong and that our ways of being are valued as highly as those of the Masculine.

Imagine a world where we innately create order that is adaptable, and build reliable structures to support what we do; a world where we are able to enter into the clear knowing of our minds, without losing the connection to our embodied ways of knowing.

Imagine a world where women view their commitments as sacred responsibilities and reliably follow through so that those around them can rest on the solid foundation of this accountability.

Imagine a world where women are the guiding architects, building the systems of a new world order.

Imagine this world and then imagine yourself shaping it!

Self-Observation Exercise for *The Father*

The purpose of this Self-Observation exercise is to deepen your ability to become an objective observer of your own experience when The Father shadows makes an appearance. It calls upon you to witness yourself in the moment, to intimately get to know those aspects of your way of being as they emerge in everyday situations.

As you become a better and better observer of your experience, you begin to see and discover things about the world inside and around you that would otherwise go unnoticed. You will in time clearly recognize when the shadows of The Father take over.

This observation exercise does not include changing anything. It just means looking at things as they currently are now . . . just noticing and writing down what you observe.

Daily Exercise

In one or two situations during the day, simply notice the presence of The Judge or The Outsider. It may arise when you are alone or interacting with others, or when at home or at work.

1. What was happening when you noticed The Judge or The Outsider making an appearance?
2. What emotions did you feel?
3. What sensations were you aware of in your body?
4. What were your thoughts/stories about the situation?
5. What were you doing or not able to do?
6. When in the grip of the shadow what were your habitual behaviors?

Weekly Reflection

At the end of the week, look over your reflections and summarize in your journal:

1. What consistent stories does The Judge or The Outsider tell you about the way the world is and how you have to be in it?

2. What are your signature emotions?
3. What connections are you making about the shadows of The Father and the felt sense and posture your body takes when one of them is present?
4. What are you learning about the way the shadows of The Judge or The Outsider are structured to provide you love, safety, or a sense of belonging?
5. How is that working and/or not working for you now?

Take some time to observe The Judge or The Outsider in yourself without any attempt to shift. Give yourself space to really see how they operate (maybe take a few days to a week). Then move into the Deep Practice.

Mysterial Change Process Deep Practice—The Father

Use this practice to turn toward the triggered reactions of The Judge and The Outsider. Depending on the level of triggering, it may take some time to bring yourself to center. It is enough to know that you are triggered and that this is not an ideal time to take any action.

SEE IT—Recognize when you have been triggered and are in the grips of The Father shadow. Notice the *state of mind* (thoughts, judgments, and stories), *emotional state* (feelings), and the *state of body* (sensations, contraction, and shape) you find yourself in.

SAY IT—Name what is happening when you recognize the familiar reactivity—the body, the emotions, the story, and the behaviors of The Judge or The Outsider—overtaking you.

STOP IT—Decline the unproductive old stories or mental attitude of the shadow by telling yourself, "Stop!"

SENSE IT—Let go of the "story" or mental attitude for the moment, bring your attention to the present by tuning into your sensation. Feel your feet on the ground, find your breath in the center of your body, and sense the reactive places in your muscles and your core. Just let them be there with recognition, but not judgment; and with no requirement to change anything in the moment. From this place, turn towards the limiting belief of The Father and say the limiting belief—*I do not belong.*

NOTICE—Observe what happens when you drop this pebble into the pond of your being. As a compassionate and loving witness simply be present with whatever arises. Allow yourself to softly touch into this tender place without trying to change or challenge what you find there.

DIFFERENTIATE—Ask yourself: Who would I be without this belief? Allow yourself to respond somatically (i.e., through body sensations and subtle postures) to this inquiry.

STAY WITH IT—Let your breath gently soften and settle places of contraction and tightening. Now call in the stabilizing and trustworthy energy of the inner Father and differentiate from the shadow by inviting the liberating belief: *I am at home in myself and naturally belong.* Allow the energizing and grounding truth of these words to resonate through every cell of your body.

COME TO CENTER—As you begin to feel a release of the emotional feelings and sensations that have hijacked you, bring yourself to center. Find your ground by feeling your feet on the ground and taking full, deep breaths from the center of your body. As you exhale, allow your muscles to relax into gravity and find yourself centered in three-dimensional space so that you become more fully present and your energy is balanced between the front and back, the right and left, and above and below.

INVOKE THE FATHER'S QUALITY OF SELF-CONFIDENCE—"What would it be like if I had a little more Self-Confidence in my being right now?"

CHOOSE ACTION—Take action or no action from this place of center. Remember to start with situations that have smaller charges and build from there so that you can get the full benefit of the practice.

Daily Practice

Select *one or two situations during the day* when you are aware that your Father shadows are activated. Deliberately go through each step above. If you were not able to stop the grab of The Father shadows in the moment, take some time later in the day and recreate the situation so that the body state is activated and you are able to move through the process. Remember that the neural network can be shifted not only through experience in the moment, but also through recreating the situation using the imagination.

Reflections

Take ten to fifteen minutes to journal on the following:

1. What happened when you were able to let go of the thoughts and stay with the emotions and sensations in the body?
2. What happened when you touched into the embodied limiting belief—*I do not belong?* How do this belief and The Father shadows influence the way you interact with others? What is possible and not possible when they are the driving force?
3. What was your experience when you brought in the liberating belief of The Father?—*I am at home in myself and naturally belong.*
4. What, if anything, was different when you came to Center (i.e., the way you feel about yourself, how you interact with others, what actions are possible now)?

Chapter 11

THE ACTIVATION OF THE MAIDEN—
Releasing Joyful Creativity

Prepare to be swept into an exciting realm of inner artistry, pulsing with a bold energy that is capable of really shaking things up. Welcome to the dynamic Flame Yin essence of The Maiden, second force of the Feminine, too chaotic and potentially destructive to unleash until The Father's capacity for structuring, ordering, and systematizing has been built.

Read this invocation aloud and see if you can feel the electrifying invitation of The Maiden tingling and pulsing in your body.

Invocation of The Maiden

Release all the tension in your body
let my energy ripple up your spine so that you can
feel my aliveness tingling through every cell of your being.

I am the electrochemical She-face of creation
and I am here to dance you into your most imaginative life.
With me you will not be afraid to make mistakes,
shake things up, or find your passion.

Make the sacred, sensual animal of your body a prayer
dedicate the pleasure of your flesh to healing the wounds of Mother Earth.

Come with me now
it is time to play
fling open the door of the birdcage
and set your song free.

Let us go into the dreamtime together
and conjure up a new world
that honors your joyfully creative Maiden self.

With the structures of The Father well built you can return to me now
and safely light the fire of your passion.

Releasing the Fire of The Maiden

To arrive here in the pulsing energy of The Maiden is a significant step forward when the healthy Father is cultivated within. Many of us have tried to access the freedom and joyful creativity that comes with our Flame Yin essence. But because we have not fully prepared the way for this fiery, volatile force, it has led to painful and unintended consequences.

Flame Yin essence is both creative and unpredictable because it opens us to the power of our dynamic Feminine life force, a libidinal surge very closely connected to our sexuality. The Maiden harnesses the flaming energy of The Hero to bring her creativity out into the world, but unlike the focus of Flame Yang, this blazing Yin archetype likes to break things open. She seeks connection and intimacy with others, unconcerned with rank, status, or differences. She rides the carrier wave of her intuition and doesn't take herself too seriously.

This, as you can imagine, constitutes a threat to the powers that be. We have created a society that honors The Father's values of order, rationality, and linear thinking. It's no wonder that The Maiden has been repressed in Modern and Traditional consciousness, domesticated into a virginal daughter or debased into a sex object. While The Maiden archetype is an ancient and universal pattern of innocent aliveness, she is a relative newcomer in terms of influencing the direction of modern society. She burst on the scene in the 1960s as flower power, sexual freedom, psychedelic art, hunger for diversity and change, and a flat rejection of the Establishment (a.k.a. *The Father*). The energy she brought created an explosion of creativity, innovation, social breakdown, and transformation.

The world would never be the same, especially for women. Almost overnight—historically speaking—women became liberated (if they chose) from the roles and traditions of a primarily patriarchal society, and the reproductive and physical constraints on their bodies. The Maiden's fertile imagination, her ability to break down barriers and connect with others to manifest new worlds, spelled the rise of The Information Age.

Awakening the healthy inner Maiden pattern allows steady, controllable access to the flow of Flame Yin essence within us. Think of Flame Yin as the dynamic, sizzling, Masculine expression of Yin in our lives. She is passionate, fun-loving, spontaneous, curious, imaginative, intuitive, and adventurous. She is full and unfettered creativity in expression.

In the maturing balance of Yin and Yang essences in an individual's life cycle—and in the evolution of society—the shift from compliance within the cerebral and steadfast systems of The Father, to deep diving into the emotively churning waters of the intuitive Maiden marks a revolutionary and potentially disorienting shift. Some leadership programs of the last quarter of the twentieth century did acknowledge this energetic turnabout and did their best to incorporate it.

For instance, the Transformational Leadership movement[1] is markedly humanistic and empowering of both follower and leader, drawing upon Emotional Intelligence, social and political sensitivity, transparency, and authenticity to tap and actualize human potential. Many of the new leadership approaches that emerged during the latter twentieth century were also trying to balance the top down, "command and control" models of leadership that had been in place for years.

A new paradigm has been emerging as many women are leaving the safety of the corporate world to strike out on their own entrepreneurial ventures, or go back to school to get training or advanced degrees in "impractical" or "alternative" fields, such as Spiritual Psychology, Creative Writing, or Shamanic Coaching. And there has been a sudden proliferation of self-help programs that promise to help us find our calling or soul purpose.

After all the hard work of building an adult life (The Father) we all want access to the same thing: **Joyful Creativity.** And that's what awakening the archetype of The Maiden liberates within us.

The Foundational Capacities of Joyful Creativity

The Maiden archetype brings with it a connection to a wilder Feminine force that liberates in us the joy of life, even with its many ups and downs: Spontaneous Intuition; Emergent Flow; Creative Mutuality; and Liberating Systems. Access to our creativity and imagination are just some of the juicy harvests of activating this second force of the Feminine.

The Promise of Joyful Creativity

> *"You were wild once, don't let them tame you."*
> —Isadora Duncan

The Maiden archetype is well worth waiting for! She will support you to boldly break apart the structures in your life and in those organizations that have kept you feeling stuck. She will give you access to the other brains besides the Head—the Heart and the Hara—as you drop you into "the zone" of effortless effort. She will enable you to be vulnerable and open in relationships so that others can meet you in that deep place where fulfillment grows.

The Maiden

INTERIOR	EXTERIOR
My Inner Experience	**How I Show Up**
Capacity: SPONTANEOUS INTUITION	**Capacity: EMERGENT FLOW**
To engage a non-rational way of knowing that arises from the body and heart intelligences giving you the ability to know something directly in the moment without analytical reasoning.	To be fully in the now and open to whatever emerges as you follow the creative impulse into action. A feeling of spontaneous joy, energized focus, full involvement and effortless effort in whatever you are doing.
Relating with Others	**Engaging the World**
Capacity: CREATIVE ENGAGEMENT	**Capacity: LIBERATING SYSTEMS**
To be intimate with and open to others, while staying fully present to your own experience and perspective. To generate a kind of "we space" with another that is dynamically creative.	To break up or let go of unnecessary and overly limiting restraints, so that a system can become more flexible, and even transform. A willingness to take Risks and make mistakes for the sake of discovering new ways of doing things.

INDIVIDUAL

COLLECTIVE

I IT

WE ITS

With The Maiden on board you work to live, not live to work. Your life becomes a creative experiment that you enter boldly into every day, curious to see what you will invent. And joy is not a fleeting experience, earned after a lot of hard work and lost as soon as you return to the grindstone. Along with an increased ability to be with the difficult moments of life, you are ready to playfully engage in the fun of living. You recognize that this is your birthright.

Think of Frida Kahlo, the artist whose surrealistic paintings were described as "a ribbon around a bomb," or Wangari Maathai, the environmental and political activist who risked her life to plant trees and became the first African woman to win a Nobel Peace Prize: risk-taking, structure-breaking, creative women in action.

The Father archetype helps you to find your purpose and stand in your own True Authority. When you bring The Maiden into partnership with your Vessel Yang essence, the passion and courage that you need to step forward in the direction of your dreams comes online.

Finally you become able to "get on your path," which can mean changing jobs, starting new ventures, or going back to school. Some set off on adventures of life and love they'd only dared to dream of before. "What will you do with this one wild and precious life?" the poet Mary Oliver asks us to consider.

You will remember that for the Flame nature of The Hero to come online safely, the Vessel nature of The Mother archetype needed to be well cultivated first. The same is true in this polarity. Once the solid and containing Vessel structure of The Father is built you can welcome the dynamic and wilder energy of The Maiden without everything being destroyed. When the shadows have been cleared and the healthy archetype cultivated, **Joyful Creativity** becomes your natural expression.

Shadows of The Maiden—The Bohemian and The Puritan

For many women who worked hard to fit into the structures of the Patriarchy, it is very challenging when this second force of the Feminine activates in the psyche. All of a sudden the world in which they were once happy feels suffocating and limiting. They don't know what happened to their joy, aliveness, and dreams, and they want them back. It is a very confusing time.

Without a developmental model that shows Flame Yin as a natural step forward, women either repress this dynamic force or totally overidentify with it. If it is the former, The Puritan shadow emerges and a woman puts a lid on her erotic energy, often extinguishing the flame by sinking into depression. If a woman jumps onto the motorcycle of The Bohemian shadow she often bursts out of the structures in her life with drastic consequences that later she regrets.

Between the ages of eight to ten we touch into the fiery nature of Flame Yang—The Hero—as we push away from our Vessel Yin essence. In the best-case scenario contact with this Flame Yang essence allows for the early expression of our uninhibited young girl energy, foreshadowing the Flame Yin essence that waits. The Maiden has a similar fiery expression but is not the same as The Hero. Often women say that they, "want to go back to find that undomesticated girl that they used to be."

But the cultivation of the healthy Maiden is actually a well-earned step forward that includes and transcends their earlier experiences. The Hero's Flame expression is like an arrow that pierces the world and moves things forward with self-discipline and focus. The Maiden's expression of the Flame essence is more like a kind of catalytic enzyme that disassembles things in unpredictable ways to create new forms.

Perhaps one of the most difficult things about this move from The Father to The Maiden is accepting what has to be surrendered. As Albert Einstein said, "I must be willing to give up what I am in order to become what I will be." It takes courage and commitment to face the shadows of The Maiden and be willing to invite this "free spirit" into your adult life.

THE PURITAN—THE PASSIVE SHADOW OF THE MAIDEN

The two poles of this shadow polarity operate in direct relationship to one another. While one of the poles will likely be stronger than the other in a woman's experience, the natural tendency will be to swing from one to the other. This is the psyche's way of trying to stabilize in the absence of the integration of the healthy Maiden archetype.

Some women have been terrified to have contact with the sparky, sensual, and catalytic energy of The Maiden. Perhaps it burned them when others expressed it in shadow in their early lives, or it exploded through them in ways that they weren't prepared for, and wound up wreaking havoc. It was just too much. So they quickly shoved their Maiden back down to the basement and The Puritan shadow appeared in her place.

CHARACTERISTICS OF THE PURITAN

See if you recognize any signs that The Puritan is buttoning up.

- ✳ When your sensual body is aroused, you feel dirty or shameful and repress it. It bothers you when other women make themselves too attractive or flirt.
- ✳ You fear that you can't survive without the security of the structures in your life—marriage, job, institution, etc.—so you stuff your feelings, toe the line, are a "nice little girl," and keep your mouth shut.
- ✳ It feels somehow wrong to just have fun and enjoy yourself, and you occasionally feel resentment toward women who do. Playful, boisterous energy (especially at work) feels counterproductive and even dangerous.

* Working in teams frustrates you, you feel conflict and mistrust and would really rather just do your own thing.
* You deny your intuition, struggling through exhaustive research when making decisions, and are mystified and skeptical when your boss/partner/co-worker/friend "goes with their gut."
* You tend to stick to routines and familiar places: eating the same food at the same restaurants, traveling to the safe places you've already been, doing things the way you have always done them.
* The exotic or unusual holds little attraction and you do everything you can to avoid uncertainty.
* Life, especially work, is hard. When a project falls into place easily, you secretly feel this is "cheating."
* When you ask yourself why you are so uncomfortable sharing too much of yourself with another, you realize it's because you honestly believe that if they really knew you they'd reject you.

These are just some of the ways in which your Maiden nature splits off into The Puritan shadow. Do any of them sound familiar? Often it is easier to recognize shadows in others, so perhaps certain people came to mind as you read over the list.

CLEARING THE PURITAN: TERRY'S JOURNEY

When we met Terry she had just turned sixty and was marching steadily toward retirement from a thirty-year career in environmental regulation with the federal government. Due to recent budget reductions, Terry's staff was cut back, requiring her to absorb additional workload. She was exceptionally serious about being disciplined and responsibly managing her staff. She was also very serious about just about everything else in her life—being a supportive wife, friend and community member, maintaining her home in tiptop shape, and protecting the environment. Her appearance was understated and modest, dressing in a way that would be sure not to be controversial or draw attention.

One Friday afternoon, after another routine week of getting up early, working hard, following all the rules and being a "good" person, Terry suddenly broke down. "I felt dead inside. I just knew that I couldn't keep living like this, but I didn't know what to do next. Despite all the positive affirmations and herbal supplements I was taking, I could not shake the feeling that I was sinking. Everything in my life was exactly as I had planned it and from the outside it all looked great. But inside something was deeply missing."

ROOTS OF THE PURITAN

Terry's childhood left little room for her to dream, explore, or color outside the lines. She grew up in a classically WASP, middle-class family of five that worked hard to keep up appearances of propriety. Her father, a banker in the days when they were cautious and conservative, was a strict disciplinarian who tightly controlled Terry's speech, dress, and behavior. No mistakes were tolerated. As the youngest child and only girl in her family, Terry was relentlessly taunted, shamed, and diminished; in other words, she grew up in the perfect environment for The Maiden to go underground!

Terry's perfectionistic and critical self-talk constantly harangued her into compliance with nearly impossible standards. "I could be so mean to myself—it was incredible," Terry observed. "No one could possibly be as hard on me as me." Early on, The Judge shadow of The Father colluded with The Puritan to prevent Terry's spontaneous, unpredictable, creative impulses from arising. Even though she was a remarkably skilled ceramicist and enjoyed quilting, these activities were discounted as frivolous.

When The Puritan shadow locks arms with The Judge a woman will tend to give her creative power away to others. Not surprisingly, Terry was drawn to a career in a very bureaucratic environment, with plenty of containment, rules and regulations, and hierarchy. She gravitated to the security and stability of the world of The Father. Because her Maiden self was so muted, Terry's natural expression in the world was overly inclined toward The Father—highly responsible, disciplined, and organized— without the mediating flexibility and enjoyment that a sufficient flow of Flame Yin would bring.

Of course, her inner Maiden had occasionally escaped from the cellar during her younger years. In her early twenties The Maiden would burst out unexpectedly (usually after a glass of wine) and she would turn into a kind of Bohemian party animal. "I couldn't let her out even just a little," Terry mused, "because I would get carried away and before I knew it, I would be bouncing off the walls and doing things I definitely regretted the next day." These experiences reinforced Terry's belief that The Maiden aspect of her being was unpredictable and very dangerous and needed to be kept under tight control.

OBSERVING THE PURITAN

From our first session with Terry we could see that it was the dynamic force of The Maiden that was pressing on her psyche for integration. And we knew that for this to occur in a healthy way she would have to do the deep work of clearing the shadows and cultivating the archetypes of the first three activations of The Mysterial Sequence. When Terry worked with her inner Mother, she learned for the first time how to really accept and be in her body.

Mary Oliver's poetic statement became Terry's mantra, "You do not have to be good. You do not have to walk on your knees across the desert repenting. You only have to let the soft animal of your body love what it loves."

Along with Embodiment, the most vital Mother capacity Terry developed was Self-Compassion. Because her own mother had remained quietly submissive to her habitually angry husband and had no sense of her own value and lovability, she didn't shield Terry from the diminishing criticisms and taunts of her father and brothers. By the end of her work with The Mother archetype, Terry became able, for the first time, to actually connect with her own preciousness as a being and could feel the liberating truth of, "I am enough just as I am."

From this connection to the sufficiency of her being, The Capitulator Hero shadow was easier to see. Her tendency to go along with whatever others wanted her to do had made her a valuable ally inside the bureaucracy at work. But this came at a cost and she began to experiment with speaking her mind and learning how to say, "No" to the demands of others. She began to feel less afraid and more daring.

After the Initiation of Empowered Radiant Presence with the first polarity, Terry was ready to take on the work with The Father's shadow expression of The Judge. The criticizing voices inside her head had been so shrill, angry, and unrelenting (a perfect replay of her father's threats and insults) for so long that they were just a natural part of her daily experience. Once she was able to see them for what they were and let them go, a sense of exciting new possibility began to arise.

"Instead of obsessively worrying that any little error could cost me my job," she said, "I began to celebrate the reality that I can retire in a few years—and do something I really love!"

Set free from the tyranny of the "shoulds," Terry was ready now to observe her inner Maiden. She instantly recognized The Puritan and for the first time considered that there could actually be other ways to be in the world that would be more satisfying. The first time she read the list of behaviors associated with The Puritan, she didn't see what the problem was with most of them.

Now that The Judge had surrendered the keys to the basement and The Maiden was starting to peek out she began to really question her worldview. She saw how she constantly shut down anything spontaneous or unpredictable at work or at home. Her meticulous systems and structures left little room for flow or pleasure.

She was surprised to notice that the only times she gave herself little treats like going to the spa, or a girl's night out were when she accomplished some big task really well. She had to earn fun, pleasure, or relaxation. Once The Puritan was flushed out of the shadows by the light of her conscious attention Terry was ready to welcome The Maiden.

Building Foundational Capacity

When you first start to welcome The Maiden archetype, you sometimes discover that she is actually quite shy. In fact, she may have been shut down completely many years ago and hasn't been invited to come out and play since then. So you must approach this energy carefully, as you might a timid wild animal in the forest, and slowly reassure her that it is safe to come out. Once your healthy inner Father is cultivated there is a protective space around your Maiden essence and you can invite her out to play!

Terry's days had historically been well programmed with little room for deviation or spontaneity. She had liked it this way because it felt safe, but now she was ready to shake things up a bit with a practice to build the foundational capacity for **Emergent Flow** (Individual Exterior—How I Show Up).

Going With the Flow Practice for *Emergent Flow*

Select a period of time such as a Saturday morning and for at least one hour simply follow the flow of your pleasure and joy. When something stops being pleasurable you stop doing it. This activity must be done alone so that you are not adjusting to someone else's rhythms or desires.

Example of one of Terry's practices: She went to a morning yoga class, then wandered around the outdoor market in her neighborhood, letting herself be drawn to various foods, objects, and conversations as they emerged naturally for her. She sat down on a bench in the park with her coffee and listened to a musician playing folk songs. In the middle of a song she got up (normally she would have been polite and waited until the end) and found herself walking away from the market and into a trendy home boutique nearby. She let the beautiful objects awaken and inspire her sensual, creative nature. As she turned down one of the aisles in the store she saw a

(continued on next page)

---

young woman *whom she had* mentored at work many years before and they had a powerful and meaningful conversation together. It nourished her soul.

Reflections:
1. What was your embodied experience as you surrendered to flow— what were your feelings, sensations, and the quality of your thoughts?
2. What was the quality of your experience after you did the practice? What did you notice about your energy and attention?

The first time that Terry experimented with this Emergent Flow practice she was stunned by how it fed a part of her that she did not even know was hungry. Stepping out of our "to-do" list allows for unfocused, idle meandering. It is deeply restorative for the brain and whole being. We describe this as generating a kind of deep Yin nectar that literally feeds the cells of our body. The latest neuroscience makes a clear case for how harmful it actually is for our well-being and our effectiveness to be constantly driving forward in doing.[2]

With the success of her weekend practice, Terry began to engage the practice of flow as a way to move through her days. She discovered that many unseen, yet vital factors to be considered in business decisions were not found on the well-beaten path of logical thought.

The ability to flow through chaos and confusion is increasingly essential in our rapidly changing world. It requires a kind of awake presence and the willingness to not drive into the future based just on experiences of the past, but rather to be open to something new happening in the present moment. Spontaneity is an important aspect of Emergent Flow because it is often this capacity that allows movement through a stuck situation. As the saying goes, "Blessed are the flexible as they will not get bent out of shape."

When you liberate yourself from the past habitual patterns and open up to Emergent Flow you make room for a very different kind of future to emerge. Synchronous events become more commonplace and a quality of *effortless effort* replaces the dirge of daily activity. The Maiden possesses a kind of serious playfulness, making it possible for her to be both engaged and carefree at the same time.

Encountering the constraining and limiting structures and system of one's life with this attitude of serious playfulness can help build the foundational capacity for **Liberating Systems** (Exterior Collective—Engaging the World). Terry's connection with her playful essence had been cut off for so long that it took some deliberate practices to really start to give her inner Maiden permission to be a little audacious, wild, and crazy.

Maiden Play Date Practice for *Liberating Systems*

Once a week schedule a play date with your Inner Maiden. It does not need to be long but it does need to be very intentional. Break out of the every day, ordinary systems that keep you safe and secure. Just as if you were taking a young girl out for the afternoon ask your Maiden self what she would like to do.

And then go and do it!

Examples:

⁕ Run around in the backyard in bare feet catching raindrops with your tongue.

⁕ Go to a movie in the middle of the afternoon when everyone else is at work.

⁕ Play hooky; leave work early and let your Maiden lead you on a spontaneous adventure.

⁕ Dance passionately to your favorite music with no concern about how you look or whether you are in rhythm.

⁕ Dare yourself to climb a tree and feel the freedom from gravity.

⁕ Call up a friend spontaneously and go for a hike.

⁕ Luxuriate in a bath and then take your time applying beautiful body creams.

⁕ Spend time coloring outside the lines.

Reflections:

1. How did you notice resistance showing up to the practice? What did you do to self-soothe so that you could nourish your inner Maiden?

2. What did you notice about the quality of your energy and attention after you indulged in your play date? How did that effect your experience in the rest of your day?

As Terry began to re-member her playful and carefree Maiden an unfamiliar inner sense of joy took up residence. It wasn't that she was happy all the time but that life was just not so darn hard, filled with only responsibilities and obligations. She didn't need to brace herself against reality anymore, but could welcome the uncertainty of life with its natural ups and downs.

She lost the fear of making mistakes or producing an unacceptable result and began to experience a joyful creativity—something that her prior tightness and fear had precluded. She discovered that all hell did not break loose if she let her hair down and had a good time.

Finally, Terry began to feel the pleasure and power of being in her woman's body. Of course, this is a subject about which The Puritan often feels conflicted! Her humanness was no longer an enemy that she had to tame. Her sexual, sensual urges and desire for pleasure were integrating now into the fabric of her whole self. When she showed up to receive an award at her workplace in a boldly colored, sensually flowing silk dress we knew the Maiden was alive and well!

For women who over identify with The Maiden and fall into The Bohemian shadow, making an appearance that dazzling is all part of the strategy.

Shadows of The Maiden—The Bohemian and The Puritan

THE BOHEMIAN—THE ACTIVE SHADOW OF THE MAIDEN

Some women respond to the crushing structures of the shadow Father by identifying full on with The Maiden. What starts out perhaps as a healthy desire to connect with the dynamic Yin essence can turn into a shadow pattern. When overly fused with the fiery, impulsive nature of Flame Yin some women break up their marriages, leave jobs, move houses. When these acts are motivated by the shadow of the wild Bohemian they do not lead us to the Joyful Creativity we are seeking.

CHARACTERISTICS OF THE BOHEMIAN

See if you recognize any of these ways in which The Bohemian may be stirring up your psyche.

* You chafe at limits. Marriage, an organization, a traditional church, etc. all seem way too restrictive. You prefer to leave things as loose and open as possible, and can be resentful toward authority figures.
* You can turn on the *femme fatale* side of yourself, sometimes subtly, to get what you want or to feel good about yourself, using your sexuality as a manipulative tool.
* You thrive on intensity and thrill to the pulsing of your life force, but

you don't know your limits. In sports, adventure, or tackling a creative challenge, you just GO, until exhaustion stops you.

* You use the power of your magnetic presence to draw others toward you yet do not experience intimacy with them. Or, you may share too much personal information too fast, overwhelming them.

* You can be dismissive of people "in their heads," or tasks that require analysis and calculation. Instead, you prefer to rely almost exclusively on your feelings and instincts.

* You can drop everything and get easily drawn into a myriad of interesting opportunities and new possibilities without thinking through the consequences.

* You are drawn to work with others mainly for the excitement factor without much desire to invest time in deeper relationships.

* When someone does something that makes you insecure, you become melodramatic, drawing attention to yourself.

* You can be a real party girl, seeking pleasure, entertainment, and even addictive substances to distract yourself from your worries, or some challenge you don't feel up to facing.

These are just some of the ways in which your Maiden nature splits off into The Bohemian shadow. Do any of them sound familiar? Sometimes a woman will be coerced most of the time by her superego into the good girl behaviors of The Puritan. Then, seemingly out of the blue, she will erupt in wild and disruptive ways when The Bohemian bursts onto the scene. This dynamic Yin force will not be kept down. It is best that we take the time to clear the shadows so that we can access it reliably and sustainably.

CLEARING THE BOHEMIAN: ZOE'S JOURNEY

Zoe, thirty-six, was a radiant, vivacious young mover-shaker in the world of philanthropy and social innovation, married to a powerful, conservative man fifteen years her senior. She worked for an iconic leader renowned for groundbreaking work to liberate the poor, especially women. Zoe rode the dynamic, innovative energy of her Maiden, with the help of The Father, into projects in exotic places around the world.

Mainlining The Bohemian's energy kept her in a constantly moving frenzy. She used her creative spark to ignite one exciting project after another: rolling up her sleeves in the rural villages of the developing world, raising hundreds of millions of dollars, meeting with heads of state, and organizing high profile global events with thousands of well-heeled attendees.

Eventually, a power struggle erupted in her organization and controversy unfairly tainted the good work many had done. At the same time as this drama was occurring she met a man, while on a spiritual retreat supposedly to connect with herself, and the two entered into a torrid love affair. They met at exotic locations all over the world and he introduced her to meditation, mountain climbing, poetry, and the countercultural experience of Burning Man. She loved the person who she became with him as much as she loved him.

She was convinced that her new lover was the soul mate she had been waiting to meet, but he was not willing to leave his wife and children. How could this be? Her already chaotic life began to spin out of control. Disillusioned, confused, and exhausted from constant travel she knew she had to do something.

ROOTS OF THE BOHEMIAN

Zoe was adopted at birth. She became the youngest child in a politically well-connected family where her parents' visibility brought significant people through the door. Bi-racial, precocious, and blessed with exotic good looks, she learned early in life how to charm and seduce others to get her way.

"The adults were always making a fuss over how cute I was and what a great imagination I had," she remembers. "I got away with a lot." The tracks for over identifying with The Maiden archetype, believing that she could get the love, safety and belonging she needed by "Being The Maiden" were laid.

As the wife of an influential mover and shaker, her mother was constantly preoccupied entertaining the glitterati, or away at meetings of one committee or another. She loved her children, but in many ways the nanny knew them better than she did. It was confusing for Zoe to experience the loving presence of her nanny and the distant affection of her mother.

Zoe's inclination was to avoid confronting the pain of never quite feeling loved or special to her parents, by seeking pleasure in diversion and wildly exciting experiences. This provided the perfect setup to stay the "eternal child." She became The Bohemian who could escape the challenges of an adult life of commitment and self-discipline by attaching herself to powerful others who encouraged her to be a smart, sexy, brash young Maiden.

OBSERVING THE BOHEMIAN

The work with The Mother archetype required Zoe to roll up her sleeves and face The Neglector head on. In her desire to follow in her parents' footsteps she had pushed so far away from the loving, self-nurturing healthy inner Mother that it required some serious rewiring of her inner operating system. Stillness was an anathema to her: a boring and dangerous place where unwanted feelings could surface. A regular meditation practice that started out as five minutes became twenty, and she began to finally quiet her idea-churning mind. Once she was able to stay centered in the present moment instead of constantly tilting toward exciting future plans, Zoe began to master the vital Mother capacity for Holding Containers. Rather than impatiently lighting fires indiscriminately, she learned to slow down, take in all the factors, empathically tune to others involved, and discern what actions to take from a more grounded place.

That work set the stage for Zoe to deal with the previously uncompromising drive of her Dominator shadow as she began to access Rhythmic Drive. She did not have to push herself and others hard all the time—she directly experienced the power of pulsing her energy on and off in a balanced way. She was able to observe the tendency of The Judge shadow of The Father to see herself as entitled and better than others, drawing her again and again into high-powered worlds of influence and questionable practices.

Once Zoe actually took the time to *be with* her direct experiences, instead of always orienting toward the future potential of things, she could see The Bohemian shadow and realized how she had become a sexy servant of the Patriarchy, channeling her substantial Flame Yin energy into seduction and manipulation. This was useful in negotiations and power brokering, but it kept her at the beck and call of powerful men.

It was a harsh wake-up call as this revelation rippled not only through her work situation but also into her marriage with Ian. She began to recognize that she had married a man who had the power and authority of The Father, which at the time she had been seeking within herself. And now she was in an affair with another powerful man who expressed the wildly creative and soulful nature of The Maiden that she was actually ready to claim herself. Ouch!

Zoe realized, as she tracked The Bohemian, that she had fused herself to her lover because she deeply wanted access to her own spontaneous, wildly creative, and soulful side. Maybe it was time now for *her* to reap the benefits of her own inner Maiden.

Building Foundational Capacity

A steady yoga practice, unimaginable before she did her transformational work, became an important feature in her life. It guided her to slow down, quiet her mind, and come into her body. With time she began to recognize the quiet voice of her **Spontaneous Intuition** (Individual Interior—My Inner Experience). Spontaneous Intuition as a foundational capacity is a way of knowing that bypasses the mind and engages the body and the heart centers of intelligence. It is very different from logical or analytical thinking and arises in the moment.[3]

For most of us, our early childhood education was focused on developing our abilities to think rationally and logically in order to fit into a cultural worldview constructed around reason and order. Our intuitive capacities were likely left to languish—undervalued, underused, and certainly unappreciated. And yet it is clear that the complexity of the challenges we face in this evolutionary moment today require that we awaken our intuitive energies, and learn to integrate knowing at a deep embodied level with rational analysis. Linear thinking only allows us to see the future as a continuation of the past, whereas intuition allows for quantum leaps in all directions that can open us up to unimaginable creative solutions.

Many researchers into the phenomenon of intuition report that it is received through two channels: as spontaneous ideas, guesses, hunches that seem to come out of nowhere, and as sensations in the body that then become feelings and images. The consistent element is that intuition is a kind of knowing that emerges from a non-thinking, quiet state of mind. In order to cultivate the intuitive capacity we must awaken the body, mind, *and* heart as organs of high perception and then learn to understand their unique languages. In essence we need to create our own IPS (Intuition Positioning Satellite) to assist us in navigating through the complexities of our lives.

In order to start accessing and trusting her intuitive powers, Zoe needed to first of all stop being so reasonable. The Vessel Yang, more rational aspect of the psyche must become a *partner with*, not a *master of*, the more intuitive Flame Yin capacity. You need to discover how intuition communicates itself specifically through your particular body-heart-mind stream so that you can recognize its signals. Is it through a feeling in the gut, tingling in the solar plexus, an ache around the heart, a block in the throat, an image, a random idea, a little voice, a nagging feeling, a repeated dream, goose bumps? Pay attention to the subtle cues and your own patterns, and learn to recognize them.

Zoe learned to trust what she called the "goose bump factor" and knew to wait through the discomfort of "not knowing" the answer about a situation until her body

Downloading the Future Practice for
Spontaneous Intuition

Select an area around which you are experiencing confusion and would like more insight.

STEP 1: Engage in some activity that naturally activates your inner Maiden so that she is alive in your body-mind. This might be going for a brisk walk with the dog, singing a song out loud, dancing to some music, rock climbing, playing with your children.

STEP 2: Do a twenty-minute period of stream of consciousness writing in which you focus your energy and attention on four questions for five minutes each. (Use a timer)

> What does my head say?
> What does my heart say?
> What does my body say?
> What do all three centers working together know?

Use the following basic principle for all of the writing:[4]

* Write as though no one is reading—uncensored.
* Don't stop to read what you have written.
* Don't delete stuff.
* Don't worry about spelling, punctuation, or grammar.
* Be willing to write things that you might not rationally agree with.
* Go wild and have fun.
* Don't hold anything back.

Reflections:
1. What did you notice about resistance from your logical mind showing up?
2. What did you notice about your experience after the exercise—quality of your feelings, sensations, and thoughts?

signaled its YES. This meant being in the present, without a past or future, or any agenda whatsoever. She had some big decisions to make about her life but when she let go of trying to figure it out mentally and dropped into her intuition she knew what she had to do. She began to set the wheels in motion that would ultimately, and in a measured and responsible way, set her on a new course in her life. She left her job, her husband, and her lover as she stepped out in the unknown territory of authoring her own life.

This meant opening up to people around her in new ways. Although she could charm others into her orbit and collect allies by trading information and favors, Zoe realized that this did not generate an experience of real intimacy with them. She had always had a Maiden-like sparkling imagination and curiosity, but would keep others at a distance with her over-the-top energy. As she relaxed into herself she was able to listen more deeply, make more space for others, be more receptive and vulnerable. This was particularly helpful as she disengaged from the people and structures of the life she had built when The Bohemian was in control. She was growing the foundational capacity of **Creative Engagement** (Collective Interior—Relating With Others).

When we add the word "creative" to "engagement" we take this capacity to yet another level. This dynamic capacity allows the Healthy Maiden to co-create a very new kind of *We Space* with another. The more access you have to Creative Engagement the more able you are to:

- ✸ Be a separate self while staying in connected relationship to others.
- ✸ Be an individual while in emotional contact with a group.
- ✸ Enhance your own welfare while not impinging on the welfare of others.
- ✸ Take a thoughtful position while staying connected to others who may disagree.

With this enhanced capacity you are open to letting the other have an impact on you—emotionally, physically, mentally, and spiritually. In essence, embracing this capacity means that you are open to the possibility of changing, of becoming a different kind of person as a result of being influenced by another.

It is also about the possibility for the materialization of new ideas, thoughts, feelings, and perspectives that emerge because of your open connection. This capacity liberates an unseen creative force found in the *We Space*, and invites the Great Mystery into the equation.

We Space Conversation Practice for *Creative Engagement*

Identify an important relationship that you would like to improve.

1. Choose something that you would like to advocate for in this relationship (e.g., "I would like to have more intimacy in our relationship.")
2. Using stream of consciousness writing, spend some time journaling on the truth about your experience of the relationship as it is now. Be brutally honest with yourself. When you have finished this, do the same writing process while reflecting on the *future desired state* that you are looking to experience as a result of taking this stand. Again give yourself permission to have a powerful intention, no matter what the current reality of your experience in this relationship actually is.
3. Now release this vision into the *field of all possibilities* so that you are still holding the intention but lightly enough so that it can shift and change as you enter into mutuality. You are allowing a feeling of trust to extend into the field between you while at the same time influencing the possible outcomes with your image.
4. Now shift your awareness to the other person, and using the same stream of consciousness writing, imagine that you are this person. Accessing your Maiden Spontaneous Intuition, envision yourself to be this person and articulate what you find challenging about the relationship (with yourself), and also what your vision is for an improved relationship.
5. Enter into a real life conversation with this person, connected to the ground of your being and the image you are holding of the future desired state. Remain open to deeply understand the other person's experience.
6. Stay present to yourself and the other, while tending to the health of the *We Space* between you. Your goal is to keep this *We Space* generative and juicy without losing contact with yourself or with the other. If you feel it shrinking or getting dry then you may want to extend some loving lubrication into the system. Or maybe soften your receptivity, which could allow the other to replenish your shared field.

Note: In this practice the *We Space* should be more generative after your conversation than before.

(continued on next page)

Reflections:
1. What did you notice about your own capacity to stay present and connected to yourself during the conversation with the other?
2. What impact did using this approach have on your relationship?

Zoe used this practice often in difficult conversations with her husband as she disentangled herself from a relationship that was in truth not serving either of them. But being in Creative Engagement with another does not mean that it is without conflict or pain. When she had considered divorce before, The Bohemian was in charge and she did not let herself feel her own pain and suffering or that of her husband. She just distracted herself with an affair, more travel, parties, and thoughts of the adventure of a new life without her husband.

Now she let herself be with the pain of ending her marriage and all that it represented. "It was not an easy split with Ian by any means," Zoe shared tenderly. "He was very angry with me and blamed me for our failure. But on my best days I was able to hear his pain and acknowledge it, while still staying true to my own experience, which was very different for me."

Zoe used the same capacity of Creative Engagement to break off the affair, facing into the winds of her own fears of being alone. With time she discovered that there was a vast difference between loneliness and being on one's own. She began to enjoy being with herself. And at the same time her heart began to really open with others—not just the superficial bubbly Bohemian expression that she was good at (which often kept others at arm's length), but she could now access the healthy Maiden's capacity for a new kind of transparency, interdependence, and intimacy.

Limiting Belief of The Maiden Shadows— "I am not free to express myself fully."

Underneath the shadows of The Maiden lies this deep belief that cuts off our innate creative expression at the knees. It holds our pleasure and authenticity hostage. Do you recognize this limiting belief in your life? Say the words, slowly and out loud, to yourself. Notice how they land in you. Do you recognize how this has lived as truth inside you? What thoughts does this belief trigger? How does it make you feel? Do you notice any subtle sensations in your body as the words are expressed?

These reflection questions provide valuable information about how you are habitually, unconsciously, and needlessly limiting your own potential. For Zoe and Terry this belief ran through their beings like a deep aquifer of polluted water. Terry was aware of it most all the time and felt tangled up in the sticky web of her superego that always had a good reason why she should hold back and not express her true feelings and thoughts. Inside her bureaucratic organization she was rewarded for her conservative Puritan ways, which made things all the more confusing.

For Zoe this belief manifested in the opposite way. She learned early on that to get attention and love she should charm and entertain others by expressing whatever she thought they wanted to hear. She became the life of the party and on the surface it looked like she expressed herself freely. But she was actually just shape-shifting herself to gain approval from others. She was deaf to her own longings, needs, and desires. The darker, difficult, or tender emotions were not available when she was in the grip of The Bohemian shadow.

When we do the deep work to metabolize the shadows of The Maiden we set this beautiful, innocent, and alive part of ourselves free. A liberating belief that supports our true expression settles into the foundation of our being.

Liberating Belief of The Maiden: "I am free to express my true nature."

Now say those potent words slowly, and out loud, to yourself. Notice how the words of this liberating belief land in you. Do you feel a subtle sense of relaxation, of relief, of freedom? Do you feel more energized, more enlivened?

What if you liberated your deeply creative genius and were able to freely express yourself? What if you knew you deeply belonged here in the world (The Father) and that your joy, aliveness, spontaneity, and unique gifts were welcomed (The Maiden)?

Once this liberating belief became a core principle of Terry's way of living she discovered many new possibilities. Her long-dormant creative nature burst forth in her quilting. She was not afraid to speak her mind and try new things and her new spirit of adventure took her to graduate school and eventually all over the world.

Zoe found a very new pathway into her true nature through the difficult experiences of loss. She turned her inner Maiden toward herself and began to create a life that was more congruent with her values. Settling into a small island community in a cottage by herself, where her glamorous persona was not the currency of connection, she began to build genuine friendships. With the money from her hard driving years and her divorce, she took a year to rest and find her true voice. And when she did, she began to write. And write beautifully!

Releasing Joyful Creativity

Did you recognize elements from your own experience in Terry's and Zoe's stories? Do you feel ready to coax this innocent, sensual, fun-loving, daring, and passionate Maiden into your embodied experience? Can you picture yourself as a creative, an innovator, someone who is here to catalyze, take risks, enjoy breakthroughs, and to live the life your soul came here to live?

The awakening of the inner Maiden invites you to recognize in yourself the joyfully creative woman that you see in others. It throws open the doors of your being and welcomes your embodied life—the difficult and the ecstatic. It opens your instinctive, intuitive, wild nature and throws you into the dance of life. You are released into **Joyful Creativity.**

IMAGINE

Imagine a world where women have access to the golden, wondrously alive essence of their Maiden innocence. Imagine how this essence has aged like fine wine, maturing into an intoxicating and spicy elixir.

Imagine a world where pleasure, play, and joy bring a productive dimension to the seriousness of work.

Imagine a world where our imaginations are boundless and our intuitive hunches are as welcome as our research.

Imagine a world where we are often in "the zone," playing with bold, creative actions that make a positive difference in the world.

Imagine a world where we can truly be ourselves with each other, where the armor that separates us dissolves and we are catalyzed together into something more.

Imagine this world and then imagine yourself shaping it!

Self-Observation Exercises for *The Maiden*

The purpose of this Self-Observation exercise is to deepen your ability to become an objective observer of your own experience when The Maiden shadows make an appearance. It calls upon you to witness yourself in the moment, to intimately get to know those parts of yourself that split off into The Bohemian and/or The Puritan shadows.

This practice cultivates your self-awareness and brings the light of your conscious awareness into the darker shadow aspects of your unconscious. As you become a better and better observer of your experience, you begin to see and discover things about the world inside and around you that would otherwise go unnoticed. You will in time clearly recognize when the shadows of The Maiden take over.

This observation exercise does not include changing anything. It just means looking at things as they currently are now . . . just noticing and writing down what you observe.

Daily Exercise

In *one or two situations during the day*, simply notice the presence of The Bohemian or The Puritan. It may arise when you are alone or interacting with others, or when at home or at work.

1. What was happening when you noticed the shadow making an appearance?
2. What emotions did you feel?
3. What sensations were you aware of in your body?
4. What were your thoughts/stories about the situation?
5. What were you doing or not able to do?

Weekly Reflection

At the end of the week, look over your reflections and summarize in your journal:

1. What consistent stories does The Puritan or The Bohemian tell you about the way the world is and how you have to be in it?
2. What are their signature emotions?

3. What connections are you making between the shadows of The Maiden and the felt-sense and posture your body takes when one of them is present?

4. What are you learning about the way the shadows of The Maiden are structured to provide you love, safety, or a sense of belonging?

5. How is that working and/or not working for you now?

Take some time to observe The Puritan or The Bohemian in yourself without any attempt to shift. Give yourself space to really see how they operate (maybe take a few days to a week). Then move into the Deep Practice.

Mysterial Change Process
Deep Practice—The Maiden

Use this practice to turn toward the triggered reactions of The Bohemian and The Puritan. Depending on the level of triggering, it may take some time to bring yourself to center. It is enough to know that you are triggered and that this is not an ideal time to take any action.

SEE IT—Recognize when you have been triggered and are in the grips of The Maiden shadow. Notice the *state of mind* (thoughts, judgments, and stories), emotional state (feelings), and the *state of body* (sensations, contraction, and shape) you find yourself in.

SAY IT—Name what is happening when you recognize the familiar reactivity—the body, the emotions, the story, and the behaviors of The Bohemian or The Puritan—overtaking you.

STOP IT—Decline the unproductive old stories or mental attitude of the shadow by telling yourself, "Stop!"

SENSE IT—Let go of the "story" or mental attitude for the moment, bring your attention to the present by tuning into your sensation. Feel your feet on the ground, find your breath in the center of your body, and sense the reactive places in your muscles and your core. Just let them be there with recognition, but not judgment; and with no requirement to change anything in the moment. From this place, turn toward the limiting belief of The Maiden and say the limiting belief—*I am not free to express myself fully.*

NOTICE—Observe what happens when you drop this pebble into the pond of your being. As a compassionate and loving witness, simply be present with whatever arises. Allow yourself to softly touch into this tender place without trying to change or challenge what you find there.

DIFFERENTIATE—Ask yourself: "Who would I be without this belief?" Allow yourself to respond somatically to this inquiry.

STAY WITH IT—Let your breath gently soften and settle places of contraction and tightening. Now call in the fiery and motivating energy of the inner Maiden and differentiate from the shadow by inviting the liberating belief: *I am free to express my true nature.* Allow the energizing and grounding truth of these words to resonate through every cell of your body.

COME TO CENTER—As you begin to feel a release of the emotional feelings and sensations that have hijacked you, bring yourself to center. Find your ground by feeling your feet on the ground and taking full, deep breaths from the center of your body. As you exhale, allow your muscles to relax into gravity and find yourself centered in three dimensional space so that you become more fully present and your energy is balanced between the front and back, the right and left, and above and below.

INVOKE THE MAIDEN'S QUALITY OF EMERGENT FLOW—"What would it be like if I had a little more Flow in my being right now?"

CHOOSE ACTION—Take action or no action from this place of center. Remember to start with situations that have smaller charges and build from there so that you can get the full benefit of the practice.

Daily Practice

Select *one or two situations during the day* when you are aware that your Maiden shadows are activated. Deliberately go through each step of the somatic awareness process. If you were not able to stop the grab of The Maiden shadows in the moment, take some time later in the day and recreate the situation so that the body state is activated and you are able to move through the process. Remember that the neural network can be shifted not only through experience in the moment, but also through recreating the situation using the imagination.

Reflections
Take ten to fifteen minutes to journal on the following:

1. What happened when you were able to let go of the thoughts and stay with the emotions and sensations in the body?
2. What happened when you touched into the embodied limiting belief: *I am not free to express myself fully?* How do this belief and The Maiden shadows influence the way you interact with others? What is possible and not possible when they are the driving force?
3. What was your experience when you brought in the liberating belief of The Maiden?—*I am free to express my true nature.*
4. What, if anything, was different when you came to Center (i.e., the way you feel about yourself, how you interact with others, what actions are possible now)?

Chapter 12

JOYFUL TRUE AUTHORITY INITIATION—
Uniting The Father and The Maiden

When we take back our power and authority from the shadows of The Father and liberate our deepest joy and creative passion from the shadows of The Maiden, a quantum shift in our experience occurs. A newfound **Joyful True Authority** is waiting for the women who do the deep work of this Initiation.

It definitely takes a leap of faith to trust that releasing the resistance to, or fusion with the powerful Father archetype will lead you somewhere more joyful. And for those who deeply desire to stand in their own true authority, The Maiden archetype seems like a stretch. But for those of us who make the leap, this Initiation marks an important step forward in not only claiming a new way of holding our power in the world, but also bringing our wildly creative selves with us into the bedroom and the boardroom.

Polarity Limiting and Liberating Beliefs

If the limiting belief of this polarity—I do not belong and am not free to express myself fully—is driving our behavior, we feel wobbly in our own authority and anything but joyful. While we might show a bold face to the world that tries to convince others that we are being authentic and do belong, deep in the layers of the unconscious lurks a different story. And this one is much older and runs much deeper than whatever new affirmations we might try to tell ourselves. Just like the iceberg whose directional movement is determined by the enormous bulk of ice under the water, so too are we driven by the shadow material in our unconscious.

When this deep belief is the guiding force, The Puritan will tend to clamp down on what feels like a dangerous creative impulse rising inside as we do our best to try to fit into a world in which we worked so hard to belong. Depression and illness will often follow as our psyche attempts to regulate things by dampening the flames of new life pushing up from the unconscious. For The Bohemian this limiting belief will drive us to become rebellious, demolishing the structures we spent years building, wreaking havoc all around. Regret and confusion often follow this path as we burn down everything that seems to be blocking our expression—only to find that we still don't feel like we belong or can freely express ourselves.

When you find the courage and commitment to go deeply into the shadow lands and make contact with the part of yourself that this shadow was trying to take care of in the early days, the old stories lose their grip. With time and deliberate work the liberating belief of the polarity arises not as a good idea, but as an embodied experience.

I am at home in myself and naturally belong, free to express my true nature becomes a way of being.

Once a woman has opened this channel, you can see in her a natural, unaffected self-confidence right down to her bones. It is congruence between who she is on the inside and how she acts in the world. She has a quality of presence that radiates strength and integrity. You just simply trust her. Although she takes her work seriously, you also catch the playful sparkle in her eye that tells you she is enjoying herself. As much as she knows and honors the value of structures and commitments, she is also open to the surprising, out-of-the-box, and spontaneous emergence of life.

She knows how to build things up, and how to stay flexible and crack things open when they become too rigid or stifling of the creative flow. She brings all her ways of knowing to important decisions, gathering information through analytical, intuitive, and emotional channels. Because she feels so good about herself, it is natural for her to extend gratitude and recognition to others, and this combination makes her a magnetic presence. She exudes a Joyful True Authority.

Joyful True Authority Emerging in Women

MEG (FATHER: JUDGE SHADOW)

For Meg, the limiting belief of this polarity drove her into demanding ways of leading in order to try to fit in and prove that she did belong as the CEO of her family business. The Puritan was the perfect ally for this harsh Yang Judge part of herself, and made sure that she would keep her creative impulses under wraps. Any time she thought about doing something fun, or spontaneous, she could hear her grandfather's voice telling her, "If you want to be successful you have to postpone your personal pleasure and let your employees see you working as hard as they do."

When Meg got The Judge to back off, she found her own authentic leadership style—which was inclusive and accepting of others, regardless of whether their views or beliefs were the same as hers. She began to rely on her own inner authority. Once she stopped feeling like an imposter at work, she began to embody the confidence commensurate with her role as CEO. She also started to loosen the tight hold on her organization as well as her son, and found out that, "all hell did *not* break loose."

Now that the healthy Father came into focus, Meg found the courage to move toward her long dormant Maiden. She understood that fear did not need to stop her from trying new things: she just had to get her "butterflies to fly in formation." She began to take more risks, deliberately moving out of her familiar and safe patterns. With the help of a good friend who was well acquainted with The Maiden she went skydiving, pole dancing, camel riding, belly dancing . . . ready and willing to stretch herself in new ways. She even took her management team on an off-site retreat that included a ropes course and country dancing.

With The Maiden, Meg began to spontaneously find ways to start enjoying everyday life with her son. "My son asked me one day if I was taking drugs," Meg said, laughing. "I knew he was teasing me, but I could also feel his pleasure in having a mother who could also relax and play with him once in a while. I am proud of myself for facing my fears, shaking things up, and growing into my own authentic leadership. I am having so much more fun in my life these days."

KIM (FATHER: OUTSIDER SHADOW)

Deep inside Kim believed that "belonging" to any group or person was too restrictive and she chafed at rules and regulations. Her Outsider shadow found a willing ally in the Puritan, and the two together made sure that things were under her control at all times. She would get overwhelmed if she was noticed or had to engage too intensely with others. Her stress would escalate when people would make emotional demands on her, wanting more of her time and energy. She used the Outsider-Puritan shadow alliance to cut off from her own inner embodied experiences and from contact with others.

When Kim began to pull back her power from The Outsider, she saw the value of creating systems and structures in her life that would give her the capacity to handle being seen by others. She let go of the belief that it was safer to just observe things from the sidelines and began to enter into experiences with her whole being. Rather than evading responsibility or recognition, she began to feel empowered and discovered that she was actually a natural leader. And as she did her networking in search of a new job, she was surprised to discover that others sought her advice and input.

With the healthy Father taking up residence, she was ready to work on liberating her vitality and aliveness. After ballroom dancing led to meeting a well-matched partner, the two of them shimmied over to the spicy rhythms of Salsa.

The sensuality of exploring dance and a loving partnership brought Kim into a new relationship with her feelings. "I am so aware now of not only what I am thinking but also what I am feeling and sensing. It is like learning a new language," Kim said. "At first it made things more complicated, but now I feel so much more confidence in myself and connection with others. I feel like I am in the Theatre of My Life, and I have just stepped out of the audience and into the movie itself."

TERRY (MAIDEN: PURITAN SHADOW)

When The Puritan shadow locked arms with The Judge it was very easy for Terry to give away her creative power and initiative to others. Her bureaucratic job was the perfect setting for these shadows. She was happy to do what she was told and she would do it exceptionally well!

She kept her home life as neat and tidy and under control as she did her professional life. After years of this setup the channel between The Father and The Maiden was so calcified that barely a trickle of her essence could squeeze through.

Now that the healthy Father had traded places with the rigid Judge, Terry's overactive superego also took a break, and she started to connect with her inner artist. In the remaining few months before her retirement she discovered a very different way of being at work. She no longer pushed herself beyond her limits and would schedule regular breaks throughout the day when she would go for walks, talk to colleagues, or work on her quilting squares. Many of her greatest creative inspirations actually seemed to occur in these "off times," so she knew she was onto something.

Terry's Maiden within, who had been patiently waiting all these years for attention, seemed to turn her into a natural comedian. She took up Improvisational Theater as a hobby and was shocked at how funny she could be and how much she loved it. When she did retire she was ready for a very exciting new phase of her life.

"I had dreaded retirement—I thought the road of my life dead-ended at sixty. Now I feel like I am just beginning and I am on a superhighway. There are so many things and places that I want to experience and so many ways that I want to contribute to my family and community. It may have taken sixty years but I am really coming into my own now!"

ZOE (MAIDEN: BOHEMIAN SHADOW)

Zoe rode both dynamic ends of this Yin-Yang polarity, grabbing hold of The Judge and The Bohemian in a Dr. Jekyll–Mr. Hyde manner. She was very good at fitting into elite circles of power and authority, both in her marriage and her profession, quickly learning the code of conduct so that she could belong. She judged others who did not toe the line and fit in. And yet, after work Zoe would often shift into her other persona and become the uninhibited party girl who had no boundaries and loved to shake things and people up. Balancing these two opposing forces within took a lot of energy, and when she began an affair with a married man her life spun out of control.

As the healthy Father took a strong stand inside of her, she accepted her brilliance and her uniquely creative way of seeing things. She stopped shaping herself around powerful men and began to take hold of the reins of her own life. Opening this polarity was such a fundamental shift inside that many of the outer structures of her life were just no longer congruent. When her marriage, her affair, and her career tumbled apart, she stayed with the pain, digesting the events of her life with a new kind of sobriety.

Her natural exuberance and visionary gifts were coming into balance with a new ability to be in the present moment and more accepting of life's difficult feelings and experiences. She did not lose the carefree part of The Maiden that was held in The Bohemian shadow. To the contrary, now that she was grounded in her own True Authority, she no longer felt the need to push her energy out in the world in dramatic displays. She knew how to slow herself down, quiet her mind, and come into relationship with others in more vulnerable ways. Her passion to change the world remained, but now she wanted to be a change agent on her own terms. Her newfound love of writing led her into a PhD program in EcoPsychology, where she explored and wrote about the effects of injustice, violence, and exploitation of women around the globe.

"I can be a voice for the voiceless now because I found my own voice," Zoe said. "My life looks totally different today from just a few years ago. It was like I was living someone else's life and now I am on my destiny path."

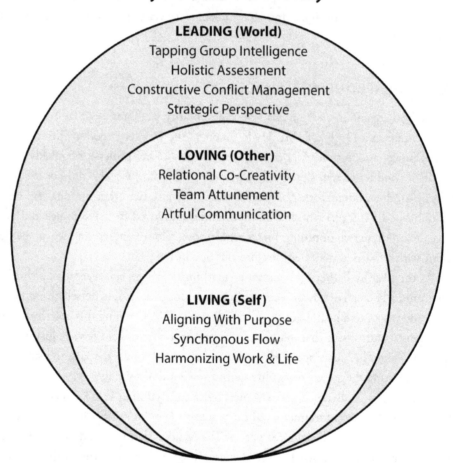

Mysterial Competencies
Joyful True Authority

LEADING (World)
Tapping Group Intelligence
Holistic Assessment
Constructive Conflict Management
Strategic Perspective

LOVING (Other)
Relational Co-Creativity
Team Attunement
Artful Communication

LIVING (Self)
Aligning With Purpose
Synchronous Flow
Harmonizing Work & Life

Joyful True Authority Embodied Competencies

It is a profound experience when a woman opens up this second Yin–Yang polarity: there is no going back to the old ways of being and doing after you have tasted Joyful True Authority. As the late poet and philosopher John O'Donohue writes, "We learn to befriend our complexity and see the dance of opposition within us not as a negative or destructive thing but as an invitation to a creative adventure."[1]

Like seeds sprouting in rich soil, when the deep capacities of The Father and The Maiden come together they transform into the new living, loving, and leading shoots of ten embodied competencies.

LIVING: Harmonizing Work & Life, Synchronous Flow, Aligning With Purpose
LOVING: Relational Co-Creativity, Team Attunement, Artful Communication
LEADING: Tapping Group Intelligence, Holistic Assessment, Constructive Conflict
             Management, Strategic Perspective

IN THE DOMAIN OF LIVING

Harmonizing Work and Life: Ability to put life events into a healthy long-term perspective that does not compartmentalize work and career, but manages them as a seamless whole.

Synchronous Flow: Ability to access an increased congruence between your inner experience and outer expression so you are able to sense what is arising, and then flow with all the factors in a way that optimizes your life.

Aligning with Purpose: Ability to rest deeply into the value of your being and allow a sense of purpose to arise naturally from this place, inspiring you into a life of fulfillment, commitment, and creative contribution.

IN THE DOMAIN OF LOVING

Relational Co-creativity: Ability to enter into deep trusting relationships with others without losing your own authority, enabling new levels of creative collaboration with family, colleagues, and significant others in your life.

Team Attunement: Ability to welcome chaos in group dynamics as a creative force and steward the collective pattern through the phase of disorder to find a higher level of alignment.

Artful Communication: Ability to articulate your unique perspective authentically and empathically, while maintaining wise timing and speaking into the listening of the other for the most creative outcome.

IN THE DOMAIN OF LEADING

Tapping Group Intelligence: Ability to cultivate the conditions in groups and systems that facilitate harmony, shared meaning, and resonance so that its creative potential is accessed and expanded.

Holistic Assessment: Ability to bring information from multiple intelligences together into one cohesive stream of knowing, leading to wise decision-making and well-timed actions.

Constructive Conflict Management: Ability to manage conflict creatively from a grounded place, seeing the partial truths and hidden strengths of an adversary, or from within a contentious situation, and leveraging those for creative solutions.

Strategic Perspective: Ability to take a global, systemic perspective with an expanded time horizon, enabling you to attune with the different social, cultural, environmental and political realities related to your work.

Taking the Next Step—
Joyful True Authority Back to The Mother

By the time we have opened this second polarity of The Mysterial Sequence, we are well on our way to Mysterial fullness. A powerful momentum naturally carries us back again around to the grounding wholeness of The Mother where we prepare to make the quantum leap to the Fifth Activation.

Similar to the period following the Initiation of Empowered Radiant Presence, making deliberate space for integration is an important part of your overall Mysterial journey. You will benefit from ensuring again that you have a clear and compelling Conscious Intention, a set of Leadership Practices that engage body, heart, mind, and soul, and a Community of Support made up of friends and family who will encourage your emerging self. These support structures are intended to keep evolving and refining over time.

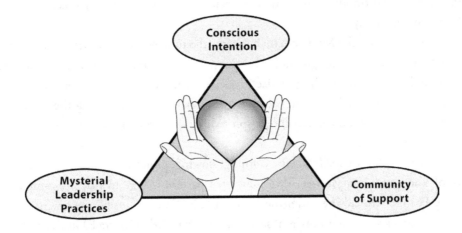

This time though, as we reground in The Mother, we are integrating all that opened up through our work with the first and second polarities. And especially after the dynamic opening of Flame Yin essence, it is important for us to turn inward and integrate the new sense of self that has been discovered. We need to adjust now to a worldview that includes a sense of grounded authority and a connection to the unpredictable mystery of being. Who are we now that we are moving beyond the paradigm of the Patriarchy?

Along with the energizing effects of this transformation there is often a cycle of grief to traverse. We are letting go of an old sense of self with its expectations, certainties, and securities, and opening into a new state of wholeness without any of the familiar landmarks. After all, we have just made a huge evolutionary move forward! It is a time to be gentle with ourselves and not be in too much of a rush to head off on our next Heroic adventure. There is something much greater awaiting us with the activation of The Crone if we take time to rest and renew here in the lap of The Mother.

The Cultural Parallel

The Return to The Mother is especially important now for reasons that go beyond our individual leadership journeys.

As we described in Chapter 2, each step of the Mysterial Sequence has a cultural parallel beginning with the Archaic consciousness of The Mother, during which humans lived as small nomadic bands of hunters and gatherers, through the dynamic breakthrough of the Postmodern age with The Maiden, where we have a globally connected Information economy.

The Return to The Mother actually marks the time we are in now: a time for taking all the wonderful breakthroughs and inventive possibilities of the Postmodern Revolution and grounding them into solid practice in society. The women's revolution, the environmental revolution, social justice revolution . . . all have occurred during the last exciting fifty years as the hot-blooded, rebellious, spirited Maiden brought her dynamic Yin energy to a Yin-starved planet.

Only now are we ready for the calming, slowing, grounding, and nourishing influence of The Vessel Yin Mother. This archetypal pattern is here to help us complete the wave of Postmodern culture. After the revolution, it is time to install the practices, structures, and policies for environmental sustainability, for worldwide social justice (especially ending hunger), and for the true ascension of women's leadership. The "glass ceiling" for women executives has been stalled at around 20 percent for quite some time. As The Mother's Vessel Yin essence strengthens, we predict this will change. Before, it just wasn't time. But now it is.

The Next Call Forward

Once you have caught your breath and stabilized in a more expanded sense of self with a return to The Mother, you will begin to feel the presence of The Crone waiting for you at the crossroads. This long repressed and forgotten archetype has been present all along, patiently waiting until you were ready to meet her. Both individually and collectively, that time has come now.

Chapter 13

THE ACTIVATION OF THE CRONE—
Summoning Alchemical Authenticity

The Crone is the forgotten and most maligned of the five primary archetypes. Forgotten, yes, but not inactive. Far behind the scenes for many millennia, this pattern has been maturing and evolving with all of life. To complete the transformation into the Mysterial Woman, the complex and inscrutable archetype of The Crone must be fully embraced.

Settle yourself for a moment and read this invocation aloud. See if you can feel the whispered invitation of the enigmatic, provocative, and insightful Crone quickening within your body.

Invocation of The Crone

Still yourself and listen carefully.
Hear my voice inside you now, arising from a well of silence.

Be, in the perfection of this moment.
Drop your past.
Drop your attempts to change, to be a better person,
drop the future that awaits you.
Drop everything.
Be in the perfection of this moment.
This is where you will discover who I am.

I will guide you into a wisdom so profound
it will weave together your many ways of knowing.
Love is here, exquisite and full enough that your heart will break wide open
into the pulsing of the whole universe within you.
Welcome my power.
I have the strength of a lion and the grace of a feather.

Prepare for my alchemy.
Mother, Hero, Father, and Maiden have done their work.
Step forward with me now,
into the Mystery . . .

At the Crossroads—Vessel and Flame Yin Come Together

In terms of essence, The Crone archetype is unusual and complex. She stands at the crossroads between the Yin and Yang polarities. She is actually a Yin archetype, with an integrated Vessel-Flame essence. However, she simultaneously has direct access to both the Flame and Vessel Yang essences, which flavors her capacities with a particular sharpness, clarity, and strength.

As the first archetype to work with both Yin and Yang together, The Crone is a very big energy to take in. This is not an archetype to activate carelessly. The ground must be well prepared with the first four archetypes of The Mysterial Sequence. If not—and sometimes even when—The Crone can instigate some major breakdowns before breakthrough occurs.

With a healthy inner Crone, an adult woman finds her ability to unflinchingly speak truth to power. Though it may be painful to be on the receiving end, her intention is to do no harm. She is both fierce and compassionate.

She brings the capacity to be with chaos and uncertainty, to be able to perceive that best next step in the unfolding of what is trying to emerge. The Crone doesn't need to know more. The Crone archetype lives in the meeting place of knowing and Mystery. Synchronicities and dreams are a normal and natural communication tool. The Crone enables us to become more spiritually awake and in tune with the sacredness of all existence.

The Crone allows us to have an open heart and to be with heartbreak—our own suffering and the suffering of others. She brings the strength and discernment to know what must die and pass away, even if it is an idea or a business. The Crone may even catalyze a major breakdown in your life, if that is what is required to help you move forward on your journey. She helps us to recognize death as a necessary and sacred part of life, not the enemy of it. And because of that, The Crone guides us to hold a space for something new and more effective to emerge from the ashes of the old. She allows us to become a true agent of transformation, an alchemist turning lead into gold.

This potent "wise woman" archetypal force of the Feminine has often nudged its way to the surface of our culture, only to be demonized, time and time again. Women's natural talents for counseling, healing, and sourcing community wisdom were suppressed in the eleventh century when university centers of higher knowledge were founded, available exclusively to men.[1]

And once public service required university credentials, women were effectively removed from the intellectual life of the community. Inside the paradigm of that patriarchal culture, women's embodied ways of knowing and their ability to speak truth to power were a clear threat to the hierarchy.

Christianity retained a limited connection with the Feminine as Maiden and Mother, but systematically eliminated The Crone. This happened most notably during the witch burning times of the fifteenth to seventeenth centuries and during the Inquisition in Europe and the Puritanism of the New World. An estimated 5 million women were drowned, hanged, or burned at the stake over a period of three hundred years—that's 16,667 women killed per year—often for no other reason than just being a woman. Even surviving to old age could get you branded as a witch; that's how threatening her uniquely powerful Feminine presence was to the social order.

In challenging times of the past, the woman in a community who exemplified The Crone was often consulted because she had her ways of seeing deeply into matters, and could even foretell the possible futures. She functioned as a kind of ambassador, shuttling between the spirit worlds and human worlds, gathering knowledge to serve her people. Her knowing extended beyond the boundaries of scientific rationalism.

You could trust a true Crone because she operated outside the political structures of her milieu; she would tell it like it was. Eminently pragmatic, resourceful, and creative, she knew how to work with the simple ingredients around her to heal the complexities of body, mind, and soul. These "dangerous women" were herbalists, artists, healers, midwives, mystics, scholars, priestesses, gypsies, and lovers of nature. But this force of the Feminine was seen as threatening and destabilizing as Yang Shadow powers gathered momentum.

We can also see The Crone archetype expressed through many indigenous cultures that value their close relationships to the unseen world of spirit, ritual, the earth and the stars, and the interconnected web of life. And we know what has happened to many of those cultures in the brutal annihilation of their ways of being for the sake of forward movement.

These painful collective memories survive in our cells. It's why we have struggled to be able to open our arms wide to the wise woman within. Of course, it hasn't helped that our still mostly patriarchal culture persistently encourages women to remain Maidens and Mothers forever. But this is not to be. The wise woman archetype is arising now, whether anyone likes it or not. This is her time, and in this activation is where you will encounter her.

The Foundational Capacities of Alchemical Authenticity

In order for the foundational capacities of The Crone to be fully understood, we must retrace the steps that have come before. This is a journey in which each step includes and transcends the last. The Mysterial Sequence began by cultivating The Mother archetype so that our *Radiant Presence* could wrap its loving arms around us as well as others. We then brought our own Hero onto the field to perform bold and *Empowered Action* to initiate our projects in the world. This awakened The Father, whose order, structure, and systems enabled us to navigate the halls of power and access the *True Authority* necessary to thrive there over time. Once solid, we could free ourselves to reclaim The Maiden and release our *Joyful Creativity*, reconnecting with our spontaneous nature and innovative genius.

Now we are ready to invite the wise, shape-shifting part of ourselves, to come forward through us and bring *Alchemical Authenticity* into the world through **Being with the Mystery, Constructive Candor, Non-Attached Compassion, and Transforming to a Higher Order.**

The Crone

	INTERIOR	EXTERIOR
INDIVIDUAL	**My Inner Experience** **Capacity: BEING WITH THE MYSTERY** To let go of control, expectation, and disappointment and accept reality as it is, comfortable with not knowing what to do or how things will turn out, while appreciating the "gold" in what is present and trying to emerge. Trusting that you are a part of a Friendly Universe.	**How I Show Up** **Capacity: CONSTRUCTIVE CANDOR** To communicate with fierce yet useful honesty in support of a higher outcome for all, free of the compulsion to punish others, to be defensive, or the fear of causing yourself or others emotional discomfort. *not fleeing the scene*
	I IT	
	WE ITS	
COLLECTIVE	**Relating with Others** **Capacity: NON-ATTACHED COMPASSION** To be present with the suffering of others with deep understanding and an open heart, without bringing your own agenda, emotional attachments, or urge to rescue to the experience.	**Engaging the World** **Capacity: TRANSFORMING TO A HIGHER ORDER** To let go of what is outdated in a creative process while simultaneously guiding what remains useful or relevant into a new and more effective insight, solution, pattern, or outcome. *implementing Jim's process - deterring when its possible.*

The Promise of Alchemical Authenticity

Alchemical Authenticity is the capacity to lovingly and astutely blend together diverse, even contradictory elements to bring about a completely new reality. With this capacity you can perceive and manifest the greatest potential held in any moment. It allows you to feel at home in the midst of chaos, uncertainty, and change, but it is much more than just managing the instability of life. You become one who can directly challenge the status quo. You become unafraid to shake things up, so that greater harmony and creative potential can arise. You become a leader with the courage to live at the very edges of systems, willing and able to push the frontiers out beyond familiar boundaries and speak the "inconvenient truth."

This quality of fierce candor is grounded in a deep concern for the well-being and health of all, and is delivered in astute and compassionate ways to those who are ready to hear the message. A student who had done the deep work with this Activation said, "When I really opened to this aspect of myself, I was sometimes shocked by what I would hear coming out of my mouth. I used to be so afraid that I would say the wrong thing or that someone would disapprove. It isn't that I am mean or rude now; it's just that I no longer dance all around an issue. I choose my timing wisely and I say what I see with a spacious invitation for others to do the same."

Those who summon the fullness of Alchemical Authenticity become a guide for the transformative process itself—in themselves, others, and the world. Imagine, without the fear of change holding you back you are free to let some things pass away and other things be born. Failure is no longer failure: it is a learning opportunity for growth and development. You realize that you live in a universe that welcomes and supports your presence, and you delight in Being with the Mystery of it all.

You also become able to synthesize complex information from many sources of knowing. You can apply rigor in your investigations while you welcome the unknown. In fact, you deliberately create conditions to ensure that you don't know everything. You have no worries about it because you remain open to new and more innovative solutions.

As the partnership of Yin and Yang begins its enthralling dance, your leadership takes on unprecedented range and depth. The healthy Crone merges your fiercely loving nature with your full spectrum of wisdom: all the centers of intelligence of body, heart, and head, with both left and right hemispheres of the head brain engaged. Your heart can hold the complexity of suffering and the heights of joy while your body becomes fully alive and uncensored. This is authentic being!

Shadows of The Crone—The Hag and The Denier

In order to breathe new life into this archetypal pattern in ourselves and in the culture, we must first traverse her shadow lands. Over identification with the powerful archetype of The Crone leads us into the active shadow of The Hag—a harsh and manipulative version of the wise woman. Conversely, when we avoid connection with this archetype, we slide into the clutches of the passive shadow of The Denier—one who denies or shuts down their inner wisdom, and can't express what they know to be true.

Let's begin with an exploration through the tendencies and behaviors that show up when you have over identified with The Crone archetype and the active shadow of The Hag emerges. Here are some of the signs that the Hag is in residence. Notice if any of them strike a familiar chord in you.

The Sword of Truth not to Wound.

THE HAG—ACTIVE SHADOW OF THE CRONE

The Crone archetype is unusual because it has access to the true sword of Yang, and knows how to wield power. However, as The Hag, this access is overdone. She cuts with the sword in a way that wounds, and uses her power in a self-serving manner. The Hag is an impediment rather than a force for women's transformation.

Today, we see The Hag occupying some of those rare positions of power in corporate boardrooms and positions of political power. In the absence of any other model of wholeness when they finally climb their way up the ladder they often assume that the only way to hold onto that turf is to mainline The Hag.

CHARACTERISTIC OF THE HAG

See if you recognize any of these signs that The Hag has you in her tower.

* You have information that might be useful for someone else but in reaction to a past hurt you withhold it.
* Under the guise of "being honest," you lash out at someone with hurtful and attacking comments, and then take no responsibility for the impact of your aggression.
* You collect extensive knowledge and information then use it to demonstrate your superiority and belittle others.

* You express defensiveness and hostility when anyone asks you a question or challenges your point of view, hiding your insecurity behind aggression.
* You manipulate circumstances and others in order to remain in control and get what you want, regardless of the consequences.
* You become irritated if others don't know what you know or are slow to fathom what you are talking about.
* You read things into what others say and do in order to reinforce your beliefs, gathering unexamined assumptions and holding them as "truth."
* You remain detached from your actual embodied experience, which makes you seem cold, impersonal, and arrogant as you steer from a distance.

Sound familiar at all? Perhaps you can relate to some of these behaviors. When it comes to how you are with others, you might tend to swing in the opposite direction—into the dampening clutches of The Denier. We will get to that tendency later.

CLEARING THE HAG: MARSHA'S JOURNEY

Marsha, forty-six, was well known in her professional field for her expertise in counseling women who were victims of domestic abuse. She poured her heart and soul into this work for many years, and pioneered several very successful new approaches to treatment. Simultaneously, she was also the busy wife of a successful CEO of a family-run company and the mother of three children ages seventeen, nineteen, and twenty. Marsha was commander in chief of a very full and complex life.

Intense, creative, and at home in the spotlight, she knew what it was to have power and worked hard to maintain it. When Marsha wanted to get things done—her way—she often used her sharp tongue, fueled by drama and deep emotions, to lash out with little concern for the consequences. This alienated friends, family, and business colleagues.

ROOTS OF THE HAG

Marsha began life as one of three children, the only daughter, in a difficult family dynamic. Her father had been wounded in combat and had given up on life. He left the parenting to Marsha's mother, who was mean and short-tempered. "I never knew what mood she would be from one moment to the next. Sometimes she seemed insightful and intuitive. Then she would lash out at us for no reason, just to knock us down a few pegs. I never felt appreciated, and spent a lot of time sulking in my room, or fantasizing about the amazing life that I was going to create.

"I was so happy to get out of the house and go to college," continued Marsha. "But no matter how far away I moved or how hard I worked, I always felt like everything could be taken away from me at any moment. I started to become just like my mother, and that really scared me."

Indeed, one day her whole house of cards came tumbling down. She woke up one morning without the drive that both maintained her life and had propelled her away from her family so many years earlier. This way of avoiding the painful truth of her life would no longer work. This realization connected her with an inner longing—a sense that there was something important missing that could make her whole. The longing intensified into an ache that became so consuming it was overwhelming her completely.

OBSERVING THE HAG

Rarely is The Crone function ready to be integrated without some experience of the active shadow of The Hag. Even if a woman primarily identifies with the passive shadow of The Denier, she will recognize times when The Hag broke loose and drove her into saying or doing things that were harsh or mean-spirited. The Crone is different from the other forces of the Feminine in that she is at home in the unconscious realm of the inchoate and the unpredictable. So when a woman over-identifies with this archetypal energy, The Hag rises up from the unconscious in an almost unstoppable way.

During the opening retreat of our leadership program, Marsha quickly assessed the power structures of the group and aligned herself more closely with the faculty than with her fellow students. She was accustomed to the safety of being the one in charge, especially in unfamiliar group situations, and defaulted to presenting herself to others behind the mask of her professional competency and knowledge. Needless to say this alienated her sisters pretty quickly.

The Hag in charge stirs up trouble! She prefers isolation and detachment, to steer things her way from a distance and stay in control. For Marsha, this shadow aspect often pushed her into confrontations, and her blunt, harsh words didn't endear her to the group. Before long Marsha had gathered ample evidence that she did not belong in the program.

Marsha's Hag shadow was protecting her territory. However, within the loving heartfield of a session with her coach, Marsha began to discern the claws of this shadow, and the consequences of its dominion in her psyche. It was a sobering moment.

Marsha recounted the story. "I was sitting with my coach after I had just walked out of a group session in judgment and irritation, and convinced that this program was not for me. As my coach reflected back to me the presence of my own Crone nature, I felt my shame melting. Suddenly I could see this new aspect of myself, The Crone, and I could also see The Hag shadow. I saw how familiar this whole pattern was. It went all the way back to my childhood . . . to the backyard tree house I would flee to whenever I felt threatened, and convince myself that I was smarter and better than everyone else.

"Ironically, I was in this program because I felt so alone in my life and wanted to have more intimate peer relationships. Yet here I was, creating exactly the opposite and blaming others. I faced my Hag for the first time and in that moment my transformative journey really began."

Once a shadow archetype is identified and seen, it seems to show up everywhere. It wasn't long before Marsha was able to detect The Hag, who had been completely invisible to her before, controlling the relationship with her learning partner Dana.

Marsha's pattern of wanting to be the all-knowing teacher met Dana's pattern of giving away her own knowing and resentfully accommodating others. It was a perfect storm. The Hag and The Denier faced off. Whenever Dana tried to share her point of view, Marsha's Hag would shoot her down. Their shadows—perfectly projected out onto each other—were actually seeking integration. They were the sand in each other's pearl-making.

It took a few explosive encounters and some careful coaching for Marsha to become a more compassionate observer of this shadow aspect in action and see how it derailed intimacy. In time, Marsha was able to offer her insights without insisting that Dana agree with them, but simply as her wisdom of the moment that included an openness to hear Dana's truth.

When The Crone first begins to push up through the cracks in consciousness, anything false or inauthentic often becomes unbearable. Without an understanding of what is happening this "truth" can often burst forth in judgment and criticism of ourselves, our situations, and others. This makes it difficult to be the partner of someone going through these kinds of deep inner changes.

Once Marsha caught sight of her Hag with Dana, she was able to notice it showing up in similar and destructive ways with her husband Richard.

"I saw how manipulative I was, withholding information about our children or larger family issues in order to stay in control," Marsha said. "It was all very under the radar and I could always claim innocence when Richard challenged me. Then I would lash out in mean and vicious ways, insisting that I was just telling the truth, until he would back down. Ouch—that was hard to admit!"

Marsha traced the evolution of The Hag in her life and lineage by first taking time to attend a weekend silent meditation retreat. It was held at a beautiful and simple monastic setting high in the mist shrouded mountains outside Puget Sound. The retreat included a number of walking meditations though the dense, primordial forests.

As her feet rolled slowly over the soft fragrant blanket of pine needles, past the fern plants and mushrooms that echoed prehistoric times, Marsha felt herself connected to the ancient wise women of the forest.

Upon her return, she delved into her family's past, now trusting that the information would find her. Her mother's older sister, who had been somewhat estranged from the family, agreed to talk.

Marsha learned that her maternal grandmother had been an extraordinary woman of wisdom and influence in her community, serving on the board of her family's foundation. A paralyzing stroke ended her tenure, and she spent the remaining years of her life embittered and frustrated. Her daughter, Marsha's mother, was an exceptionally bright, intuitive young woman who entered medical school with the intention of learning how to heal others from such traumatic damage to the brain. She faced the brutal Dominator hierarchy of medical school and the open bias against female medical students. And when her young husband was injured in combat, she ended her medical career.

Like her own mother, she became embittered and frustrated, her powerful combination of intellect and intuition distorted into the manipulation, control, and mean-spiritedness of The Hag.

Feeling a deep wave of compassion move through her being, Marsha committed herself to ending this painful family legacy. She was determined to clear The Hag and welcome The Crone. It was time.

Building Foundational Capacity

One must fearlessly embrace the unknown to tackle the shadow aspects of The Crone. And the healthy Crone within must be cultivated simultaneously. Yet to embrace the big Crone energy, the previous work of The Mysterial Sequence needs to be very solid. Marsha first learned to soothe her exaggerated emotional states by clearing The Devourer; then to calm her relentless, destructive overdrive up the ladder of success by clearing The Dominator. As an Empowered Radiant Presence began to take the place of her demands for attention, she became more naturally magnetic. Clearing the demanding, self-righteous Judge made it easier to be in the room with Marsha, and as the drama settled down with the clearing of The Bohemian, then Joyful True Authority opened the way for an exciting new phase of innovation and transformation in Marsha's organization. She was now being called to the subtler and even spiritual capacity for **Non-Attached Compassion** (Collective Interior—How I Relate to Others).

In Marsha's case, building capacity for Non-Attached Compassion was essential for anchoring the healthy Crone pattern. She was already fierce enough: she needed to balance that with the deep and unconditional embrace of the suffering of the world.

The Hag's harsh shadow expression, "I've got to speak my truth and too bad about the consequences" has often been mistaken for The Crone's constructive communication. Certainly, the integrated Crone knows how to wield the sword of truth, but she always does so with compassion and timely wisdom, while at the same time not being attached to any particular outcome and willing to let the chips fall where they may. In fact, whenever you compassionately tell the truth rather than stay silent you can be sure The Crone is present.

As Marsha began to see the difference between The Crone and her shadow expression in The Hag, she cultivated a quality of Non-Attached Compassion for others that was not predicated on her position as the therapist, board member, or teacher. It emerged from the simple connection to a shared humanity and the desire to relieve suffering.

Tonglen Practice for *Non-Attached Compassion*[2]

According to Tibetan Buddhist nun and teacher Pema Chodron, Tonglen practice is a method for connecting with suffering—ours and that which is all around us—everywhere we go. In her words, "It is a method for overcoming fear of suffering and for dissolving the tightness of our heart. Primarily it is a method for awakening compassion that is inherent in all of us, no matter how cruel or cold we might seem to be."

* Begin by sitting in a comfortable meditation position. Gently close your eyes and let your body and mind settle. You want to feel relaxed and open.
* Bring to mind a loved one who is suffering.
* Imagine their suffering as hot, dark, polluted smoke. Breathe this hot smoke into your heart. Take it in willingly and with kindness.
* Send them in return a deep, cool, light, and spacious healing breath.
* Let this connectedness open your compassion toward yourself and them. The Dalai Lama says that you cannot be compassionate to-

ward others unless you are able to be compassionate with yourself. Do this practice until you feel intuitively that you are done.

* Repeat this practice with someone that you perhaps dislike or have a challenge with.
* Repeat this practice again for the suffering of the world. Keep the rhythm of your breathing steady, breathing in hot, heavy smoke that dissolves into the vastness of your heart. Remember to be gentle with yourself.
* Breathe out through every pore of your body the coolness, clarity, kindness and healing to the whole world.

As she developed the capacity for Non-Attached Compassion, Marsha also started to clear the skeptical, controlling Hag by cultivating the capacity for **Transforming to a Higher Order** (Collective Exterior—Engaging the World). We develop this capacity over time by being open to the complexity of existence. It emerges as we encounter person after person, experience after experience, trusting that although we may not know how something is going to turn out, we are moving forward with a positive intention for transformation.

Marsha was asked to chair a section at a major professional conference, something she had not done previously. Although she was scrupulously prepared, on the day of the conference so many things were changing and happening at once that she knew things would not go exactly according to her plan. She stopped resisting, opened herself to the experience, and began to notice how factors were coming together.

When a key speaker failed to show (and his message about that did not arrive) Marsha nearly panicked. *What on earth will I do for the next hour,* she thought, *with this restless audience expecting a talk?* She took some deep breaths, centered herself, and thought, *Okay, this is what is. Given that, what is possible here?*

She spied a couple of the most expert and respected members of the section in the audience. On the fly, Marsha explained to the audience what had happened, and asked the expert members if they'd be interested in having an impromptu panel discussion with her facilitating. They and the audience agreed that would be a good idea.

The panel discussion was a great success, and Marsha was hailed for her graceful leadership under pressure.

To deepen this emerging capacity Marsha engaged in a practice of Chaordic Embodiment. "Chaordic"[3] simply means to be at the edge of chaos and order, an extremely creative place.

Chaordic Embodiment Practice for *Transforming To A Higher Order*

Set aside approximately forty-five minutes for this activity. You may want to play some relaxing music to enter a state of receptivity.

Gather together a number of magazines with enough variety to provide a diverse array of images. You can also use the Internet as a place to gather images from if you prefer that format.

1. Begin by reviewing your Intention. Form a question in your mind about which you would like some insight. This could be as simple as, "What should I be aware of in regards to x?"
2. Spend fifteen minutes cutting out images that you are intuitively drawn to in the moment. This is not a mental exercise. You are just cutting out the images that appeal to your senses. Perhaps it is the color or the shape or the emotion the image evokes.
3. Once you have your pile of images you will then spread them out on a table in front of you and begin moving them around. Let your attention be open and soft. Keep moving the images around in relationship to one another. Enter into a kind of creative chaos flow state with your images—until you begin to sense an order emerging. You will know when this happens in your body . . . things will slow down and you will connect with (in a felt sense way, not just as a mental preference) the collage in front of you. This is not a permanent collage (as in glued down).
4. Stand up from the table where you have been arranging your images and take a few minutes away from the collage. Make a cup of tea or go for a walk. See if you can stay in soft, open focus—aware of all of your senses, with a sense of space and timelessness.
5. Come back to your collage, and now see what wisdom there might be for you in this pattern of images. What might they be telling you about what is important for you to pay attention to or take care of at this time? This is where you allow your mind to come back in as a useful tool in the pattern-seeking process.

Reflection: Journal your thoughts and insights from the collage.

You may choose to save these images to use in a similar way at another time.

Marsha began to recognize the building blocks from other activations of The Mysterial Sequence now starting to come together in the alchemy of The Crone. She saw that it was possible for something better than she imagined to fall into place as long as she did her part by remaining open and mutable, while also holding a clear intention.

Shadows of The Crone—The Hag and The Denier

THE DENIER—PASSIVE SHADOW OF THE CRONE

Next we swing to the opposite pole of the Crone archetype shadow, from active to passive. Under-identification with the transformative, truth-telling, mysteriously compassionate, world-bridging, multi-perspectival, archetypal energy of The Crone leads a woman into the passive shadow of The Denier.

When The Hag shadow is operating at the crossroads of Vessel and Flame Yin and Yang, your Yin river is running low, while your grasp of the Yang levers is too tight. Your expression is harsh, bitter, and manipulative.

When The Denier shadow is operating at the crossroads, your Yin river may be too muddy and deep, and your grasp of the Yang levers too tenuous to pull you forward. Your expression is suppressed, muddied, confused, and frustrated.

CHARACTERISTICS OF THE DENIER

See if you recognize The Denier cowering in you.

- ✳ You get easily frustrated when learning new things, expecting that knowledge should come easily and without effort.
- ✳ You tend to experience constant confusion and find it very difficult to connect with your inner wisdom.
- ✳ You fear the chaos of a creative change process and shut yourself down—contracting and withdrawing—rather than staying with it until clarity emerges.
- ✳ You are easily overwhelmed by intense energy, which can collapse you into helplessness or depression.
- ✳ In a group process you hide what you know by withholding information or input that might be useful.

* You fear rocking the boat and find it hard to speak clearly and directly about things you know to be true.
* You have a difficult time letting go of relationships, projects, things, and ideas that are ready to be released.
* Your personal relationships are filled with frustration and anger. When things reach a boiling point, you explode in an irrational diatribe then recoil and withdraw, blaming others for not understanding you.

These are just some of the ways in which your healthy Crone nature splits off into the shadow of The Denier. Do any of them sound familiar? Often it is easier to recognize shadows in others, so perhaps certain people came to mind as you read over the list.

CLEARING THE DENIER: CHRISTINA'S JOURNEY

Christina, fifty-five, was a loving grandmother, and a senior engineer with an established IT firm. Well-liked for her calm, reassuring manner and an uncanny ability to read a group, she appeared to have a peaceful, comfortable life.

Even though she never drew attention to herself, people often sought her out for guidance which she was pleased to offer no matter how busy she was. Her ability to settle disputes among the fractious technical experts was legendary, and she seemed to need nothing in return.

On the inside, however, Christina was feeling increasingly cut off from herself, and overwhelmed by the powerful energies and signals she was receiving internally. It was so easy to sense into other people's feelings and what they needed in the moment. When it came to herself, Christina drew a blank. Everyone else turned to her, but she could not turn toward herself. Feeling frustrated and overwhelmed by the tsunami of information that she was picking up all around her, she began to shut it down and deny it. She avoided sharing her intuition in public. At times the somatic signals were so urgent that she feared having a panic attack.

As her children grew up and her business responsibilities became more complex, Christina felt more and more detached from herself, and not in control. Life grew increasingly confusing. She didn't understand what was going on inside, other than it didn't feel good or safe. She worried that she was not going to be able to keep a lid on things. Her frustration sometimes boiled up into uncharacteristic angry outbursts.

ROOTS OF THE DENIER

Christina's father had left the family when she was four years old, and her connection to him had always been distant. Her relationship with her indigenous Native American mother, who had a history of substance abuse, was difficult and tumultuous. In the face of her mother's unpredictable behavior, Christina learned how to make herself invisible.

Early in life Christina discovered that her knack for sensing into what others were thinking, feeling, or needing could either be an asset or a liability in securing the love, safety, and belonging that she needed. Hard experiences convinced her that most people didn't really want to hear the truth as she understood it. Her response was to go numb to the messages in her body, and retreat into the background.

Christina's personality was organized around staying comfortable, and pleasing others to keep things peaceful and harmonious. She handled stress by numbing out, blending into the background, and attending to everyone else's agenda except her own. Even though she had demonstrated excellent technical competency in her projects and had exceptional people skills, Christina did not have a strong expectation to be promoted into a more visible management position.

Not one to push herself, Christina had always had difficulty exercising or paying attention to her body's signals. Her disassociation from her body helped her to endure a traumatic childhood but was not serving her now.

On those rare occasions when Christina dared access her deepest wisdom, she was afraid to express it. Her unacknowledged fear of what others might think would become anger toward herself for not having the courage to speak up, and then resentment of those she blamed for shutting her down. Along with her personal experiences she was also shaped by the cultural repression and denial of the Native American experience of brutal oppression of her people. All this provided the ideal conditions for The Denier shadow to flourish.

OBSERVING THE DENIER

Christina had learned early on in her life that she saw and felt things that others didn't. Because these insights often caused her more pain than pleasure she split off the clear-sighted, insightful Crone into the shadow of The Denier. "In meetings at work I used to go into such a state of confusion when we were working on relatively straightforward things. I discovered that just prior to getting confused, I usually had an insight or an idea that was different from the mindset of the group. Bam! The Denier would show up and drop a wet blanket over my knowing."

With the help of The Mysterial Change Process, Christina first learned to stay connected to herself by grounding and centering in her body. This simple practice began to dissolve the sense of invisibility, and the fear in her body of standing out that had gripped her all her life. Fueled with these new understandings, Christina began to learn how to hold more energy in her body, while she opened her heart to others.

Christina quieted the impulse to flee from intensity within herself. The energy actually became exhilarating and she learned to ride it through to a deep heart-connection with others. "I sometimes felt that my heart would burst with compassion as I let myself experience others so deeply. So much energy would move through my body but now I knew that I could handle it. I could feel myself shape-shifting right in the moment—transforming The Denier into the free flow of The Crone."

As her journey unfolded, Christina discovered that The Denier had a long history in her family. She had little connection to her Native American roots save an older cousin she would see from time to time at family gatherings. According to the cousin, when Christina's mother was younger she used to be a very sensitive, lovely woman with artistic talent and big dreams. When she fell in love with a young man Christina's grandmother did not bless the union, and so she cut the ties with her family and set off into her new life.

Living in the basement of her in-law's rural Midwestern home, her mother's indigenous ways of being and speaking were ridiculed. Her husband became tyrannical and abusive and ultimately the marriage fell apart. Christina's mother slipped into a deep depression, using addictive substances to cope with the increasingly difficult circumstances of her life.

Christina wondered why she hadn't known or remembered this information until now. Perhaps her Denier had been blocking it. It was clear that her mother's instinctual, Feminine ways of knowing had been completely suppressed. It was no wonder that she had passed on The Denier. Christina felt warm cleansing tears sliding down her face, and onto her journal as she wrote out these words.

Building Foundational Capacity

The Crone is a complex Feminine archetype that has a strong connection to both Yang essences. The Denier tends to align with the passive Yang shadows—The Hero's Capitulator and The Father's Outsider. Thus Christina learned to appease, capitulate, and withdraw into the background, focusing attention on others rather than herself in order to create the harmony she craved.

By working her way through The Mysterial Sequence, Christina first learned to stay present in her body by clearing The Neglector, then to take a stand and pierce the world with her intentions by clearing The Capitulator. Her newfound Empowered Radiant Presence actually harmonized well with her natural peacemaker ways. Emboldened, Christina stepped up her game to clear The Outsider and The Puritan, gaining a quality of Joyful True Authority that started to bring her notice.

With major holes in her foundation filling in, Christina was now willing to practice the more demanding challenge of embodying the capacity for **Constructive Candor** (Individual Exterior—How I Show Up). This is a way of communicating that is fiercely honest yet delivered constructively, in support of a higher outcome. Constructive Candor is not motivated by The Hag's compulsion to punish others, or by The Denier's fear of causing emotional discomfort. It is motivated by love.

Difficult Conversation Practice for *Constructive Candor*[A]

Think of someone with whom you have or have had a challenge. Notice the feelings and body sensations, such as tension or fluttering, that this brings up.

Prepare yourself to begin a difficult conversation with a sixty-second opening statement that sets the stage for Constructive Candor.

1. Name the issue—and stick to only one. Resist the temptation to make it about everything that is wrong with the relationship. (For example, "You frequently cut me off in conversation and interrupt me.")

2. Select a specific example that illustrates the behavior or situation you want changed. For example, "During our staff meeting yesterday, I was describing my point when you cut me off with a joke and proceeded to talk about your department after that."

3. Describe your emotions about the issue. Avoid saying things like, "You made me feel _____." No one can make you feel anything. Your feelings are entirely your own. Instead, use "I" statements. For example: "I feel shut down, unheard, unimportant, belittled, devalued, and disrespected when you interrupt me at staff meetings."

(continued on next page)

4. Clarify what is at stake. Is it trust? Respect? Authenticity? "I want to have a good, mutually respectful working relationship. I value your contribution to the team, but this behavior makes me not want to work closely with you. We have the opportunity to collaborate on some future projects, and I think the unique combination of our different gifts could be a real strength, but I feel afraid of entering into a collaboration, because I'm dreading feeling unseen and not treated as an equal. I am afraid that my contribution won't be heard or valued."

5. Identify your contribution to the problem. Nothing diffuses the rising heat of defensiveness like taking responsibility for our part in the issue. We are ALWAYS a factor in the conflict, and finding our contribution suddenly gives the other person permission to find their own. It's a way of saying, "I'm sorry—I was part of this, too. I could've made it better and I didn't. I should have come to you sooner, instead of letting this boil over for the past few months. I also could've spoken up and told the team that I wasn't finished with my report. I didn't choose to own my own power to redirect the conversation and the attention back to what I had prepared. Instead, I simply stopped talking."

6. Make a simple direct request about what you would like changed. "I'd like you to wait until I'm finished with my entire presentation before commenting. I would really appreciate you not interrupting me or making jokes or wisecracks during staff meetings, while I'm presenting. Other times are fine. This would help me feel a mutual respect between us and give me a desire to collaborate with you in the future."

7. Invite the other person to respond.

Reflections: Prepare each step and then imagine yourself delivering this.
1. As you imagine that person sitting in front of you, allow a response from them to emerge. What did they say?
2. Allow a natural response to arise within you that will help to bring this conversation to a constructive close. What did you say?
3. Notice your feelings and body sensations now. Are they any different? Journal on your experience.

Through this and other practices, Christina discovered that it was possible to skillfully speak her truth in mutuality. With practice she was able to voice insights that sometimes led to a breakdown before the breakthrough. In the past, her peace-seeking nature couldn't have tolerated that, and the insight would have been repressed.

Those who were accustomed to her compliance did not welcome this at first either. "It took a while for my daughter Jana to accept me as a truth-teller," Christina said. "That gradually changed, when insights that I would normally have held back actually proved helpful to her. The same thing happened at work."

For The Crone to activate fully, Christina also needed to build her capacity for **Being With The Mystery** (Individual Interior—My Inner Experience). This capacity allows us to comfortably fluctuate between the known and the unknown. Through a steady meditation practice, and by engaging with some Process Art[5] practices and other non-rational ways of learning, she began to trust the experiences that were beyond her rational mind.

Simply Being With What Is Practice for
Being With The Mystery[6]

Choose a period of time, maybe two hours or half a day, to not resist anything that you experience. Assume that nothing you encounter "should" be any other way than it is, even if it is very unpleasant.

For example, you are driving to work and the traffic is much worse than you expected. In fact, it is making you late for an important meeting. Notice when the resistance arises, "I can't be late! This traffic is ridiculous; why is everyone driving so badly?! . . . I've got to get out of here!" Notice how much you resist what is.

There are so many ways that we resist what is. You may wake up with a sore back, or to a cranky child, with the belief that "this is a problem, a setback, and should be different." You may hear of a dear friend's cancer diagnosis. At work you may be sitting in a meeting that drones on, resisting it with intense frustration. It goes on all day. Just notice how much of your life energy and attention goes into resisting what is rather than accepting it and moving forward.

Reflection: For deepening, you may choose to journal on your experience.
1. What thoughts came up? What feelings were generated? Are there any particular body sensations or postures you take when you are resisting something?
2. How might your life be different without this resistance to what is?

In fact, after decades of alienation from her Native American roots, Christina began to feel drawn back toward her mother's beautiful lineage and its traditions. She recognized the intergenerational trauma that was still present in her tribe and in her own experience. With The Crone coming online she was ready to heal her own wounds and turn back toward her lineage to be a voice for others.[7]

It was not easy and there were many times when she doubted whether she should have even started down this path. Yet at the same time, when she reflected on who she was before she began her Mysterial journey she said, "If I had known what I was going to need to go through to heal all of myself, including my indigenous roots, I probably would have been too afraid to start, but I am so thankful that I did. I am now able to look back at my former self with compassion and although I am far from finished with my healing, I would not go back to the me who was asleep safely nestled in the arms of The Denier."

Ritual is an important language of The Crone and as Christina began to activate the archetype she discovered that it was as natural to her as her native tongue. She began each day with lighting her candle and meditating at her altar where she had laid out meaningful objects that connected her to her own wisdom and power and to that of her indigenous roots. She would consciously send healing energy to her family and friends today and to those in her historical lineage.

Synchronously, someone Christina met at a technical conference invited her to join the Native American Diversity counsel at work. This kind of "coincidence" is something we have seen happen over and over again with many students. As they connect with the truth of their own authentic expression, the outer world responds appropriately. What we call the "Friendly Universe" reacts in unimaginable ways. The Crone force of the Feminine links us to this Friendly Universe and brings us into an understanding of the interconnection of all things.

Having integrated both her healing and corporate diversity experiences, Christina then went on to become a public speaker, sharing her personal story about the intergenerational trauma and internalized oppression of her people, awakening others to the issues facing indigenous people today. As she shared her unique insights, colleagues looked to her for leadership and guidance. The self-forgetting, comfortable invisibility cloak that Christina had wrapped around herself was replaced with a willingness to be heard, and to flow with whatever reality presented. The sensitive intelligence of her embodied nature was no longer frightening and foreign, but a natural way of being.

She made peace between the two parts of herself—the rational engineer and the intuitive, openhearted seer. As The Crone emerged, Christina became the teacher and sage guide that she had always secretly felt herself to be.

Limiting Belief of The Crone:
"I don't have enough knowledge, connections, or influe

At the root of clearing the active Hag shadow driving Marsha, and the passive shadow driving Christina was the dismantling of the unconscious limiting b   ⌐⌐ the Crone.

Do you recognize this limiting belief in your life? Say the words, slowly and out loud to yourself. Notice how they land in you. What additional thoughts does this belief trigger? How does it make you feel? Do you notice any subtle sensations in your body as the words are expressed? These reflection questions provide valuable information about how you are habitually, unconsciously, and needlessly limiting your own potential.

Marsha recognized that the belief, **"I don't have enough knowledge, connections or influence,"** was driving her need to hoard knowledge and fight for power as protection against her own feared insignificance. She had never truly felt seen at her essence, and the only way to make sure she got the attention and regard she needed was to fight for it.

Christina immediately saw that "I don't have enough knowledge, connections, or influence" was the mantra that played in the back of her mind and kept her hidden. As an engineer, she had learned to value her rational knowledge as the only valid truth and this made her hesitant to speak up with any intuitive insights. And the actual experience of her Native American ancestry certainly reinforced this deep limiting belief.

Liberating Belief of The Crone:
"I am an evolving source of wisdom, love, and power."

As both women worked to clear the shadows and cultivate healthy Crone capacities, the Liberating Belief of The Crone unfurled its beauty within them. Marsha could let go of her fierce grip on reality and allow things to unfold. Christina opened the channel for not only her own deep heart and wisdom to be shared but also that of her cultural lineage. Although The Crone can emerge in a relatively young woman, this liberating belief perfectly suited the mature season of life that both Marsha and Christina were entering. This paved the way for them to take their place as wise women in their communities.

Summoning Your Alchemical Authenticity

Perhaps you recognized elements of your own experience in Marsha and Christina's stories. Maybe you even felt the burn of familiarity in their shadow expressions, plus the unique part of yourself that has been struggling to get your attention. Do you sense that you might be ready to midwife this woman into being? Can you see yourself as an alchemist, here to transform the raw materials of your human existence into an awakened life of conscious purpose? If so, then you can be certain that The Mysterial is calling you toward **Alchemical Authenticity**.

IMAGINE

Imagine a world where women are unafraid to express the fullness of themselves, joyful and sad, afraid and courageous, chaotic and ordered, beautiful and ugly, autonomous and interconnected—the whole paradoxical mix of being real.

Imagine a world where we don't take ourselves too seriously and yet are deeply serious about those things that matter most to us.

Imagine a world where women are at ease with uncertainty and paradox and can remain present and peaceful as leaders in the midst of it all.

Imagine a world where women bring their deep multi-dimensional knowing into expression through fierce candor, delivered with compassion.

Imagine a world where we are dynamically guided by women who are partners with The Great Mystery and who know how to unfold the emergent, revealing breath-taking beauty and harmony.

Imagine this world and then imagine yourself shaping it!

Self-Observation Exercise for *The Crone*

The purpose of a Self-Observation exercise is to deepen your ability to become an objective observer of your own experience when The Crone shadows make an appearance. It calls upon you to witness yourself in the moment, to intimately get to know those Hag or Denier aspects of your way of being as they emerge in everyday situations.

As you become a better observer of your experience, you begin to see and discover things about the world inside and around you that would otherwise go unnoticed. You will in time clearly recognize when The Hag or The Denier is online.

This observation exercise does not include changing anything. It just means looking at things as they currently are . . . just noticing and writing down what you observe.

Daily Exercise
In one or two situations during the day, simply notice the presence of The Hag or The Denier. It may arise when you are alone or interacting with others, or when at home or at work.

1. What was happening when you noticed the shadow making an appearance?
2. What emotions did you feel?
3. What sensations were you aware of in your body?
4. What were your thoughts/stories about the situation?
5. What were you doing or not able to do?

Weekly Reflection
At the end of the week, look over your reflections and summarize in your journal:

1. What consistent stories does The Hag or The Denier tell you about the way the world is and how you have to be in it?
2. What are your signature emotions?

3. What connections are you making between The Hag or The Denier and the felt sense and shape or posture your body takes when she is present?
4. What are you learning about the way The Hag or The Denier is structured to provide you love, safety, or a sense of belonging?
5. How is that working and/or not working for you now?

Take some time to observe The Hag and The Denier without any attempt to shift. Give yourself space to really see how they operate (maybe take a few days to a week). Then move into the Deep Practice.

Mysterial Change Process
Deep Practice—*The Crone*

Use this practice to turn toward the triggered reactions of The Hag and The Denier. Depending on the level of triggering, it may take some time to bring yourself to center. It is enough to know that you are triggered and that this is not an ideal time to take any action.

SEE IT—Recognize when you have been triggered and are in the grips of The Crone shadow. Notice the *state of mind* (thoughts, judgments, and stories), *emotional state* (feelings), and the *state of body* (sensations, contraction, and shape) you find yourself in.

SAY IT—Name what is happening when you recognize the conditioned tendency—the body, the emotions, the story, and the behaviors of The Hag or The Denier overtaking you.

STOP IT—Decline the unproductive old stories or mental attitude of the shadow by telling yourself, "Stop!"

SENSE IT—Let go of the "story" or mental attitude for the moment, bring your attention to the present by tuning into your sensation. Feel your feet on the ground, find your breath in the center of your body, and sense the reactive places in your muscles and your core. Just let them be there with recognition, but not judgment; and with no requirement to change anything in the moment. From this place, turn toward the limiting belief of The Crone and say the limiting belief—**"I don't have enough knowledge, connections, or influence."**

NOTICE—Observe what happens when you drop this pebble into the pond of your being. As a compassionate and loving witness simply be present with whatever arises. Allow yourself to softly touch into this tender place without trying to change or challenge what you find there.

DIFFERENTIATE—Ask yourself: Who would I be without this belief? Allow yourself to respond somatically to this inquiry.

STAY WITH IT—Let your breath gently soften and settle places of contraction and tightening. Now call in the stabilizing and trustworthy energy of the inner Crone and differentiate from the shadow by inviting the liberating belief: **"I am an evolving source of wisdom, love, and power."** Allow the energizing and grounding truth of these words to resonate through every cell of your body.

COME TO CENTER—As you begin to feel a release of the emotional feelings and sensations that have hijacked you, bring yourself to center. Find your grounding by feeling your feet on the ground and taking full, deep breaths from the center of your body. As you exhale, allow your muscles to relax into gravity and find yourself centered in three dimensional space so that you become more fully present and your energy is balanced between the front and back, the right and left, and above and below.

INVOKE THE CRONE'S QUALITY OF TRUST—"What would it be like if I had a little more Trust in my being right now?"

CHOOSE ACTION—Take action or no action from this place of center. Remember to start with situations that have smaller charges and build from there so that you can get the full benefit of the practice.

Daily Practice
Select *one or two situations during the day* when you are aware that your Crone

shadows are activated. Deliberately go through each step of the somatic awareness process. If you were not able to stop the grab of The Crone shadows in the moment, take some time later in the day and recreate the situation so that the body state is activated and you are able to move through the process. Remember that the neural network can be shifted not only through experience in the moment, but also through recreating the situation using the imagination.

Reflections
Take ten to fifteen minutes to journal on the following:

1. What happened when you were able to let go of the thoughts and stay with the emotions and sensations in the body?

2. What happened when you touched into the embodied limiting belief—*I do not have enough knowledge, connections, or influence?* How do this belief and The Crone shadows influence the way you interact with others? What is possible and not possible when they are the driving force?

3. What was your experience when you brought in the liberating belief of The Crone: *I am an evolving source of wisdom, love, and power?*

4. What, if anything, was different when you came to Center (i.e., the way you feel about yourself, how you interact with others, what actions are possible now)?

PART III

Chapter 14

AUTHENTIC MYSTERIAL
EMERGENCE INITIATION—
Sacred Union of Yin and Yang

When sleeping women wake, mountains move.
—Chinese proverb

Like unraveling the complex structure of our DNA code to reveal the mystery of life, our journey through The Mysterial Sequence brings us to the naked edge of all we have known as we get ready to step forward into a whole new way of being. In some ways even the journey itself does not prepare us for the experience of the world that opens up through our new eyes.

Once the 3rd force of the Feminine—The Crone—comes into The Mysterial Sequence, bringing not only her unique capacities but also her role as integrator in the psyche, the stage is set for the deeper inner union that gives birth to the fullness of the Mysterial Woman. This fifth synthesizing archetype carries with it the alchemical conditions necessary for a sacred inner union to occur between all of the Yin and Yang essences. It is a moment of grace after much hard work!

The channel is open and the natural unfolding of your creative genius will inexorably occur. Life itself wants you to express your full potential, often more than you do. As you unblock the self-sabotaging shadows that have held your essence back, the complex beauty of your Mysterial self can't help but emerge. You are once again turning on the developmental tap. The fresh water of your life force simply seeks to move in the direction of more wisdom, love, and power: this is the evolutionary imperative. You just need to keep letting go of how you think your life should be and make room for the life that is actually trying to come into being.

Sacred Inner Union

> *"When it's over, I want to say: all my life*
> *I was a bride married to amazement.*
> *I was the bridegroom, taking the world into my arms."*
>
> —Mary Oliver

Now that you have cultivated access to the healthy archetypes of The Mysterial Sequence, they will continue to resonate as active forces in the psyche until they catalyze a deep inner union. It is this inner union, sometimes called a sacred marriage, that gives birth to the new capacities of the Mysterial Woman. And just as the birth of a child is a kind of miracle that arises from an interpersonal union, so is giving birth to our Mysterial nature. It represents an extraordinary quantum leap in our development.

It is as awe-inspiring as the butterfly emerging out of the body of the caterpillar; including yet transcending all of the raw material of the earlier form. The Mysterial Woman, carrying the DNA of the whole Mysterial Sequence within her, emerges with capacities that her caterpillar self could never have imagined.

This upgraded inner operating system and the subsequent new options for action that become possible, are unprecedented in human history. These capacities are coming in now for the first time because we need them to take on the challenges of a complex society that is outstripping what we constructed with our earlier meaning-making structures. So, in essence we have a kind of evolutionary tailwind pushing us forward, if we can just stop resisting it and start sailing.

The Way of the Mysterial Woman

Many women have found that a deep comfort and strange familiarity occurs when their Mysterial nature begins to come into expression—like meeting someone for the first time and feeling like you have known them forever. And that makes sense, as the seed of the Mysterial has been in us all along, waiting to emerge and spread its branches into a way of living, loving, and leading that would be a deeply fulfilling match for the complex challenges of life today.

So let's meet this old friend inside and imagine together what the way of the Mysterial woman looks and feels like . . .

First of all, there is a deep relaxation that occurs when you realize why you have felt so out of place for so long inside the cultural paradigm. You recognize yourself as part of a new wave of consciousness that is coming in now, through all the turmoil and confusion, to shape the emerging future.

With the assurance of the liberating belief of The Mother-Hero polarity—*I am enough just as I am and empowered to do what is mine to do*—you rest into a deep sense of sufficiency from which your actions then arise. With the Father-Maiden affirming—*I am at home in myself and naturally belong, free to express my true nature*—you know you are a vital part of this world and are boldly bringing forth your creative voice. And with the guidance of The Crone's belief—*I am an evolving source of wisdom, love, and power*—you are ready to show up in your wholeness and make a difference in the world as a co-creative partner with the Great Mystery.

With the channel now open you settle into a more consistent state of centered presence from which you can engage fully with any of the Yin or Yang capacities as needed in the moment. Over time even the very distinctions of Feminine and Masculine fall away in the experience of oneness that occurs as your Mysterial nature unfolds. The Way of the Mysterial Woman is simply more than the sum of its parts.

You have developed enough free awareness to recognize when you fall into the shadows (and, yes, this will happen!) of any of the archetypes. And you know how to be with the shadow material as you integrate those split off parts of yourself back into your wholeness.

When your Mysterial nature arises you naturally feel compelled to bring yourself into the world with a quality of artistry, compassion, intelligence, embodiment, and creative action that is a match for the challenges of this evolutionary moment. You can't help but become a Mysterial woman who leads. It is not something that you even have to choose. You naturally become an inspiring guide for others, simply by your presence and your clear actions. And because you know that you are intimately woven into the great fabric of life with all other beings, you deeply desire to make a difference in our troubled world.

A Mysterial Woman Who Leads

There is a lot of talk today about the leadership vacuum in every continent on the planet. And as it is said, nature abhors a vacuum. Women leaders are emerging now all over the world, who are not yet visible because their ways of leading do not fit the paradigm of leadership as we know it currently. So we need new eyes to see and a new courage to step forward as Mysterial women who are willing to *lean in* to the vacuum and redefine leadership in these times.

This budding quality of leadership is not based exclusively on roles, power, and command over others. It is an integral way of being that takes into account your vibrant inner world, your outer capacity for effective action, your co-creative relationships with others and your understanding and influence of the systems and structures of the world.

This definition of leadership manifests in the smallest, most mundane activities in your life, as well as the profound and consequential actions you may take. It is about how you get up in the morning and do what needs to be done even though you might be feeling your own fear and anxiety. It is about making wise decisions in the press of your professional responsibilities and the ambiguities of conflicting information. It is about taking the time during a busy day to stop and be with a good friend who is struggling, as much as it is stepping forward with a new policy that could change the way health care is funded.

A Mysterial woman who leads is committed to ongoing development as a way of life. Knowing that she is a "work in progress," she accepts failures and feedback as part of her ongoing learning adventure. Mysterial does not mean a fixed way of being or behaving. The capacities that arise when our Mysterial nature is unlocked are constantly expanding and growing to meet the needs of the moment.

A Mysterial woman who leads is able to bridge between the old worldview in which the majority of the world exists and the new worldview that she is here to bring. She is a kind of shape-shifter who can be *in the world, but not of it.* When you engage this quality of consciousness and courageously show up in the world you are able to embrace a wide range of differences while maintaining a grounded connection to your own unique experience. You recognize your relationship with Mother Earth, not just as a resource for you to use, but also as a dynamic partner with whom you are on this co-creative evolutionary journey. You tenderly care for her and her creatures just as you count on her for the food, air, water, earth, and fire that you need.

A Mysterial woman who leads is consistent in her authenticity, as present and genuine at a boardroom table as she is with the bus driver on her morning commute. She knows the power of a dynamic collective and takes the time and effort to tend to the energetic field of any group she is in. She is willing to be vulnerable and open in a quality of dynamic mutuality with others that naturally creates a trusting environment where everyone brings their best selves forward.

A Mysterial woman who leads draws upon all her ways of knowing. She allows things to manifest in natural and unpredictable ways so creative solutions arise that are vastly more complex than anything that could have been invented through a predictable process. She is open to the mystery of life and welcomes uncertainty, ambiguity, and change as necessary aspects of any creative endeavor.

A Mysterial woman who leads knows how to pace herself and others as she engages in her well-lived life. She values being as much as she does doing; stillness as much as action. She tunes herself to coherence, order, harmony, and beauty at the same time as she recognizes and embraces the incomplete, chaotic, conflicted, and ugly dimensions of reality.

A Mysterial woman who leads understands the current world pattern of "power over" and how to navigate through it, and yet is committed to a life of "power with and for" others. She knows that true wisdom is not something she can glean only with her rational mind but rather is something that emerges when she is open at all levels—body, mind, heart, and soul—in any moment and fully present to all that streams through her.

Love is her deepest motivating impulse, guiding her to more and more wholeness and compassionate connection with herself, others, and the world around.

Sound good? Sound familiar? Read on to find out about the Eight Mysterial meta-capacities that allow for this way of being to express in the world.

Eight Meta-Capacities of a Mysterial Woman

The picture we painted above of a woman living, loving, and leading as a Mysterial is drawn from the co-arising of eight key meta-capacities that we have identified. No doubt, in the years ahead, as we explore more fully the dimensions of what it means to be a Mysterial woman and as the problems in the world become more complex, other capacities will emerge.

Indeed we, the authors, see ourselves as the mapmakers who have charted a route to a new land but are only just beginning to explore the dimensions of this new territory ourselves. While each of these capacities is individually expressed, in general many of them will tend to co-arise in response to situations.

Just as we needed to create the word Mysterial to represent this new way of being that is so newly emerging now in our culture, so too have we come up with names for the

The Mysterial Woman

	INTERIOR	EXTERIOR
INDIVIDUAL	**My Inner Experience** Capacities: MULTI-DIMENSIONAL KNOWING EMBRACING PARADOX	**How I Show Up** Capacities: AUTHENTIC PRESENCE ENERGY STEWARDSHIP
	I	IT
	WE	ITS
COLLECTIVE	**Relating with Others** Capacities: GENERATIVE MUTUALITY TENDING THE FIELD	**Engaging the World** Capacities: INFLUENCING SYSTEM RESONANCE UNFOLDING THE EMERGENT

Mysterial capacities that may not be familiar to you at first glance. We invite you to begin by reading the words in **The Mysterial Woman** chart above and experiencing what they evoke.

To understand these capacities more fully let's look back into the stories of four of the women you met earlier as they worked their way through The Mysterial Sequence. Although all of the capacities will naturally co-arise as ways of being and doing once our Mysterial nature starts to awaken, we will show each woman expressing just two of the capacities so that you can see how they feed into one another.

TERRY'S MYSTERIAL EMERGENCE

Remember that we first met Terry as she wrestled with The Puritan shadow of The Maiden. Once The Father's Judge, Hero's Capitulator, and Mother's Neglector shadows were integrated, she was ready to find her joy, aliveness, and spontaneous creative expression. When her inner Maiden was set free and she saw just how strongly The Crone's Denier had a clamp on her generative capacity, Terry was ready to make a difference in the world and have fun at the same time!

After deeply sitting with the question of—*What will best serve my growth and my ability to be of service and feed my creativity?*—Terry reconnected with her deep desire to return to graduate school to study art therapy. This was an opportunity she had passed up years before, believing she would need to abandon her career with the federal government and forfeit her years of service. Using her capacity for **Embracing Paradox,** Terry was able to hold the tension between her desire to grow and learn in a field that would be soul nourishing and her practical need to earn her retirement benefits. She trusted that there was some possibility out there beyond "abandon my job" or "abandon my dream."

Embracing Paradox (My Inner Experience)

To embrace the polarities of paradox is to be able to hold the tension and complexity of seemingly contradictory or opposite elements at the same time. There is no need to quickly reduce everything to one pole or the other—either black or white, right or wrong. With this capacity to embrace dilemmas and paradoxes that are in essence unsolvable, you open the space for creative outcomes that arise from the synthesis of the differences. You are also able to hold a space for variances in yourself, others, and the world around. You can be happy and sad, clear and confused, confident and uncertain, trusting and afraid all at the same time. You can focus a clear intention and dynamically steer your way through situations as needed, be a change agent and an advocate for stable structures, work hard with discipline and be playful and spontaneous. And with the ability to embrace many conflicting points of view you have the possibility of arriving at the simplicity on the other side of complexity.

Terry doggedly researched possibilities, eventually finding her way to three programs she liked at different institutions. All were designed to accommodate students with full-time careers. It would be hard work, but Terry could feel the strength of her desire rising to meet this challenge. But which program would be the best choice? It was a major life decision. Using her capacity for **Multidimensional Knowing,** Terry first made a comparison of all the objective data—time, cost, travel, faculty quality, reputation—and eliminated one institution.

Multidimensional Knowing (My Inner Experience)

The complexity of our leadership challenges today requires the ability to access information from many diverse sources beyond the rational mind. Multidimensional Knowing combines carefully cultivated intuition, body cues, and feelings along with the rational capacities of logic, analysis, and planning to assess situations and make decisions. When you are using this capacity you are comfortable with not knowing everything—able to Be With the Mystery—and this opens up a space of curiosity for new ideas and solutions to arise. You are naturally alert to the signs, signals, and synchronicities that arise around you and give you information about where to direct your attention in any given moment. All levels of yourself—mind, heart, body, and spirit—are actively engaged, and you have the capacity to be present and discriminating in the midst of this ongoing stream of awareness.

She then traveled to California and Colorado to visit the two remaining campuses and meet with faculty and students, carefully monitoring her feelings, impressions, and body reactions during the visits. Still she could not feel a clear "yes" and felt her old anxiety begin to gnaw away at her; the applications were due soon! Yet she knew she needed to wait until she had full clarity.

It was during a "time out of time" quilting session late one afternoon that Terry suddenly felt the pleasure, as opposed to just the fear, of plunging into art therapy. She could feel her body relax and lighten as she digested the decision. As she drove to work that morning, Terry noticed the sporty little car in front of her had California license plates. She smiled.

RACHEL'S MYSTERIAL EMERGENCE

We first met Rachel tightly bound in the arms of The Mother's Devourer shadow. It took time and effort to bring back her power and authority from the grip of The Hero's Capitulator, The Father's Judge, The Maiden's Bohemian, and The Crone's Hag shadows. But once she had done it, she was ready to step forward as an empowered agent of change.

After years of raising her children and volunteering, Rachel was hired for a paid position as a community organizer with a fast growing startup NGO working to halt the destruction of the Amazon rainforests. This was Rachel's first experience as a virtual team leader, meaning she had to learn on the fly, working from scratch to build a team of young activists around the world who had to travel and work long hours for a small stipend.

Using her capacity for **Tending the Field**, Rachel thoughtfully built personal relationships with her team members using phone calls, texts, and video conferencing and created opportunities for the members to get to know and appreciate each other as beings and as contributors to a common mission. She also worked at the subtle level. Every morning as a practice, she would pause and bring into her heart-mind each of her volunteers, briefly tuning her attention to each of them. Then she would extend her loving attention to the whole community, the whole organization, and finally out to the rainforests. This invisible practice also worked well to replace her tendency to be the caretaker when she was in regular daily contact with someone.

Tending the Field (Relating With Others)

When you are Tending the Field, you attune to the symphony of emotions, concerns, expectations, challenges, and joys of a collective, taking appropriate action or non-action to best serve the whole system and the overall purpose of the collective. You know how to create a deep well of shared meaning and are able to guide others to it so that the inherent wisdom of the collective may be sourced from this place. When you Tend the Field, you are cultivating an ongoing heart connection with another or a collective that encourages a resonant heart field to emerge more powerful than the sum of its parts. You pay attention to the gross (material), subtle (emotional, imaginal, energetic), and causal (Great Mystery, spiritual, Higher Self) levels of the collective field and know how to nourish each one. You understand that conflict and chaos are natural elements in any dynamic community and you are able to hold the space for new order and harmony to arise naturally. Appreciation and gratitude flow freely through you as a natural part of your leadership.

This capacity was also a necessary way for Rachel to stay connected with her children and husband while not being available all the time as she was before. She had the capacity now to be with her children's challenges without taking over—quietly and subtly creating the conditions around them that would help them learn how to deal with life's challenges themselves. In many ways her relationships at home and with her extended family and community were actually deeper than when she had more time.

As the interpersonal and subtle connections deepened both at work and at home, Rachel was able to tune into the emotional undertones, noticing what issues were bubbling under the surface, and gauging her response. At work she could sense a tension building between the activists in the field and the staff at the head office who managed the resources. When a financial emergency at the head office meant that her young team would not be paid and faced immediate disbandment, Rachel discovered her capacity for **Generative Mutuality**.

She was completely transparent with her team, staying grounded in her own feelings while she made space for their anger, grief, and feelings of betrayal to be expressed. Rachel connected with the executive team, acknowledging their pain, and the courage it was taking to make hard decisions to preserve the organization. "My first impulse was to help out by offering to volunteer my services again," she recounted. "But I realized that was The Devourer showing up and it wasn't going to move any of us forward."

Generative Mutuality (Relating With Others)

To be in Generative Mutuality with others is to bring all of yourself into relationship with one person or a collective in a way that is transparent, undefended, compassionate, and intimate. This way of being in collaboration allows the greatest good for the most people to arise. It is built on a foundation of integrity in thought, speech, and behavior between everyone involved so that the relationship can withstand the inevitable storms of reactivity that may arise in difficult conversations. To be in Generative Mutuality with others requires that you serve as an ambassador between different worldviews and types, cultivating and catalyzing shared meaning and common vision without being attached to particular outcomes. You recognize that you are part of an interconnected and "Friendly Universe" and that you can let go of control and surrender into relationships with others. You are able to have deep appreciation for and empathy with others, while standing your ground and being willing to confront and dissolve, with love and candor, what doesn't serve.

By working with both sides to minimize fear and blame, and staying centered so that she would not be pulled into the strong emotions on either side, Rachel was able to open a space of creativity and collaboration. Her team prepared a proposal to run their own local fundraising event and asked for support from the head office. The proposal was accepted, and the fundraiser was a huge success, leading her team to financial independence over time. Rachel glowed, "As it turned out, we've been able to make a larger contribution to the organization and to our mission . . . and I didn't have to give myself away."

GABRIELLA'S MYSTERIAL EMERGENCE

We last saw Gabriella standing in her Empowered Radiant Presence after claiming her sufficiency from The Mother's Devourer shadow and her capacity to act from The Hero's Capitulator. From there she was ready to face The Father's Outsider shadow and The Maiden's Puritan so that she could let herself be seen in her natural leadership power and creativity. The Crone's Denier hardly stood a chance as Gabriella came so gracefully into her truth-telling, compassionate way of being.

The channel was open now and she could never go back to the old Gabriella. After several years of hard work with her partners trying to get her entrepreneurial consulting business off the ground, Gabriella could feel the energy draining out of the enterprise. In the old days this would have been enough for The Capitulator to kick in and she would just given up. Using her capacity for **Energy Stewardship** she was able to assess the situation with all levels of her being. She could see that in the last few months every time she tried to move forward she would run into a roadblock of one kind or another and it was draining all of her energy. And when early one morning she tried to start the car and the battery was dead she realized she was getting messages on all fronts that she was running out of juice.

Energy Stewardship (How I Show Up)

Energy Stewardship is the capacity to wisely guide the movement and flow of energy both within yourself and in your outward expression. All levels of yourself—mind, heart, body, and spirit—are awakened and actively participating in the ways that you choose to guide and direct energy in any moment. This capacity requires the ability to both contain and release the life force moving through you. When you have this personal capacity you are able to bring it into groups and skillfully guide the flow of the creative process. You value stillness as much as you do action, and you know how to move wisely between the two as needed. This allows you to be very accomplished and productive in a sustainable way.

Even though her friends were encouraging her to keep pushing forward, Gabriella recognized that there was actually no energy in her body or in the organizational system to do that. Something else was trying to show itself and she was paying attention so that she could be **Unfolding the Emergent** in whatever next step seemed right. So she spoke frankly and compassionately with her partners about her sensing that perhaps their business venture had reached a place of completion.

"I was really surprised that when I got up my nerve to speak with them," she reported, "that although they were disappointed, they both had new situations arising in their own lives that made them also question the wisdom of continuing on with the business."

Unfolding the Emergent (Engaging the World)

When you are Unfolding the Emergent, you are creating the conditions and discerning the right timing to midwife an outcome that conveys the greatest good, even if the result is very different than your original intention. You are comfortable with ambiguity and not knowing, and are able to allow things to unfold in unpredictable ways. You are also awake to the internal and external factors of the situation as they arise, paying attention to synchronicities, and dynamically adjusting in the moment to take the next best step. When you Unfold the Emergent you are able to honor rhythms and cycles and have a sense for the sacredness of life, knowing that some things require patient gestation before they can emerge, and other things require quick and decisive action, even if it means reassessing your original intention and changing course. You know when to let things dissolve and when to bring things into a new synthesis. Your intuitive understanding of the nonlinear nature of most problems that we face allows you to flow through life.

Together, Gabriella and her business partners decided to close things down and it was a relief to them all—another sign that this was the right decision, even though she had no idea what was next. A few weeks after this shift in focus an unexpected invitation came to Gabriella's husband that would require their family to move to a completely different city for a job opportunity. She knew in her bones that this was the right decision to make.

Even though she did not know where it would lead her personally, Gabriella had tremendous faith in the process. If she had pushed forward with her business and taken other steps to keep it growing, this would have been a very difficult decision to make. Everything now flowed easily toward this unexpected new future. Gratitude filled her heart.

MARSHA'S MYSTERIAL EMERGENCE

We met Marsha in the last gateway of The Mysterial Sequence as she took her true wisdom and power back from The Crone's sword-wielding Hag shadow. She had already done the difficult work of shaking herself loose from The Mother's Devourer, Hero's Dominator, Father's Judge, and Maiden's Bohemian—an unholy active shadow convergence if ever there was one!

Marsha was always a powerful woman and her physical beauty and natural charisma would light up any room. When her Mysterial nature began to arise there was a new spacious invitation for the radiance of others to emerge as well. She no longer needed to overshadow others. Her capacity for **Authentic Presence** made her not only interesting but also *interested*. As she was listening to one of her friends tell a story, she caught herself about to plunge in with her even more dramatic version of the same experience. She settled back, putting her full attention back on her friend. Her grounded connection to herself made it possible for her to stay curious and present with the other and not indulge in her old, familiar desire to grab all the attention.

Authentic Presence (How I Show Up)

To be Authentically Present is to be sourcing your moment-to-moment expression from a deep connection to the ground of your being. There is no gap between your inner experience and your outer behaviors, resulting in a genuine way of engaging with others. Presence emerges when the masks are dropped and your true essential nature beams through without either grandiosity or false humility. Moving from a deep self-love and empathy for others, you have the capacity to speak clearly and candidly about things. There are no games, falsehoods, or manipulations needed to communicate with others. You are in touch with your true self at all levels—body, mind, heart, and spirit—and share that in easy, confident, and congruent ways.

Of course, expressing more and more of your authentic essence does not always mean that those around you will be happy. Marsha was surprised to find that one of the people most challenged by her new way of being was her husband. She thought that he would be happy for her to stop her pushy, controlling ways. In fact, when she was not taking care of everything and everyone all the time it changed the dynamic between them dramatically. They had married young and Marsha's growth spurt was cracking open the structure of their relationship.

What began as a small fissure between them moved to a trial separation, and with painstaking work on Marsha's part, ended in an amicable divorce. She was an integral part of her husband's family business, and she knew that the dissolution of their marriage would require her to develop the capacity of **Influencing System Resonance**. She understood that she was like a kind of tuning fork in the family system and the company, and that she needed to be very mindful about what note she was sounding.

Influencing System Resonance (Engaging the World)

When you are Influencing System Resonance, you are bringing a subtle alignment and harmony to the culture, systems, and structures around you, so that the net effect is to convey the greatest good to the most people possible. You embrace the complexity of multiple systems, appreciate the capacities and limitations of each, and recognize what they bring to an overarching vision and purpose that may extend far beyond your lifetime. You wisely influence rather than force systems to come into resonance. Working co-creatively through others you prune, nourish, dissolve, synthesize, and revise in order to increase the coherence, beauty, and effectiveness of the overall ecosystem of any endeavor.

Marsha knew that she needed to move slowly through the changes in her relationship with her husband so that the systems they were embedded in together would be able to disentangle without unnecessary dissonance and suffering. She also knew that how she went through this dissolution would have everything to do with what would emerge next for both of them and their children.

In other words, the seeds of the future were being planted in the ground of the present moment. There was a lot at stake. "I am so grateful for my Mysterial women friends who stood with me through this time of transition. They kept reminding me that I was not alone and gave me the courage to keep showing up fully as I made my way through the rocky shoals of rearranging just about everything in my life."

Completion—The Ten Competencies of Authentic Mysterial Emergence

Once The Crone comes online all the archetypal forces are activated within. The Mysterial Sequence, the Source Code that optimizes the flow of your Yin-Yang essences, is now complete. Everything is in place for the deep inner alchemy of the Authentic Mysterial Emergence Initiation that brings forth the Mysterial Woman.

> *The Way of the Mysterial Woman is a wise, loving, and powerful way of being that arises when our unique Yin and Yang essences are moving freely through mind, heart, and body in a creative partnership with the mystery of life.*

As the eight foundational capacities of the Mysterial Woman gather substance within us and are consistently accessible, they become the fuel source to develop the associated ten embodied competencies, like muscles to exercise in a practical way in our lives. It's the very same process we experienced with the Empowered Radiant Presence and Joyful True Authority Initiations.

Competency building happens through Deep Practice, by focusing your awareness on a competency you intend to build, making incremental attempts to try out a new behavior or mindset, and consciously adjusting to try again when things don't work out the way you envisioned. It happens over time, with persistence and patience (a sense of humor also helps). We can't be afraid to laugh at the inevitable missteps that will happen in this ongoing life experiment to construct new neural pathways.

You may be doing the math, and realizing that twenty-eight capacities and thirty embodied competencies are a lot to track. Who has time for all this Deep Practice? Now we discover and can truly appreciate the simplicity on the other side of complexity. The capacities and competencies of The Mysterial Emergence include and transcend everything that came before. The earlier ones get baked into the final celebratory cake, becoming much more than flour, eggs, milk, baking powder, and chocolate. The ingredients are all in there, but the higher order result is far more refined and palatable.

In short, once you've made it this far, all you really need to do is keep your eye on the ten Living, Loving, and Leading competencies of the Mysterial Woman. Not only will you experience deep satisfaction with this final "cake," you'll find over time that those in your circles of influence will appreciate being served a slice!

Mysterial Competencies
The Mysterial Woman

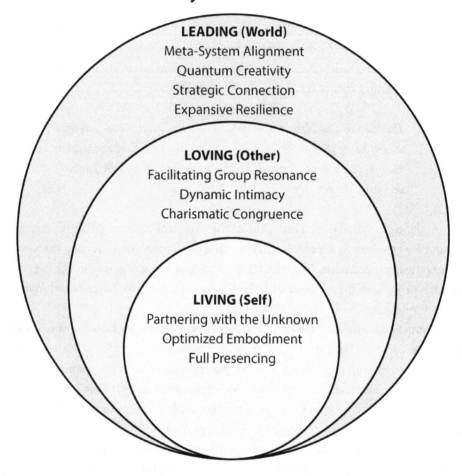

LEADING (World)
Meta-System Alignment
Quantum Creativity
Strategic Connection
Expansive Resilience

LOVING (Other)
Facilitating Group Resonance
Dynamic Intimacy
Charismatic Congruence

LIVING (Self)
Partnering with the Unknown
Optimized Embodiment
Full Presencing

LIVING: Full Presencing, Optimized Embodiment, Partnering with the Unknown
LOVING: Dynamic Intimacy, Facilitating Group Resonance, Charismatic Congruence
LEADING: Meta-System Alignment, Quantum Creativity, Strategic Connection, Expansive Resilience.

If you've committed the appropriate time, energy, and attention to each step of The Mysterial Sequence, your life will unfold with an exquisiteness that you couldn't have imagined at the start. The ten Mysterial Woman competencies offer you ways of being and acting that can elegantly meet the manifold demands of your own rich and evolving life. What's more, they are ideally matched for the leadership needs of a world of increasing complexity, accelerating change, and near constant uncertainty—our emerging future.

IN THE DOMAIN OF LIVING:

Full Presencing: Ability to be fully engaged with your present moment experience so that nothing is excluded and you are flowing with all that is arising in a deeply interconnected pattern of wholeness.

Optimized Embodiment: Ability to be in direct relationship with the changing needs of your physical being as you move through the different phases of your life so that you are able to constantly tune yourself toward the optimal conditions needed for a sustainable and healthy life.

Partnering With the Unknown: Ability to suspend the need to know everything, so that from a place of curiosity you can invite the unknown to lead you into creative solutions beyond your current experience.

IN THE DOMAIN OF LOVING:

Dynamic Intimacy: Ability to create and maintain close, open-hearted, and deep relationships with others without becoming emotionally fused with or needing to control them so that the relationship can continue to change and grow.

Facilitating Group Resonance: Ability to create alignment and harmony within family, work, and community systems by engaging in transparent and heartfelt conversations, leading to greater connectedness and trust.

Charismatic Congruence: Ability to show up authentically in a public or performance situation, where your words match your actions, in a way that naturally creates a sense of personal and inspiring connection with others.

IN THE DOMAIN OF LEADING:

Meta-System Alignment: Ability to harmonize key individuals, groups, processes, and structures within a system, and align them with economic, social, and environmental goals such that the overall system functions as a seamless, sustainable, and intelligent whole.

Quantum Creativity: Ability to engage your multiple ways of knowing in a fearless approach to rapid experimentation where you are willing to learn from your mistakes and do things differently.

Strategic Connection: Ability to identify stakeholders inside and outside one's own family, group, or organization that have an influence on its success and well-being, and build effective partnerships with them.

Expansive Resilience: Ability to remain grounded and maintain a baseline of inner well-being in the face of adversity or great setbacks, quickly recovering full functionality and even thriving, while also supporting one's partners, families, organizations and communities to do the same.

Stepping onto the Path—Walking The Beauty Way

When these ten competencies are embodied you are living The Way of the Mysterial Woman. And this way of being and showing up in the world can also be called The Beauty Way. It is a way of seeing in which you are awake to the beauty of your own being, and therefore vulnerably open to being touched by the beauty in others and the world around. You value creating, expressing, and enjoying beauty as a language that bridges between the soul and the outer world.

Think about a time when you were caught up by the experience of something truly beautiful: a rainbow in the midst of a mighty storm, crashing surf on an open beach, a woman wrapped in a colorful sari, the scent of jasmine on a hot afternoon. When you perceive anything as beautiful it opens the gateway to your senses, evokes your feelings, and brings you into the present moment. It generates an inner coherence.

The Beauty Way is not a pathway to perfection. It is about being with yourself, just as you are, with forgiveness, compassion, and tenderness. It is about being with "what is" with acceptance, equanimity, and non-attachment. And it is about seeing with eyes that ripen what you behold as you shape a new world order.

A few years ago the Dalai Lama said, "The world will be saved by Western women." His quote stirred up a lot of attention at the time and shone a light right on those of us who have the luxury to be considering things like growth and development. He was saying that we are needed! It is our belief that it is not, however, gender alone that will change the world.

It will require women who are willing to go *down and in* and do the shadow work needed to reconnect with our authentic essence and cultivate the capacities required to show up in the world as true Mysterial Women who are leading the way.

It will require women who are able to respond and not just react to the challenges of life; women who have gathered up all of themselves and are an inspiration for others to do the same. Women who are ready to upgrade their internal operating systems and start to express some unprecedented ways of living, loving, and leading.

It will require us to give up playing small and staying stuck, and recognize that evolution really needs us to, "Be the change [we] want to see in the world."

Chapter 15

THE MYSTERIAL FUTURE

Another world is not only possible, she's on her way.
On a quiet day, I can hear her breathing.

—Arundati Roy

The awakening of a woman's Mysterial nature is a momentous personal event that will irrevocably change her life and those she influences. The elegantly complex and artfully refined Mysterial capacities that come online cannot help but move her in a direction of making a difference.

With that awakening comes the insight that this difference needn't be made alone, and almost surely won't. There are other Mysterials awake now, and many more on the way.

You are History in the Making

We are inviting *you* to consciously join with like-minded others, to participate in the earliest stirrings of something profound and historically significant. Women today are just beginning to come into their own Mysterial nature. We saw it in the women you met through our stories in Part II, we are seeing it in ourselves, and nearly everywhere we look.

The Mysterial Woman is quietly, organically coming forth around the world. It's her time.

If you have made it to this final chapter and can feel a current of resonance vibrating within, then you are surely playing a part in this historic emergence. You are on the threshold of what could become a sea of change in the way we live, love, and lead. This has a tremendous bearing on our future, and the world we are seeding for our grandchildren and beyond.

Arundati Roy poetically foreshadows that another world is on her way, yet that doesn't tell the whole story. The time we are in can be thought of like this: you are looking out your bedroom window enjoying the encouraging glow of sunrise at the horizon. It is that magical moment just before the orb of the sun actually appears.

You have a choice. You can turn over and go back to sleep. Or, you can choose to awaken and enthusiastically meet the promise of the day with everything you've got.

In other words, you can choose to actively participate in this time of emergence—to grow.

The sun will rise whether we're awake or not. But it doesn't dictate what kind of day we'll have. If we greet the sun with full, conscious participation and clear intention it will make for a much better day for us and for those with whom we are connected. A new world is on its way, and if many of us choose to awaken into our Mysterial nature, a brighter future can come sooner.

The Mysterial Woman is not something we, the authors, invented. We simply recognized and named the phenomenon, and created the conditions to encourage and accelerate it. A woman's full Mysterial nature arises naturally once her inner Crone is awakened, and the healthy Mother, Hero, Father, and Maiden are reasonably embodied. These primary archetypes are part of our ancient and enduring human legacy, our evolutionary story. And given the opportunity, they want to come forth.

You don't need to work with a coach, attend a program, or find a community to awaken your Mysterial nature, although doing so can greatly accelerate the emergence. The psychoactive patterns of The Mysterial Sequence will naturally start to come alive in your psyche the moment you read and resonate with them, and will build strength and vibrancy as you work with them.

As an emerging Mysterial Woman you will not only experience personal changes but the way you choose to live, love, and lead will shape the world for future generations.

The Time of The Great Transition

A hundred years from now, maybe sooner, our descendants will look back on the time we are in currently as something like The Great Transition. Far-seeing thought leaders such as evolutionary futurist Barbara Marx Hubbard and eco-philosopher Joanna Macy have said as much. With the perspective of history and a basic understanding of how consciousness develops, it's easy to see what we are transitioning from: that five-millennia cycle of civilization built in the image of The Hero and The Father. Without those powerful Yang patterns having operated in our past, we could not be here today. But if we continue on that same course, we won't be here tomorrow. Or at least we won't be in very good shape. That's evolution in a nutshell.

It's not a straightforward or easy path, nor is the outcome a given by any means. We women as a global cohort have spent the last fifty-odd years in a relentless and sometimes harrowing climb up history's steepest learning curve. Before we could truly join in and co-create a world that is more inclusive, caring, and healthy, we had to pick up the reins and learn to master the Yang world that had already been created. It has taken an incalculable investment from our collective minds, hearts, bodies, and spirits just to adapt to the Yang-saturated workplaces, institutions, infrastructures, lifestyles, expectations, and beliefs that The Hero and The Father bequeathed us.

We even had to adapt to that first taste of Maiden Flame Yin essence, when the global floodgates finally opened to women taking positions of power, influence, and contribution traditionally held by men. Like water poured into a hot, dry pan left too long on the stove, the revolutionary Maiden's spicy nectar of Flame Yin essence had to hiss and boil furiously before a steady simmer could be maintained. It's been a wild ride.

With most of us still catching our breath, we are unlikely to register the full magnitude of this grand historical achievement by women. The bottom line is this: It is only now that we women are collectively poised to take our rightful and needed place in partnership with men, and bring forth our full contribution. Together we can, with intention, help shape a positive future.

So what could this positive future look like? And how long will it take? What happens next? That's harder to say, but gazing ahead we can make some informed predictions.

Fortunately we have a wonderful tool available to us. Given that The Mysterial Sequence has mirrored transformational changes in culture and mass consciousness at every step, we can use that as our possibility guide. It can help us to imagine a Mysterial future.

What's next? The return to The Mother archetype, with a corresponding influx of Vessel Yin essence on a mass scale.

It's worth noting that the sudden influx of a new essence and archetype on a historically large scale across the world is not magic. It simply means that from an evolutionary and developmental perspective, this is the next step humans are compelled to take in order to solve the pressing problems of existence. For that reason, the inner pressure to develop begins to press on a large number of individuals in a similar time period. As these individuals make their marks on the world, these patterns in the psyche become more accessible and familiar to everyone.

Before we move into this, let's take a step back and view the larger pattern. Although we are over five decades into the Second Feminine Epoch, we are just now completing our passage through the turbulent transition zone leading out of the culmination of The First Masculine Epoch. That epoch consisted of three successive influxes of Yang essence: Flame Yang, Vessel Yang, and Flame+Vessel Yang. It manifested as three distinct cultures that still exist today in some form around the world: Warrior, Traditional, and Modern.

We propose that the Second Feminine Epoch from here on out will be experienced in two stages. First, the presence and influence of Mysterial Women in society will rise significantly with the collective Return to The Mother. However, the full flowering of the Mysterial Woman will not happen until the collective embrace of the third force of the Feminine—the long hidden and much maligned Crone archetype. That will be an interesting time indeed.

Overview of The Second Feminine Epoch

The Postmodern revolution—the arrival of The Maiden archetype into mass consciousness in the 1960s—signaled that the Second Feminine Epoch had begun. Like the First Masculine Epoch, we can expect it to unfold for a significant stretch of history. If the pattern holds—and for now let us assume that it will—it will likely come in three sequential waves of Feminine essence: Flame Yin, Vessel Yin, and Flame+Vessel Yin.

We've had a couple of generations to collectively soak up the vibrant and volatile Flame Yin essence of The Maiden. The Mysterial Sequence suggests that collectively we are due to return full circle, next touching into the Vessel Yin essence of the archetypal Mother. This is not the same as the primordial Mother of the Archaic Age, but a complex and highly conscious expression of Vessel Yin that is appropriate to our time.

What might the world be like when a highly conscious and complex expression of the Vessel Yin Mother archetype starts to be felt, embraced, and accepted by mass consciousness? Let's actually drop into the body right now and draw upon our multiple intelligences to sense into it. This activates our intuition, which has always been a woman's way of seeing into the future. Bringing our intuitive sight together with our rational pattern-seeking ability can make for a powerful combination for connecting with the future.

You can start by feeling into the whole historical Mysterial Sequence within you. Observe what arises as you allow yourself to follow the flow of energies through the figure eight of The Mysterial Sequence.

Guided Visualization through *The Mysterial Sequence*

Let your thoughts drop away and begin to notice the feeling of your body pressing against the furniture or ground.

As you read these words, start to imagine yourself at the edge of an ancient, primordial forest that provides everything you need. Facing north, you take in the warm and nourishing embrace of the ancient Yin Mother, feeling such gratitude for her abundant sustenance and shelter.

As if startled from a delicious daydream, a sudden urge compels you to explore beyond the boundaries of this safe known world. Mounting your horse, you feel compelled to ride east, joining forces with the fiery, willful conquering Yang Hero to claim new territory.

You are stopped by a mountain upon which sits an imposing castle. You claw your way up through the burning obstacles of a fiery initiation to the stabilizing, controlling, rationally steady Vessel Yang Father.

As the Flame Yang Hero matures under the watchful eye of this Yang Father, you stop for a while to witness the miracle of rising technology, affluence, democracy, and human rights. You feel compelled to join in, find your place. You work hard and enjoy the fruits of your efforts.

After awhile, you begin to feel trapped and overworked. Gazing out west over the cliffs, you spy the irresistibly sparkling waters of a vast ocean. You can't help yourself and cast off your stuffy clothes, taking a deep dive into the creative, sexual, spontaneous, imaginative, adventurous waters of Flame Yin Maiden. The very depths are resplendent with treasures galore.

Clutching treasure, swimming furiously upward through a watery initiation, you finally break through the surface for a glorious breath of air. Moments later your feet touch down on Vessel Yin Mother land.

You reground and rest here after your journey—realizing that you are not the same person who left so long ago. You see through new eyes now—you have new gifts.

As you gaze around in wonderment, you find that you have somehow landed in a new and advanced society. How amazing it is!

With The Mysterial Sequence alive in your body, ask yourself the following: What is out beyond this return to The Mother? What has the journey prepared us for next? What can we anticipate about the future?

First, let's discuss the big things. We can expect that women as a group or collective (and men who have developed their Yin essences) will make a general shift from occupying the margins into a more central role in society. In the First Masculine Epoch, men—with their higher likelihood for carrying a core Yang essence—were naturally at the forefront. As the Second Feminine Epoch stabilizes with the fortifying influence of The Mother's Vessel Yin, we can anticipate women moving rapidly toward full participation as citizens of influence, and into much greater power and numbers as leaders.

While few will be full Mysterials, many of these women will be expressing some measure of Empowered Radiant Presence and Joyful True Authority. As they begin to reground and restore with the Return to The Mother, they will become a magnetic and confident force in society—able to bridge gaps, come up with innovative solutions, deal with conflict and uncertainty, and keep themselves healthy and working with "effortless effort" and flow for the long haul.

The influx of grounded Vessel Yin essence will be experienced as a supportive and energizing force for many women with a Yin core essence—like fresh wind in their sails. That stubborn 20 percent glass ceiling for women in senior leadership positions will become a happily forgotten artifact of the past, like corsets or chastity belts.

Although it is tempting to imagine, this will not likely be a time of power reversal with women now staking their claim as king of the mountain. Such hierarchical thinking is an old Yang concept. The more contemporary Yin expression will be to share power—to be co-creative with men and Yang ways in general. Formerly Hypermasculine activities will tend toward more balance with the Feminine.

For example, in organizations and institutions where intense competition was the norm, employees will be supported and compensated for their ability to both compete and collaborate as the situation requires, to use their rational faculties as well as their intuition when making decisions, and to navigate hierarchies as well as network laterally. Dress codes will combine professional identification with Feminine flow and natural comfort, with wearable technology that will support us to be in tune with our biological rhythms and overall health.

We will demand that people take vacations and naps, and tend to their health to ensure their well-being and ability to contribute healthily over the long term. With a much longer view of the future, we will recognize that investment in human and natural capital pays off in myriad ways over time.

The Return of The Collective Mother

Will the return to The Mother mark the rise of an entirely new culture, on the order of the historic shift from Traditional monarchies of feudal landowners to Modern democracies fueled by industrial commerce? At this point, we think not. Here's why: The Mother is not a new archetypal pattern arriving on the scene. Her fundamental essence is deeply known to all humans. What is more likely is that a contemporary re-infusion of The Mother archetype will stabilize and expand the Postmodern culture that has already sprung up in pockets, with values that are more humanistic, environmentally sensitive, and spiritually-oriented than Modern culture.

Movements still on the edge—such as "green" MBA degrees, "Conscious Capitalism," alternative mind-body medicine, Transition Towns,[1] permaculture, co-housing, gift economies—these will become more the norm. Over time we expect they will overtake Modern Yang culture and become "the mainstream," with institutions, policies, and infrastructure that are more enduringly sustainable and in balance with the needs of human beings and the natural world.

As the driving edge of global culture shifts from Modern Yang to Postmodern Yin, our collective memory of life under Yang dominance, at least in the most developed parts of the world, will fade. It will seem quite normal, and we might become oblivious to the fact that women on the whole (along with more Yin-essence men) are having greater influence on our institutions, workplaces, built environments, beliefs, and styles. Society will organically become more Yin.

The Vessel Yang Father of the Medieval era tamed the destructive adolescent wildness of the Flame Yang Hero who had dominated the city-state Empires. Similarly, the Vessel Yin Mother will ground the dynamic impulses of the Flame Yin Maiden, toning down the excesses. This will help turn the relational idealism of caring for the environment and for all beings, especially the most vulnerable and oppressed, into grounded, practical, everyday reality.

There are few of us who are happy living frantic and fractured lives. As the Postmodern wave becomes the natural dominant force in consciousness and culture for our world milieu, we will likely notice some settling of the chaos and more coherence in general.

The emerging future is calling for the stabilizing Vessel Yin container of The Mother, for a time to create sustainable (as well equitable and nurturing) systems and structures. In other words, we are being called to start walking our talk in a big way. The planet needs to be kept clean and healthy; everyone needs a pathway to contribute to society and be appropriately compensated; no one should go hungry or have their basic human rights violated.

The archetypal Flame Yin Maiden, initiator of the Second Feminine Epoch, had a crucial role in breaking the ossified grip of the old Yang pattern. History shows us that revolutions are never meant to last. They occur in narrow windows of time, and eventually their gains need to be integrated into society. During the Modern wave, for example, the gains of the American Revolution—breaking the grip of Traditional Monarchism—were integrated through the structures of the US Constitution and the formation of the world's first stable democracy. This we know profoundly influenced the trajectory of world events. That will be true again.

Vessel Essence—Slowing down, Finding Stillness

As we know, the Vessel essences, both Yin and Yang, are by nature slow and still compared to the dynamic Flame essences. When Modern productivity (Flame Yang), with its narrow focus on financial profitability and growth joined up with Postmodern connectivity and speed (Fueled by Flame Yin), human life turned into a race inside an unsustainable hamster cage of demands. We need to slow down and restore our collective general well-being. We need to encourage more of The Beauty Way in our culture, even if it doesn't appear to increase profits. The issue of work-life balance will likely ascend to a top priority as we come to grips with the fact that an unhealthy and overworked society is costly and ultimately less productive.

The slowness of recovery from the Great Recession of the late 2000s may indeed have been early indication of Vessel Yin influence, in the collective unconscious, putting on the brakes in preparation for massive structural change. By comparison, the early days of the Vessel Yang Father were marked by the hard stop of the Dark Ages and the slow recovery of civilization through the Medieval period. Fortunately we have learned much in the intervening time.

It's not surprising that full and/or living wage employment remained a challenging issue around the globe for years after the Great Recession, even though large corporations seemed to be doing relatively well. Employment is a means to nourish and shelter ourselves: an issue of the archetypal Mother. Yet a relatively narrow set of roles in the economy were actually well compensated, and they tended to be quite Yang in nature.

Futurist and green economist Hazel Henderson describes the economic "cake" (in contrast to the traditional economist's pie) as consisting of a top layer of a paid economy— the private sector with all the icing resting upon the public sectors—and the two unpaid bottom layers supporting everything above it. The first unpaid layer is the "love economy" of mostly women taking care of children and households, providing nurturing and counseling, building community, volunteering, and generally maintaining the social fabric. The very bottom layer is nature's productivity, which supports everything above, and is not only currently not supported and compensated, but is exploited and harmed.

In the return to The Mother, there is likely to be a massive structural rethinking of how we view employment and compensation in society, and how we value and invest in supporting nature. It's possible that ideas considered far out today, such as a guaranteed minimum income for all citizens, may become viable in this time to come.

A look at the Scandinavian countries of Denmark, Norway, Finland, and Sweden, for better and worse, give us some early indication of the nature of a more stabilized Postmodern culture. Although living costs can be high, bureaucracy overbearing, and gender equality militantly enforced, The World Happiness Report 2013 ranked Denmark the world's happiest country. Many reasons can play a part, and among those commonly cited are the lengthy maternity care, low cost or free child care (resulting in a high percentage of Danish women feeling comfortable enough with the well-being of their children to return to work), efficient and universal health care, high gender equality, a proliferation of biking as transportation, some of the highest voting percentages in the world (and thus a strong democracy), and a strong sense of collective responsibility to each other. Although the Scandinavian countries (compared to the US) have small, racially homogenous populations with high per capita income, the contemporary Mother is clearly at work in Denmark today.

An intriguing early "smoke signal" of the return of The Mother is being sent aloft by one of the most patriarchal institutions in world history—the Catholic Church. As of this writing, Pope Francis is preparing a "papal encyclical" on the subject of climate change and human ecology. A papal encyclical is a rare event, a formal letter to all the Roman Catholic Bishops and through them to the 1.2 billion Catholics worldwide, using the highest level of the pope's authority. In the months prior to the planned encyclical, Pope Francis had been making a case for a radical new financial and economic system to avoid human inequality and ecological devastation. When Pope Francis focused world attention on caring for the poorest of the poor and planet Earth herself, he spoke the language of The Mother.

Don't Expect It To be Perfect

If you ever have a chance to read futurist scenarios or just pay attention to futuristic movies, you'll notice that they have a tendency to swing idealistically positive (utopian) or frighteningly negative (dystopian). We're either all singing "Kumbaya" in a veritable heaven on earth, or we're all toast. One of the most valuable capacities of a Mysterial Woman is her ability to be with what is, to be comfortable with the Mystery. Even in a relatively positive scenario, she accepts that life is inherently messy—especially if you want to change something—and will dish up challenges. That's how we grow! This is as true personally as it is collectively.

It is likely that the shadows of The Mother will show up in our cultural pattern. Imagine a US Congress or British Parliament, with its heavy load of active shadow Dominators and Judges, replaced with a majority of Devourers. There would be less direct fighting and desire to blame and vanquish the opposing party, but things could bog down and stagnate. Imagine them leaning so far and holding on to each other so tightly that nothing gets done, or using passive-aggressive manipulation and campaigns of blatant victimization to push forward an agenda. Overregulating industries and overprotecting individuals to the point that they can't grow . . . it could be rough.

We can't forget that the Yang essence cultures (Modern, Traditional, and even Warrior) will still be alive and well on the planet and within US society even if they aren't at the leading edge. Our planet will likely become even more diverse, not less. Having a Yin Postmodern culture in the planetary driver's seat will bring some greater inclusiveness and sensitivity, but the stress and strain and vast disagreement between these very different cultures will still be present.

Further, developmentalists who study these structures of consciousness and culture point out that Postmodern consciousness still feels that its beliefs are the "right" beliefs and has no problem imposing those on others. A good example is the ongoing "culture war" between these factions in US culture (especially evident in the political scene). Traditional social conservatives struggling with Modern business conservatives and libertarians, both of whom pitch furious, to-the-death battles with Postmodern liberals.

As the Postmodern Information economy overtakes the steel and smoke stack Modern Industrial economy (which surpassed the Traditional Agricultural economy in most of the developed world), it is likely that everything about everyone will be known. And that is a powerful card to hold, requiring even higher cultural ethics and greater sensitivity to human needs. And the more collectivist ways of Postmodern culture, as evidenced by more socialist leaning cultures in Scandinavia, will no doubt continue to clash with the ardent free market/capitalist ways of Modern cultures.

From an evolutionary point of view, an imposition of Postmodern power to stop the more egregious violations of Modern capitalism may be entirely necessary to protect the planet and its most vulnerable and oppressed denizens from further destruction and exploitation. A collectively imposed Vessel Yin Mother "time out" may be entirely appropriate to prevent us from going over the brink until better solutions emerge.

Now let's stretch out in the future a little further. Let us continue to use The Mysterial Sequence as our viewing portal—we see a significant number of women are now emerging Mysterials and influencing the perspectives, traditions, and institutions of our society.

At the Close of The Return to The Mother

This is a world, perhaps of our grandchildren or their children, where the Vessel Yin essence of the contemporary Mother gathered enough strength that we were compelled from a place of love for the earth and all beings to find ways to slow down some of the runaway problems. Standing in Joyful True Authority, we finally mustered sufficient collective will and creativity to stop some of the most egregious forms of harm to the planet.

The previously unquenchable hunger for endless upward growth was finally tempered. With the Empowered Radiant Presence of many influencers, we began to collectively appreciate and value time for being, for reflection, and for investment in our well-being and that of those around us. We continue to make time and space for that in public life.

We find ways to bring together our reverence for and enjoyment of the natural world with sophisticated designs and advanced technologies that can mimic the gifts of nature. The "built world" around us becomes green, socially connected, and energy efficient with off-the-grid energy sources, rooftop gardens, water catchment, net-zero housing, and whole new ways of organizing decentralized, energy efficient, connected living.

It has become the norm to create lives of fulfillment and purpose without needing so much stuff or to rack up so many personal achievements. We are inclined to live more simply and communally, sharing resources with each other. Caring for the needs of others and empathically connecting beyond our own family, community, and even nation—while also tending to our own needs—has become a strongly held societal value.

Most working environments are now designed to adapt to the unexpected contingencies of a busy family life. The artificial separation of work and life has dissolved. There is just life, and a clear intention to make that healthy and fulfilling for everyone.

The creativity that has been made possible, and the continued integration of ever more intelligent information systems with the greatest gifts of everyone has resulted in unprecedented productivity in many sectors. We look back on the Great Transition days of 24-7 frantic activity, and corporate environments that routinely burnt people out, with the same horror that we held for forced child labor and indentured servitude.

Yet it is far from a perfect world. Devourer shadow tendencies have created stagnation that accumulated over time. The tendency to overprotect the environment and the vulnerable has generated a cascade of unintended consequences and constrained some needed growth. It can be very hard to get a new enterprise started.

An acceptance of martyrdom in service to others has attracted violence and discord from the more Yang-infused subcultures. Neglector shadows express themselves in the homeless and sick who continue to populate the ghettos and margins of societies, and fill the more sensitive and loving but still overtaxed healthcare system. There is an unremitting sense that the clock is winding down, that things are slowly disintegrating.

Bringing in the Collective Crone and Integral Culture

Now we have reached a place where a new kind of dynamism is needed, when a truly new, radically different form of culture can emerge. This will be the time of the collective Crone. When the inner Crone comes online within a woman, and the other primary archetypes are reasonably embodied, then a woman's Mysterial nature arises. Likewise, when the complex and inscrutable Crone pattern starts to take hold in mass consciousness through a substantial number of women, that truly will be a tipping point for the full flowering of the Mysterial Woman collectively.

This Crone pattern will carry the integrated essence of Flame and Vessel Yin—a more complex, nuanced, and mature Yin different from either the quiet womblike feel of Vessel Yin, or the passionate creative adventure of Flame Yin. It will also be able to connect easily with assertive Flame Yang and organizing Vessel Yang, wielding the "the sword" and "the hammer" as needed.

This sophisticated and powerful new Yin-Yang of the wise Crone archetype will ascend from the ghetto of history, where she has lived as the outcast witch for millennia. Her ways were too unfathomable, and her complex abilities to heal, to walk between worlds, and see beyond the veil too threatening to be allowed into regular society.

Until now.

It is here that The Mysterial Sequence departs from what had seemed like a satisfying infinity loop of Mother—Hero—Father—Maiden—Mother, around which we would go forever. But that is too simple. The Crone compels us to take a vertical leap in complexity, elevating us to an entirely new pattern and world of possibility.

Once again, return to that place inside where you can feel the pattern of The Mysterial Sequence.

You have had an opportunity to engage in the wonders of the advanced new world of the contemporary Vessel Yin Mother. You feel nourished and satisfied; but in time you begin to notice that you are feeling a bit sluggish.

A mysterious magnetic force starts pulling you into uncharted territory. You cross hauntingly beautiful landscapes with rivers, lakes, mountains, deserts, and seas. You are not sure if they are from the past or the future. These landscapes are different than anything you recall, and the experience calls upon everything within you to navigate them. Yet surprisingly it is not that hard; you feel buoyed as if gravity had become somehow slightly reduced.

You reach a place you intuitively know is "it." Looking upward, you spy very high, a distant hovering platform glinting in the sun. Instantly, you are transported onto it, looking down upon the blue and green sphere of the Earth. What a vista to take in! Your body, heart, mind, and soul are brimming with love for this planet, and for all the Yin and Yang places and experiences that you have had. Each is an irreplaceable jewel in its own right.

You know down to your bones that another world has truly come.

Where the Return to The Mother has stabilized and expanded the Postmodern wave of culture that The Maiden initiated, The Crone will be associated with the rise that developmentalists have been anticipating since the mid-twentieth century: Integral culture.

What might this be like? For the previous cultures we identified, we had solid existing examples that we could experience and study. Integral culture is something that is just beginning to emerge at the edges and under the surface of global societies.[2] It is estimated that this particular pattern of consciousness is active in only about 2 percent of the population, and only 4 percent of leaders.[3] It is from those few that we can begin to imagine what such a culture might be like in the future.

In December 2013, in a welcome speech to a group of participants of the Integral movement in Russia, Integral theory pioneer Ken Wilber[4] wrote:

> *In particular, we are facing, for the first time in human history, the emergence of a truly holistic or integral consciousness—meaning a consciousness that is all-inclusive, embracing, caring, pervading, outreaching, enveloping. Never before in humankind's history has this significant a transformation occurred. All previous transformations—each important, to be sure—were nonetheless partial, fragmented, and excluding—whether magic, mythic, rational, or pluralistic. And yet, starting just a few decades ago, developmentalists began observing the emergence, in rare individuals, of an entirely new type of awareness or new type of consciousness—one that fully appreciated and embraced all earlier stages of development, and did not exclude, marginalize, or attempt to suppress them, but transcended and included them all. Maslow called this self-actualizing; Gebser called it integral-aperspectival; for Loevinger, it was autonomous and integrated; Graves called it systemic. But by whatever name, this consciousness was radically new and altogether revolutionary.*

This new integral consciousness and culture will be about *harmonizing* all that has been in conflict in the previous waves, breaking through the embattled impasse of the culture wars to find realistic, practical solutions for our global problems. With an appreciation for the values of all the previous stages, and a discerning eye for those elements that are harmful to life, something new, that actually includes the important wisdom and intelligence of all time and all peoples has a possibility to come into being.

A highly efficient and necessarily sustainable global systems economy powered by collective wisdom could, eventually, surpass the information economy of the Postmodernist wave. With technology breakthroughs that always come with a new wave (in this case, possibly free forms of energy) we could have entirely new ways of meeting our material needs, and resolving deep conflicts.

Whatever happens, we expect to be surprised.

Mysterial Field Work

The ability to harmonize such divergent patterns of consciousness will require a consciousness that transcends one individual being. A distinguishing trait of the Mysterial, which is a direct inheritance from The Crone, is her ability to attune to and read the group or collective field. She can actively cultivate it to grow more coherent and resonant—essentially more alive with collective wisdom. We are all familiar with a group experience that amplifies our own, for example at an exciting sporting event, a political rally, or a moving memorial service.

What is a group field? In a sense, it is a metaphor for a complex human bio-psycho-social phenomenon that cannot yet be measured directly, but that we can observe and experience. Borrowing from classical physics, the field transmits a quantity of matter, energy, or information through a force, such as gravity or electromagnetism. The force can often be represented by waves of energy that ripple out in space beyond the object of its source.

Think of Senator Obama's campaign stops right before the historic election, Princess Diana's funeral procession at Westminster Abbey, the spontaneous global outpouring of emotion for September 11th victims, or for the shooting of young Malala Yousafzai. We can literally feel the abundance of emotional, physical, mental, and even spiritual energy shifting the quality of the atmosphere around us. As social media becomes a fixture in our lives, we are shaping, and being shaped, by collective fields as never before, even when we participate virtually.

Fields can also be a way that new forms, such as the Mysterial Woman, emerge and become commonplace. In the 1980s, biologist Rupert Sheldrake made the startling proposal that the particular forms that living things take (e.g., molecules, cells, or organisms to societies and even galaxies) are shaped across space and time by "morphic fields." You can think of morphic fields as the cumulative memory of similar systems through time. Species of animals, plants, and even humans thus "remember" from generation to generation how to look and how to behave. According to Sheldrake, morphic fields are a scientific way of explaining Jung's archetypes and the collective unconscious.

Have you ever seen a tuning fork start to vibrate just because a nearby tuning fork of the same frequency has been struck? The two tuning forks are resonating with each other. Morphic fields operate through "morphic resonance," the influence of *like upon like*.

One of the interesting phenomena that Sheldrake's theory predicts is that when a member of a species learns or invents a new behavior, for example, Mysterial behavior, it is easier for those following in their footsteps to learn that behavior.

Sheldrake was able to demonstrate this with rats learning a brand new maze. Once one rat had figured it out, subsequent generations of rats, and even rats in different places around the world, learned the same maze more and more quickly. The morphic field created by the first rat's mastery of the maze appeared to become reinforced and more coherent with repetition.

Scientists and engineers have observed this phenomenon in the synthesis of crystals. When an entirely new crystal structure is synthesized for the first time, it is a challenging and slow process. With repetition, it happens more quickly and easily. You might argue that of course the scientist would learn to do it better with practice. Yet the speedier synthesis is observed to happen in labs around the world where a completely different scientist may be giving the recipe their first try. Something else is going on.

Once an organizing field has come into existence, it is possible to "tune in" and bring something into form, or learn a behavior, with more ease. As with Sheldrake's rats, we have observed firsthand that succeeding "generations" of our students learned to embody Mysterial capacities with more speed, ease, and solidity. We have described our decade of work to crystallize the Mysterial within our students as our "petri dish," so to speak. It really did take a full ten years.

A new morphic field for Mysterial Women has come into existence. From now on, it will become easier and faster for women around the world to embody these capacities. In fact, we see it as our responsibility to encourage and invite women to begin to participate in building and strengthening this Mysterial field. This book is a part of building that field.

Where Are the Mysterials?

Now that we've had a chance to dance in a possible future, let us return to deal with the present. The women who we worked with, some of whom you met in Part 2, will be the first to admit that the Mysterial is just beginning to arise within them, and much of the time they backslide. Even (and especially) in ourselves, she is nowhere near fully developed. We each have a long way to go.

That's part of being a Mysterial Woman: you are able to be with your own unfinished and unpolished aspects without beating yourself up, even laugh at your imperfect humanness—and then step forward knowing that you have it in you to be wiser, more loving, and powerful. The channel is open and the water of your own developmental potential is flowing again through you.

Where are the Mysterial women and Mysterial leaders out there? There are plenty, but you will not see many examples of full-blown Mysterials who have risen to iconic stature, or are recognized globally.

Most Mysterial leaders today are working their magic in quiet corners, appreciated by those just around them. Our cultural eyes are not yet fine-tuned enough to pick up her uncommon frequency. Even the word "leader" brings to mind a particular image that was shaped by The Hero and The Father, equating leadership with institutional authority and formal position. Most women who have risen to world stature are exemplars of the last two waves of consciousness: Modern Hero + Father, and Postmodern Maiden.

Look at three US first ladies, spanning the period from the last decade of the twentieth century into the early twenty-first century: Laura Bush, Hillary Clinton, and Michelle Obama. Now, this is not a comprehensive analysis of the first ladies' psychological maturity or leadership capacities and not in the order that they served. It is simply a broad-brush generalization based on the public impression that they project, a stylistic look for the sake of illustration.

We might think of Laura Bush as representing a Traditional First Lady. Her leadership and personal style is classically feminine in the sense of being a traditional mother figure to the country, alongside the commanding father figure of President Bush.

Hillary Clinton represented a Modernist first Lady. She attended law school with her husband and made it clear that she had her own "territory" in the White House. Her leadership and personal style, which continued into her position as Secretary of State, had a distinctly masculine, sometime militant, feel and rightly so as she came up through the early battles for women's liberation.

Michelle Obama, having come of age after the women's movement had broken the trail, represents a Postmodern First Lady. We might say that she is at the point of her own inner Return to the Mother. Like Mrs. Clinton, Mrs. Obama also attended law school with her husband. She then became a successful senior executive in her own right.

Mrs. Obama's leadership and personal style, compared to Mrs. Clinton, is distinctively more feminine, and far more sensual and adventurous than the Traditional Mrs. Bush. Mrs. Obama did not give up her well-earned masculine capacities that allowed her to rise to positions of authority, and at the same time, she is comfortable in her femininity, and in her own individual style and skin. Mrs. Obama's focus and modeling of eating good, organic, whole foods and getting plenty of exercise—and bringing that to school programs—indicates that she is embodying the Vessel Yin Mother in a mature and complex way.

It is possible that all three of these First Ladies are in some ways Mysterial, especially with their inner circle. However, we needn't limit ourselves to such highly visible positions to find representatives of the Mysterial Woman acting as a leader.

The Mysterial Future

The future has a stealthy tendency to come into being long before most of us are aware of it. It lies hidden in the quiet margins, just out of sight of the mainstream, waiting for its moment in the sun. "The future is already here—it's just not very evenly distributed," declared sci-fi novelist William Gibson. His 1984 novel *Neuromancer* gave readers an anticipatory glimpse, an image of the future of life in the exotic world called "cyberspace."

Back then, hardly anyone had a home computer, and very few even used computers at work. People sat at desks writing on paper with pens, or dictated to someone else (almost always a woman) who captured their words in little hieroglyphic squiggles called "shorthand." They replicated those words by punching metal typewriter keys against a ribbon of ink pressed against a piece of paper. People talked to each other on rotary-dialed phones tethered to the wall, paying burdensome long distance rates even for calls inside the same country.

But the adventurous, freedom-loving, free-flowing archetypal Maiden longed to express its relational and creative energy, to be in connection with everyone, every idea, everywhere, all the time. Three decades later, we spend much of our time immersed in this mysterious non-physical cyber reality. It's normal; it's old hat. And such an assimilation of a new reality will be true again.

We believe the emergence of the Mysterial Woman is a potentially powerful "image of the future" that could shape the world that is coming. Image of the Future research is actually an area of academic study. In the aftermath of World War II, a number of social scientists were motivated to figure out what factors would lead to a positive cultural transformation, and which might lead to collapse. Dutch sociologist Fred Polak initiated the field in the 1950s with a groundbreaking comparative analysis of 1500 years of European cultural change (imagine doing all that without computers).

After searching through and testing many possibilities, Polak was surprised to conclude that the lone causal factor he could find that determined the future outcome of a culture *in transition* was the images of the future most resonating with a significant group or "creative minority." In his words, "Their enkindling spiritual power radiates out over the course of history, via the creative minority . . . as long as they have a convincing mass appeal."

In short, Polak found that if there is a small but significant number of individuals in a transitioning culture (a creative minority) that can hold a positive, motivating, shared image of the future, then the image itself was magnetic. It would behave as an attractor, drawing the whole system toward a desirable future state. And this appeared to hold true despite the dire state of existing circumstances that the creative minority was experiencing.

On the other hand, pessimistic, negative images invariably led to decline and stagnation.

In the 1990s, Susan's doctoral dissertation focused on the positive image of the future of leaders who demonstrated a Postmodern or Integral consciousness. This vision prepared Susan for her meeting with Suzanne, who had also recognized women's role in shaping the future. The rest is history. And now you can see that this book is intended to provide an inspiring and liberating image of the future for (and with) you: The Way of the Mysterial Woman.

A quarter century ago, leading edge researchers were predicting inspiring scenarios of Feminine leadership and consciousness that seemed far-fetched, yet have since greatly come to pass. It seems that the future is constantly being shaped by the visions of a culture, and the coherent image exerts a "magnetic pull" on a people, drawing them into the future. Doesn't that sort of mutual causality have an interesting, paradoxically Mysterial feel to it?

Our Final Invitation

A part of our invitation to you is to begin to notice and encourage your own Mysterial nature emerging. Notice who around you is already a Mysterial—a woman who has come into her Mysterial nature and naturally shows up in the world as a Mysterial leader, whether or not she is in a position of formal authority.

We want to hear from you, we want to meet these women, to learn about how they live, love, and lead, and how they became who they are. We the co-authors recognize it is time for us to expand beyond our own little petri dish and quiet Mysterial sanctuary. We are asking for your assistance in this next phase of our work. This is how we will continue to understand how best to support the arising of the Mysterial nature in women.

As more Mysterials are seen, and seen in effective action, our cultural eyes become more tuned. As our cultural eyes become more attuned to the Mysterial, we will collectively invite more of them to serve in positions of influence. The collective field of the Mysterial Woman will build in strength and coherence, which will have an amplifying effect, making it easier for future generations of Mysterials to develop.

The second part of our invitation is to begin to cultivate—and to help us cultivate—a collectively held positive image of the Mysterial Future. If you are interested in participating formally in such a venture, stay in touch. We will be offering ways to do this.

Paraphrasing the words of poet Mary Oliver, what you choose to do "with your one wild and precious life" has impact far beyond you. During this remarkable window of history, the outcomes of the path you choose will be greatly magnified and radiate across generations to come.

We hope that this book serves as a catalyst for your continued Mysterial emergence. May your descendants be thanking you from the future for your wise, loving, and powerful choices on their behalf.

We invite you to connect with us and join the Mysterial Emergence.
www.thewayofthemysterialwoman.com

NOTES

Introduction

1. For a thoroughly readable and well researched account of how much the world has changed for American women, read New York op-ed columnist Gail Collins' 2009 book *When Everything Changed: The Amazing Journey of American Women from 1960 to the Present.*
2. The term "Medial" was first coined in the early 1900s by Toni Wolff in her paper, "Structural Forms of the Feminine Psyche," *(1956) C.G. Jung Institute.* She was a psychotherapist and longtime lover, muse, and collaborator of Swiss psychiatrist Carl Jung, and the first to describe this unique aspect of a woman's psyche.

Chapter 1

1. For a comprehensive yet accessible aggregation of evidence-based futures-relevant books, reports, and articles, see Michael Marien's *Global Foresight* books. See especially the Book of the Month archives that include Marien's insightful reviews.
2. The concept of emergence—how new order arises from chaos as the existing order is disrupted— can be pretty abstract. In her award-winning winning book *Engaging Emergence: Turning Upheaval Into Opportunity*, author Peggy Holman translates these concepts into heartfelt, useful practices and possibilities that can help individuals, communities, and organizations manage change.
3. For an excellent distillation of the current leadership challenges and why we are ill prepared to meet them, see the white paper "The Future of Leadership for Conscious Capitalism" by developmental scholar Barrett C. Brown.

4. See the report by Development Dimensions International & The Conference Board: "Ready-now leaders: Meeting tomorrow's business challenges. Global leadership forecast 2014| 2015.*"

5. Swiss psychiatrist and psychotherapist Carl Jung, a successor to Sigmund Freud, first proposed that men and women both have masculine and feminine aspects of their psyche that co-exist and require development as part of the healthy maturation process.

6. Some of the Traditional leadership qualities were adapted from Maureen Metcalf's *Innovative Leadership Fieldbook*, kindle version, loc 168.

7. The naming convention for these waves of consciousness and culture was borrowed from integral evolutionary scholar Steve McIntosh, from his book, *Integral Consciousness and The Future of Evolution.*

8. The mapping of Masculine and Feminine essences and archetypes with the historical stages or waves of culture and consciousness are described in more detail by psychologist Gareth Hill, *Masculine & Feminine: The Natural Flow of Opposites in the Psyche (2001),* and by psychologist and award winning writer Anodea Judith, *Waking the Global Heart: Humanity's Rite of Passage from the Love of Power to the Power of Love (2007).* Both authors stop at the Postmodern wave and do not include the emerging Integral wave.

9. For more about this cultural overthrow of the archaic Feminine by the emerging Masculine, see award-winning social scientist Riane Eisler's groundbreaking book, *The Chalice and the Blade: Our History, Our Future.*

Chapter 2

1. We are deeply indebted to the groundbreaking work on women's development that Carol Gilligan articulates in her book, *In A Different Voice.* And the book *To Be A Woman: The Birth of the Conscious Feminine,* edited by Connie Zweig, provided us with a broad range of perspectives on the birth of the conscious Feminine.

2. In *Uniting Sex, Self and Spirit,* psychologist Genia P. Haddon arrived at a similar conclusion and reinforced her ideas with the insight into the four-fold physiological correlations in female and male bodies.

3. In *Masculine and Feminine: The Natural Flow of Opposites in the Psyche,* Jungian analyst Gareth Hill's writing greatly inspired our thinking with his similar findings on the quadrated nature of Masculine and Feminine. He outlines a developmental progression through these four forces that aligns well with our own experience.

4. Ibid.

5. In *Waking the Global Heart,* Anodea Judith tracked a similar pattern through the waves of consciousness and culture arising throughout human history.

6. We drew from many sources to deepen our understanding of archetypes: Susan Rowland's *Jung: A Feminist Revision*; Jean Shinoda Bolen's *Goddesses in Every Woman: Powerful Archetypes in Women's Lives*; Marion Woodman's *The Ravaged Bridegroom: Masculinity in Women*; June Singer's *Boundaries of the Soul*; and Nor Hall's *The Moon and The Virgin: Reflections on the Archetypal Feminine,* to name just a few.

Chapter 3

1. Many of those who followed Carl Jung elaborated on his insights: *Owning Your Own Shadow: Understanding the Dark Side of the Psyche* by Robert A. Johnson; *A Little Book on the Human Shadow* by Robert Bly; *Meeting the Shadow* by Connie Zweig and Jeremiah Abrams; *Romancing the Shadow: A Guide to Soul Work for a Vital, Authentic Life* by Connie Zweig and Steve Wolf; and *Integral Life Practice: A 21st-Century Blueprint for Physical Health, Emotional Balance, Mental Clarity, and Spiritual Awakening* by Ken Wilber, Terry Patten, Adam Leonard and Marco Morelli.

2. Suzanne had the opportunity to work with Robert Moore and Doug Gillette in the creation of a leadership program based on archetypes. She was profoundly impacted by the good work they had done in articulating four primary archetypes and their active and passive shadows in the male psyche in their book *King, Warrior, Magician, Lover: Rediscovering the Archetypes of the Mature Masculine.*

Chapter 4

1. See journalist Daniel Coyle's *The Talent Code: Greatness Isn't Born. It's Grown. Here's How,* pg. 32. His book provides an accessible synthesis of current neuroscience in the service of optimizing human potential and enhancing performance.

2. See *The New Feminine Brain: Developing Your Intuitive Genius* by Mona Lisa Schultz MD, PhD. Dr. Shultz is a neuroscientist and medical intuitive who offers deep scientific insight, relatable case studies, and practices for optimizing the full gifts of the feminine brain.

3. The popular idea of a left and right brain is more a simplifying metaphor than factual reality given the complexity of brain function. However, for our purposes this left-right metaphor is a useful illustration pointing to distinctions that humans do experience.

4. In her book *My Stroke of Insight,* brain scientist Dr. Jill Bolte Taylor describes her personal

and profound experience of the differences of the two hemispheres of her brain as she suffered a massive stroke.

5. See the Institute of Heartmath, especially the downloadable e-book, *The Coherent Heart: Heart-Brain Interactions, Psychophysiological Coherence, and the Emergence of System-Wide Order* by Rollin McCraty, PhD, Mike Atkinson, Dana Tomasino, BA, and Raymond Trevor Bradley, PhD. The Institute of Heartmath is a treasure trove of published scientific research and accessible information for the layperson pertaining to the Heart center of intelligence.

6. For more about how our body and posture can affect the way we think and act, see Wendy Palmer's work on Conscious Embodiment, a somatic (body) practice informed by mindfulness and the non-violent martial art of Aikido. We have drawn especially from her 2008 book *The Intuitive Body: Discovering the Wisdom of Conscious Embodiment and Aikido.*

7. For more about the relationship between body posture and power, see the research of social psychologist Amy Cuddy, Associate Professor at Harvard Business School. Her work showed that assuming body postures that convey power for as little as two minutes can change testosterone and cortisol levels, relating to increased openness for risk, better performance in job interviews, and greater ability to cope with stress.

8. We wish to bring attention to two powerful transformative frameworks embedded in our work. First is the Enneagram personality typology, specifically the work of Don Riso and Russ Hudson at The Enneagram Institute, and David Daniels and Helen Palmer at Enneagram Worldwide. The second is the systems innovation work by MIT Sloane School of Business senior lecturer Otto Scharmer.

Chapter 5

1. Read more about this phenomenon in the landmark study in *Psychological Review*, "Biobehavioral responses to stress in females: tend-and-befriend, not fight-or-flight" by Taylor, S. E., Klein, L. C., Lewis, B. P., Gruenewald, T. L., & Updegraff, J. A.

2. Michael Murphy and George Leonard were early pioneers in articulating the power of an integral approach to transformative practices with their Integral Transformative Practice. This comprehensive approach was elaborated on later in *Integral Life Practice: A 21st-Century Blueprint for Physical Health, Emotional Balance, Mental Clarity, and Spiritual Awakening* by Ken Wilber, Terry Patten, Adam Leonard and Marco Morelli

Chapter 6

1. In *The Heroine's Journey* Maureen Murdock addresses what is missing in the Hero's journey and outlines a spiritual and psychological journey of becoming whole that integrates all parts of a woman's nature.
2. We drew from many texts to end up with this particular version of the Kore myth. Several that stand out were *The Homeric Hymn to Demeter* by Helene Foloey, *The Road to Eleusis*, by G. Watson, A. Hofmann, C. A.P.Ruck, *Persephone Unveiled* by Charles Stein, *The Long Journey Home*, edited by Christine Downing, and *Mysteries of The Dark Moon* by Demetra George.
3. Charlene Spretnak's *Lost Goddesses of Early Greece* draws from ancient and scholarly sources to re-imagine the myth without the addition of the violent abduction by a Masculine force.

Chapter 7

1. We are deeply indebted to Ken Wilber and others for the groundbreaking five-element Integral Model, which distills all major thought and wisdom systems across all time and cultures down to the most essential pattern. This gave us a powerful map to ensure that our Mysterial Sequence was truly comprehensive. One of those five elements, the Quadrants, are the four irreducible, most fundamental perspectives or dimensions of any aspect of reality: the inside and the outside of the singular and the plural.
2. NIA is a worldwide phenomenon and a wonderful way to get connected to all levels of yourself – body, heart, mind and soul. Go to their global website to find classes near you. www.nianow.com.
3. This version of Centering Practice was refined by Dr. Julia Smith, a physician and specialist in Somatic Embodiment who worked with our students. It draws on the work of Richard Strozzi-Heckler and Wendy Palmer.
4. See Julia Cameron's *The Artist's Way* for other suggestions for opening the channel of your creativity and joy.
5. Drawn from Kristin Neff's *Self-Compassion: The Proven Power of Being Kind to Yourself.*
6. Suzanne worked with consultant and author Elaine Gagne *(ENGAGE!: Roadmap for Workforce-Driven Change in a Warp-Speed World)* on this model of the Creative Cycle that integrates Yin and Yang energy.

Chapter 8

1. See Sandberg's acclaimed 2013 book, *Lean In: Women, Work, and the Will to Lead.* We acknowledge the importance of her role as an accomplished and inspiring woman leader with a well-developed healthy Hero.
2. For more on the research supporting the biological need for and enhanced productivity through alternating cycles of work and rest, see *The Power of Full Engagement: Managing Energy, Not Time, Is the Key to High Performance and Personal Renewal* by Jim Loehr and Tony Schwartz (2003).
3. See *Autopilot: the Art and Science of Doing Nothing* by Andrew Smart, 2013, for an in-depth study of the value of stillness and simply being.
4. In *Hardwiring Happiness,* Rick Hanson makes the powerful case for the importance of directing our attention away from negative experiences to reinforce the positive ones.
5. See *Buddha's Brain* by Rick Hanson (2009) pg. 69. This book provides many insights on why and how the brain programs us to experience the world, and how we can use the properties of neuroplasticity to decrease negative emotions and create more happiness and fulfillment in our lives.
6. See *Wishful Thinking: A Theological ABC* by Frederick Buechner (1973).

Chapter 9

1. For more information about how polarities work as an interdependent system and their value in organizational development and leadership, see Dr. Barry Johnson's work: www.polaritypartnerships.com/ beginning with his seminal book, *Polarity Management: Identifying and Managing Unsolvable Problems.* You might also check out a further development of this work, Polarity Wisdom©, by Beena Sharmer and Dr. Susanne Cook-Greuter: www.cook-greuter.com/Sharma%20Cook-Greuter%20 paper%20EAIF%20SUNY.pdf

Chapter 10

1. This practice was adapted from one developed by University of Pennsylvania research psychologist Martin Seligman, a leading advocate of the field of Positive Psychology. Seligman's version of this practice was empirically validated to produce a measureable increase in happiness and decrease in depressive symptoms after one week of daily en-

gagement, lasting for six months. According to Seligman, humans are evolutionarily biased to magnify the bad and diminish the good things in our life. Such Positive Psychology practices help people shift from depression to happiness, from pessimism to optimism and lead to more Self-Confidence and greater resilience in life. For more about the work of Dr. Martin Seligman and the field of Positive Psychology, see http://positivepsychology.org/and www.ppc.sas.upenn.edu/articleseligman.pdf

2. One of the inspirations for this practice was current day mystic Brother David Steindl-Rast. For more about Brother David and his work with gratitude, see http://www.gratefulness.org/

3. Once again, see the Heartmath Institute for excellent research on the physiological benefits of generating positive emotions such as gratitude.

4. For a powerful clutter-clearing process that is intuitive, light-hearted, and potentially transformative, we recommend Marie Kondo's 2014 book *The Life Changing Magic of Tidying Up: The Japanese Art of Decluttering and Organizing*. Kondo's central question "does it spark joy?" encourages you to keep only those things in resonance with your being, and frees you to lovingly retire or recycle all the rest.

Chapter 11

1. For an excellent comparison of leadership movements see *The Integral Leadership Manifesto* by Brett Thomas and Russ Volkmann. It can be downloaded at http://integralleadershipmanifesto.com/manifesto/the-problem-with-leadership-theory/

2. In Andrew Smart's *Auto Pilot: The Art and Science of Doing Nothing*, he explains the critical function of the resting-state network of the brain, and how constant busyness erodes its robustness.

3. For more on developing the capacity for Spontaneous Intuition, check out Sophy Burnham's 2011 book, *The Art of Intuition : Cultivating your Inner Wisdom*.

4. Writing in this way was inspired by writing and creativity author Natalie Goldberg's process for letting your inner creator have a say.

Chapter 12

1. See page 39 in John O'Donohue's 2005 book, *Beauty: The Invisible Embrace*. This book is a lovely companion for anyone who wishes to follow the "beauty way."

Chapter 13

1. In her book, *The Crone*, Barbara Walker takes us on journey through history of how culture has repeatedly responded to the emergence of this powerful energy.

2. This practice was adapted from a Tonglen practice created by Joan Halifax, a Buddhist teacher, Zen priest, anthropologist, and pioneer in the field of end-of-life care. See more about Joan Halifax at the Upaya Zen Center website where she is the Abbott and Head Teacher: www.upaya.org/about/roshi/

3. The word "chaordic" was coined by Dee Hock, former CEO of VISA International and a pioneer in organizational development. He argued that traditional organizational forms could no longer work because organizations have become too complex. He advocates a form that is chaordic, or simultaneously chaotic and orderly without either dominating. For more, see his book *The Birth of The Chaordic Age*.

4. This practice was inspired by Susan Scott's Fierce Conversations and adapted from a Fierce Conversation practice presented at The Aurora Crossing http://www.theauroracrossing.com/fierce-conversations/.

5. Process Art is an artistic approach where the importance is not focused on the final product (the art or craft) but the creative process through which the art emerged. We find it a valuable methodology. For more information check out Stewart Cubley at www.processarts.com; Michele Cassou at www.michelecassou.com; and Aviva Gold at www.paintingfromthesource.com.

6. For excellent and more involved practices for accepting reality as it truly is, we recommend The Work by Byron Katie, and ActiveInsight, a derivative of The Work, developed by Andrew Bernstein, a student of Byron Katie.

7. Eduardo Duran's powerful book, Native American Postcolonial Psychology, was a great help to Christina as she opened up the Pandora's box of her lineage.

Chapter 15

1. Transition Towns are grassroots community projects that seek to build resilience in response to impending challenges such as peak oil, climate change, and economic instability. For more information, see the Transition Network website: www.transition-network.org/support/what-transition-initiative

2. See *The Integral Leadership Review*, April-June 2014 article by Russian bureau chief Eugene Putoshkin, "The integral movement in Russia: Bigelow, Fuhs and Wilber."

http://integralleadershipreview.com/8062-the-integral-movement-in-russia-bigelow-fuhs-and-wilber/_

3. See the leadership research of David Rooke and Bill Torbert. In their 2005 Harvard Business Review article, "The Seven Transformations of Leadership," the term "Strategist" is used interchangeably with the Integral level or stage of development: https://hbr.org/2005/04/seven-transformations-of-leadership

4. Philosopher Ken Wilber is often credited with catalyzing and creating a map for the emerging integral movement around the world. His Integral Life website is one gathering place and repository of information: www.integrallife.com/

ACKNOWLEDGMENTS

When we, the co-authors, synchronously met each other 15 years ago at a women's leadership conference we couldn't have imagined how significant that encounter was to be. Our collaboration together over the years has been a steady thread woven into the fabric of our complex lives. Sometimes destiny called us closely into partnership and sometimes it pushed us further apart. Yet the ever-present call of the Mysterial pattern seeking to be seen and named kept drawing us back together. Our collaboration, like any long-term partnership, has been extremely challenging at times and sweetly fulfilling at others. We are thankful to one another for sticking with the creation, gestation and finally the birth of The Way of the Mysterial Woman.

We are deeply grateful for all of the courageous and committed students who joined us over 12 years in our many women's leadership programs. We are especially indebted to our Women's Integral Leadership Advanced (WILA 3) women who helped us decode the final steps of The Mysterial Sequence. Your surround and support for our work has been extraordinary and crucial. Without you we simply would not have discovered the Mysterial pattern and the pathway to access this next level of our evolutionary capacity. Thank you to all our student collaborators for pushing and pulling us forward.

We extend a most heart-full thank you to Deborah Kennedy for your deep commitment to this work and your contribution at so many levels. Your generosity of heart and substance was a nourishing river running through our years of collaboration. Without you we would not have discovered the potency of the Mysterial pattern, nor would we have articulated it into a manuscript. You have made all the difference.

With deepest gratitude to Julia Smith MD for your co-creative contribution in shaping the very bedrock of this work as an embodied journey – without the foundation of your somatic sensibilities the Mysterial could not have emerged. N'Shama Sterling we thank you for your wise, soulful partnership and stewarding of the catalytic Enneagram thread carefully woven into all our programs. And an enormous bow of appreciation for the extraordinary faculty with whom we were fortunate enough to work over the years. Your expertise and friendship shaped so much of what has emerged in this book. Thank you Kim Church, Jamie Selby, Sarah Keenan, Sharleen Chesledon, JoAnne Lovascio, Martha Enson, Peggy Holman and Nota Lucas.

A huge thank you to Antioch University, Bastyr University and LIOS Graduate College of Leadership Studies at Saybrook University for your partnership with us in our years of research into a developmental pathway for women that could unlock the next level of women's leadership capacity.

Thank you to Harmony Hill Retreat Center (http://www.harmonyhill.org/) for hosting so many of our student cohorts in your exquisite and sacred retreat center.

Will Wilkinson you are a true brother on the path who arrived as our writing coach at just the right moment. Thank you for your generous contribution and encouragement to keep on going when we were slogging through the mud of our first draft. Thank you Gail Hudson for believing in us and so skillfully taking our manuscript from draft into reality through your brilliant developmental editing. We have been inspired by Lynda Lowe's artistic expression for years and we are deeply grateful for the use of her painting Boundless as the evocative, Mysterial image on our cover.

Finally, we want to deeply thank every one of our many Indiegogo supporters who patiently and generously made it possible to turn the manuscript—our great labor of love—into this book. First we wish to acknowledge the WILA3 Circle: Lisa Fryett, Carolyn Blackler, Carlee Casey, Birdena Leininger, Roberta Pendell, Amy Schottenstein, Vickie Strand, Claudia Thompson, and Ginger Wilkinson. We are also delighted to acknowledge Albie Beannacht, Kippy Messet, Julie Speidel, Michelle King, John Roland MD, Theresa Soukup, John and Deborah Swain, Amy Schottenstein, Carlee Casey, Marla Fenske, Jamie Selby, Katherine Diamond, Peter and Karen Anderson, Chilina Hills, Norie Marfil, Cliff Penwell, Barbara Alexander, Lori Ambrose, Doreen Bingo, Carolyn Blackler, Allyson Brown, Yvonne Brown, David Cannon, Tom Catarra, Richard Chadek and Dianne Grob, Sharleen Chesledon, Rosemary Daszkiewicz, Beth DiDomenico, Wendy Fraser PhD,

Ann Guthrie, Marilyn Hamilton, Valerie Manusov and Hestia Retreat, Peggy Holman, Michelle King, Kathy Koenig, Barbara Krauss, Nota Lucas, Lynn Hagerman, Mirium Mason Martineau, Katie McEachern, Dana McPherson, Andrea Saunders Moore, Krissie Patterson, David Pfeiffer and Daniel Klein, Kristina Preedy, Melissa Ransdell, Virginia Rhoads and John McConnell, Jane Charles Savarise, Julia Schechter, Betsy Schwartz, Sarah Schwartz, Susan Siegmund, David Smith, Sonya Wilkins, Will Wilkinson, Kimberly Williamson, Mike Wombacher, and Lois Wyse. A deep bow and heartfelt thank you to all!

Susan's gratitude: I am deeply grateful to David Cannon for the encouragement, support, and understanding you generously extended over the years as this book evolved from cloudy first draft toward its crystallized radiance, and to John Roland, M.D. who even during our raw teenage years recognized and encouraged my budding Mysterial nature. Thank you for your continued support, blessing, co-generativity, and love. To my parents, Jud and Jane Russell, I will always be grateful for the love and stability you selflessly provided and the freedom you gave me to be myself—foundation stones for my path. And finally to my ancestral womanline, I deeply honor the gifts that have passed from you to me, often in circumstances of pain and hardship. I feel your supportive and mysterious presence with me every day. Thank you.

Suzanne's gratitude: I simply could not have written this book without the rock solid support and love of dear friends and family who came in around me as the bottom fell out of my world when my beloved husband tragically died right as we finished the first draft. Thank you to Dianne Grob and Richard Chadek, Antonia Greene and Rob Synder, Sharleen Chesledon, Deborah Kennedy, Julia Smith and Rick Head, Sarah Keenan, Lynda Lowe, David Pfeiffer and Daniel Klein, Pam and Don Avriett, Claire and Chris Tirtoprodjo, Virginia Rhoads, Julie Speidel and Joe Henke, Vicky Adams and Tom Amorose, Daniel O'Connor, Michael Meade, Catherine Johnson, Susan Hormann and Barbara Cecil for holding me until I could hold myself. To my loving family—dearest siblings Hannah, Peter, Kathy and their deeply supportive spouses Brian, Karen and Kirk and their children; especially nephews Justin, Simon and his wife Kelly; cousins, Sarah Schwartz and Nora York—thank you for steadying my capsized ship so that I could eventually return to the book. To my guide Erica Helm Meade I thank you with all of my heart for walking with me every step of the way before, during and after the tsunami of loss—without the light of your seeing and your loving presence this book would not exist. And to my First Flock of allies—thank you for being with me not only in the years of Kore programs but also for circling around me as I put myself back together and completed the book: Carlee Casey, Adriana Chmiel, Kim Church, Arlene Fairfield, Pattie Hanmer, Deborah Kennedy, Nota Lucas, Amy Schottenstein, Jamie Selby and Jacqueline Van Paassen.

I am also deeply grateful to my first husband Robert Marcus for your support and encouragement in the early bushwhacking years of the research. The path we walked together was a powerful contributing force to the understandings that are in our book.

Although sadly my parents are not alive to see this book published I deeply acknowledge the ways in which their love and support shaped so much of my life journey. Thank you Mother for your unconditionally loving acceptance and seeing of my true essence. And Father thank you for inspiring me to be an explorer on the edge of the known and for challenging me to stay true to myself.

And finally I am infinitely grateful everyday for the 10 years spent with my beloved husband David Smith. You provided a deeply loving sanctuary within which this work and I could bloom. Your loving and your leaving have been the two great transformational forces in my life.

Both co-authors deeply bow down to the Great Mystery herself who has guided us forward every step of the way. While this journey has certainly not always been easy it has always felt deeply guided by a force greater than ourselves. We sincerely hope that our book captures the radically upgraded wisdom, love and power that is the hallmark of the Mysterial Woman, and the promise of the future.

ABOUT THE AUTHORS

SUZANNE ANDERSON, MA, is a global citizen who has worked for the past thirty years in the field of transformational leadership development in North America and Europe as a senior management consultant, educator, executive coach and motivational speaker. She was the co-creator of a highly acclaimed women's empowerment program that launched her research into women's development. The owner of Kore Evolution, she facilitates transformational university certificate leadership programs for women worldwide. Combining her graduate studies in women's developmental psychology together with her well developed intuitive, artistic, and soulful sensibilities, she is a change agent for the change agents of the world.

SUSAN CANNON, PhD, is a visionary scholar-practitioner, executive coach, futurist, and artistic intuitive who loves the intimacy of guiding innovative influencers. Her transdisciplinary career includes engineering management and executive positions in the semiconductor, defense, construction industries and historic global change projects; co-creating highly successful university certificate women's leadership development programs, as well as producing and co-hosting a weekly radio show for TalkSpot Studios. She is a media guest and presenter, a certified Integral Master Coach,™ founding affiliate of Kore Evolution, senior associate with Vollett Executive Coaching, co-facilitator of The Shift Leadership Academy, the owner of Evolucent Consulting, and a professor of Organizational Development and Leadership at Fielding Graduate University.

SELECTED TITLES FROM SHE WRITES PRESS

She Writes Press is an independent publishing company founded to serve women writers everywhere. Visit us at www.shewritespress.com.

The Thriver's Edge: Seven Keys to Transform the Way You Live, Love, and Lead by Donna Stoneham. $16.95, 978-1-63152-980-1. A "coach in a book" from master executive coach and leadership expert Dr. Donna Stoneham, *The Thriver's Edge* outlines a practical road map to breaking free of the barriers keeping you from being everything you're capable of being.

Think Better. Live Better. 5 Steps to Create the Life You Deserve by Francine Huss. $16.95, 978-1-938314-66-7. With the help of this guide, readers will learn to cultivate more creative thoughts, realign their mindset, and gain a new perspective on life.

Stop Giving it Away: How to Stop Self-Sacrificing and Start Claiming Your Space, Power, and Happiness by Cherilynn Veland. $16.95, 978-1-63152-958-0. An empowering guide designed to help women break free from the trappings of the needs, wants, and whims of other people—and the self-imposed limitations that are keeping them from happiness.

The Clarity Effect: How Being More Present Can Transform Your Work and Life by Sarah Harvey Yao. $16.95, 978-1-63152-958-0. A practical, strategy-filled guide for stressed professionals looking for clarity, strength, and joy in their work and home lives.

The Complete Enneagram: 27 Paths to Greater Self-Knowledge by Beatrice Chestnut, PhD. $24.95, 978-1-938314-54-4. A comprehensive handbook on using the Enneagram to do the self-work required to reach a higher stage of personal development.

People Leadership: 30 Proven Strategies to Ensure Your Team's Success by Gina Folk. $24.95, 978-1-63152-915-3. Longtime manager Gina Folk provides thirty effective ways for any individual managing or supervising others to reignite their team and become a successful—and beloved—people leader.